Systematic Security

In today's rapidly evolving digital landscape, safeguarding critical data and systems has never been more vital—or more challenging. *Systematic Security: A CISO's Playbook* by Timur Qader offers a groundbreaking guide to building a resilient and scalable security practice from the ground up. Blending real-world experience with practical insights, this book lays out a phased approach to security implementation.

Timur begins with describing the current state of security and the landscape security professionals find themselves in that offer both opportunity and risk. He goes on to systematically address strategic design, operational efficiency, risk-based modeling, and a rapidly growing regulatory landscape. This essential resource provides step-by-step strategies for implementing a comprehensive security framework. Whether you're launching a new security program or transforming an existing one, this book delivers actionable insights on governance, compliance, and advanced security operations.

Drawing on years of hands-on experience, Timur shares practical advice on:

- Establishing a structured roadmap with clear milestones and deliverables.
- Building effective governance and compliance teams to address evolving regulations.
- Developing security operations through advanced techniques like Zero Trust and Data Protection Capabilities.
- Navigating complex relationships with stakeholders, executives, and regulators.
- Creating metrics and scorecards to measure and continuously improve security posture.

More than just a technical manual, *Systematic Security* is a leadership toolkit for today's security executives. It highlights the mindset, collaboration, and communication skills needed to succeed in high-pressure environments. With tips on presenting to boards, handling audits, and managing compliance, this book prepares readers for the challenges of modern cybersecurity leadership.

Whether you're an aspiring CISO, a security professional, or a business leader looking to fortify your organization's defenses, *Systematic Security* delivers the strategies and tools to create lasting security excellence.

Timur Qader's candid, experience-driven approach ensures this book is not just informative but indispensable for anyone serious about protecting data, systems, and reputations in a world of escalating security threats.

Prepare to lead with confidence, foster innovation, and build a future-proof security strategy that aligns with organizational goals and industry best practices. With *Systematic Security*, success isn't just a possibility—it's a repeatable process.

Systematic Security
A CISO's Playbook

Timur Qader

CRC Press
Taylor & Francis Group
Boca Raton London New York

CRC Press is an imprint of the
Taylor & Francis Group, an **informa** business

Designed cover image: Shutterstock Image ID 2501608715

First edition published 2026
by CRC Press
2385 NW Executive Center Drive, Suite 320, Boca Raton FL 33431

and by CRC Press
4 Park Square, Milton Park, Abingdon, Oxon, OX14 4RN

CRC Press is an imprint of Taylor & Francis Group, LLC

ISBN: 978-1-041-01273-3 (hbk)
ISBN: 978-1-041-01812-4 (pbk)
ISBN: 978-1-003-61652-8 (ebk)

DOI: 10.1201/9781003616528

Typeset in Sabon
by SPi Technologies India Pvt Ltd (Straive)

Contents

Author Biography

Born 1976 in Afghanistan, Timur Qader, the youngest of four, left the country in 1978 as a result of the coup d'etat and Russian invasion. His father secured a position with the United Nations and the negotiated terms were that he would go on assignment and in return the UN would extract his wife and four kids to meet him in his first assignment. For the next 10 years, the family lived in several countries and had the opportunity to experience different cultures along the way.

In 1985, Timur's father was reassigned to headquarters in New York and the family moved to Westchester, New York. After graduating from Lakeland High School in Shrub Oak, NY, Timur attended the University of Buffalo where he received his B.S. in Mechanical Engineering. Right after college Timur moved to the Capital Region of New York (Albany), where he started work not in engineering but telecommunications with Bell Atlantic that shortly became Verizon. Along the way, he completed his MBA, MS in Information Security, and met his wive Vanessa Qader with whom he had two boys named Xavier and Darian Qader.

Over 25 years, Timur has held multiple positions as CISO, and worked for the security think tank Center for Internet Security (CIS). He spends his time with family, exercise and education. Timur received what he deems as his greatest achievement short of family, his black belt in Brazilian Jiu Jitsu in 2022, and he continues to practice the martial art as part of his exercise regimen.

Chapter 1

Lay of the land

Zero Trust!!!

Okay now that we got that out of the way, we can begin. There's so much noise out there with people and companies trying to capitalize on the next big thing that it can become hard to know what is vital and what is just a hustle. A fundamental element that speaks to my perspective on things is that there's no such thing as an expert. Look, I don't pretend not to be cynical and while there's value to be found in the pitches and hustles and advertising and promotions that run the worlds drive for consumerism, we need to apply some good common sense and reason in the things we do. On the topic of experts, none of us are that. I've come to realize that everyone is trying to legitimize their position in some manner and they're all guessing; some are better at it than others.

Guessing is the foundation of most people's basis for expertise; it's just a matter of how you convey it. Say 'it' with confidence and without hesitation, and someone somewhere will believe you know what you're talking about. Say it with conviction! Even if you have no clue what you're talking about. Sadly there are a lot of people who talk about things they don't have an inkling of knowledge about, but we believe in them. Now, I don't deny some have more history and experience that makes them a more reputable source but just watch the next apocalyptic story on the news on any topic: the stock market is going to crash, this stock will rise and another will fall, predictions of faith and science, everyone having an opinion about everything with no basis for most of what they say. You see many would-be experts fail miserably in their predictions, and they fall into the shadows hoping no one remembers their adamant statements about the future of the world.

So what's this got to do with this book and me? Well, I fall in the latter; I have history and experience and have a repeatable practice instituting the concepts captured in this book in multiple environments and companies. I'm not an expert and avoid the label as a vampire avoids the sun (attempt at being overly dramatic), but I have a success story tied to installing strong security practices in private and public companies. So with a conscious eye on knowing that everything we talk about is probabilistic, I can say with pretty good confidence that if you institute the things we will go through,

DOI: 10.1201/9781003616528-1

your chances of establishing a pretty strong security operation is good. But hey, it could all come crashing down around you as well...sorry but that's unfortunately the reality of everything. So the last thing I'll say about this is to apply concepts and recommendations with common sense. What works for your organization, what works for your personality, what works for your team's culture. Most of what I present should be universally applicable but there are those elements that require the voice of reason to ensure they apply to your conditions.

Okay one more last thing... watch out for falling for the next big thing. Every time I hear someone speak about 'zero trust' I get this pain somewhere deep in my chest that I have to push down and swallow. We as humans love to latch on to things and then blindly parrot them to feel part of the story. That's not to say they don't have some merit but it goes back to what I said earlier... apply some reason on where things fit and how.

In the following introduction, I cover some of the general concepts that will be addressed in more detail in the subsequent chapters. The intent here is to lay the foundation for how to think about your role in security, and to install a realistic view of what you're up against and how to effectively navigate the challenges that can be at some times, overwhelming. Make no mistake, there is a lot to process as a security leader, and the road is laced with potholes along the way, but if you do it right, the benefits and ultimate impact you can have on the health of your company and in some cases, and sometimes in your industry, nationally and even globally, can be the most rewarding work one can do.

1.1 THE 'RIGHT' PERSONALITY TYPE FOR SUCCESS

There used to be this idea that type A personalities depicted strength, confidence and had the highest chance for success in corporate environments. If you wanted to succeed in that environment, you needed to be aggressive, intense, and show no weakness. In the days when corporations were dominated by male authority, there was this admiration of those who portrayed authority in this manner. They were admired, feared and used as models for behavior.

Well, I'm here to tell you the world today has changed and in my opinion, become more balanced. Gone are the days when the employer had all the leverage and the employee had to accept abuse because that's just the way it is. Today there's a clear movement towards balance and employees are growing in their influence and ability to influence the terms of employment. The old school thinking of 'lead through authority' is quickly fading and allows for more constructive leadership to rise that takes care of both the companies interests and the employees.

There is no such thing as a 'right' personality. What you find is those who exhibit alternative personalities to an A bring forth elements of compassion, empathy and thoughtfulness. The concept of emotional intelligence and emotional IQ are used today to speak to an individual's ability to drive success through constructive relationships, their own self-awareness, and empathy. This does not debunk the idea that type A characteristics are not important, but a well-balanced leader can adjust their leadership across all personality types because they have a firm grasp of the right approach for the right conditions.

If you've been in corporate environments, you've likely been exposed to some of the personality and behavioral modeling tools like DISC or Talent Dynamics or Myers-Briggs. These tools tell you what your dominant personality type is, where you gain energy and conversely what drains your energy. They tell you how you like to communicate and your natural tendencies. They are interesting but what a leader should strive for is to bridge the different types depicted in say DISC, to apply consciously, all the different types at the right time. There is a time to assert authority, there's a time to defer and there's a time to drive consensus. When taking these tests, we should find out what is our dominant style and then work over time, to develop in the other areas that aren't as natural for us.

What this means is a strong leader will sometimes put themselves in positions that will drain their energy but they do it consciously and selectively because in those times, the team, the individuals and the company they support requires it. Take myself as an example. When I started my career as a young graduate from college, I was energetic, ready to conquer the world but relied mostly on myself to get things accomplished. I had no interest in public speaking or frankly, interacting to a large degree with others because in my own cocky way, I looked around and didn't see the same level of intensity in others, so I judged the world and said they are a bunch of slackers.

Public speaking was a big problem for me; I would get anxious if I had to do anything beyond staff meetings or small teams. I knew right then that for me to grow in my career, I would have to resolve a few things 1: become more accepting of different styles of work and people in general, and 2: address this public speaking thing because as leaders you will have to address teams and groups as part of your path to 'success' so you better get used to it. Over the course my career, I became less judgmental, I became pretty good at presenting because my anxiety forces over-preparation, which votes well for conveying concepts in a competent fashion. I became more tolerant and all of these in turn improved my empathy towards others. To this day, my interactions are constructive and genuine but they drain energy because my natural tendency is to be quiet, and prefer alone time. However because I lead teams, I make it a point to have multiple channels of communication with my team and their teams because I know direct and personal relationships are a fundamental pillar for driving strong culture. The point here is that you can be any type of personality, and each of them have strengths; when you lead teams, your self-awareness of your energy is vital and a willingness to balance across areas that are not natural is essential. You don't have to be a Type A and they don't have to be any other type either; you just have to grow that insight into what individuals, teams and leadership needs to develop trust and grow your credibility.

1.2 JOB SECURITY... OR JAIL

A little bit about the job outlook for those starting out or currently working in the information security space. The outlook is very positive and will only grow over time. As the world becomes more connected and digital services grow, the need for information and cyber experts will grow as well. The more uses for networks and integration grows, the more opportunities for the bad actors to attack.

Think about the big push on integrated solutions today. The value proposition of connecting multiple products to one another; mapping hardware and software into comprehensive solutions has never been so sought after. Apple did it with its iPhone connected to iTunes connected to every other product that made seamless transfer of data, account information and user experience intuitive. The merger of products and software is taking hold everywhere and will make the job of security that more complex.

We see it with cars. Today's cars come standard with a sophisticated set of electronics that are more and more connected to networks. The future of automotive will see more electronics and autonomous driving, something that will heavily rely on networks and software. Your home is a growing platform of intelligent solutions as well and will continue to expand. Smart homes are a real thing and well, in my career I have seen first-hand the emergence of how interconnected devices in the home will offer homeowner's a lot of neat new ways to perform preventative maintenance for critical systems such as water, heat, air conditioning and others.

The thing about integrated systems in homes and autonomous driving and an even greater push in digitization is that they are all now accessible or exposed to some network or cloud service. Think about security cameras, today most of the do-it-yourself or professionally installed cameras offer some form of cloud storage. You no longer need to have local storage that needs to be maintained, but rather, you connect via Wi-Fi or cellular and push data to whatever cloud platform that is offered. The same holds true for many of the other home solutions noted here as well: energy management, HVAC health monitoring, intelligent appliances, they are all being interconnected. That means our attack surface is growing at an unprecedented pace. That also means more is at stake; life-safety becomes something that can be infiltrated and attacked in ways never before seen.

What does this mean for the security professional? It means the profession is not going anywhere soon. We may see certain roles and functions move to automation and artificial intelligence-based solutions such as analytics and monitoring but security engineering, architecture, leadership is only going to grow. For those who have worked in security, you will likely agree that there seems to be more to do than you can get to at any given time. Sometimes it feels overwhelming at how many dimensions there are to security and how many times you feel you're playing whac-a-mole as you work towards maturing a practice. In some ways it's frustrating, but in other ways, it truly is job security (no pun intended).

So if there's so much opportunity, why are some exiting the profession? Well, the stakes are never higher, if you happen to be leading a security organization, you should check to see how much liability insurance the company carries for you, especially if your company is public. In the United States, the Securities and Exchange Commission (SEC) continues to increase the requirements and demands on security organizations. Some argue the SEC doubling down on cybersecurity reporting is good, some say they are excessive, but from a practitioner's perspective (talking about myself here), I can see how some would look for an exit strategy because of the personal liability placed on CISOs that can lead to jail time!

Imagine a person who did everything right in their lives (doing 'right' is subjective I get it), but they were a model student, treated their parents with respect, maintained a high sense of ethics at the workplace, put their best foot forward in working to do the right thing for their teams and company, but along the way, they missed something. At any given time, a security leader has to juggle numerous 'opportunities' for security improvement against funding availability and a team's capacity to execute. So this leader did the right things; they had a risk management practice and in one of those reviews, something amongst a bunch of other stuff was listed as a potential gap but from prioritization, and this item got lost amidst all the other initiatives and was left unaddressed or through prioritization was pushed down the list for a later date. Well sometime later, a breach happens taking advantage of that particular gap and leads to a major incident. This becomes a reportable event to the SEC, and an investigation ensues. During that investigation it becomes evident that the risk was known but nothing done about it, never mind all the other things that were being improved and matured, but this particular one was left unattended. Well, all roads lead to the CISO; you most certainly will find him/her in the hot seat for their job, but now also depending on the impact, they can be held liable personally for negligence.

It is a scary place to be, and while some will say, Timur, CFOs and CEOs have this type of liability amongst others as well, so stop being overly dramatic. Well, it's very true, but I would argue that there are ways to buffer a CEO from liability with probable denial. The CFO has one of the most important roles in a company but there is a focused aspect to their role tied to financials. When dealing with security, it can apply to any and all aspects of the business: products, operations, systems. The CISO has a massive surface to cover. So, before deciding to take a job as a CISO, make sure you understand how your company will protect you (insurance) and what type of culture exists at the company; are they supportive, do they have a strong connected culture, or could you find yourself on an island when the brown stuff hits the fan?

So, how do you mitigate the SEC requirements, the growing EU mandates, and the land mines? Structure and efficiency. For me, in order to combat the growing sensitivity, you need to beef up your SOC, incident management practices, and communication protocols. Make active stress testing your SOCs ability to recognize and identify anomalies something routine. Assess your incident management practice from identification to notification to ensure it becomes reflex that any anomaly that is outside of normal routine security alerting is immediately reported to a security leader to assess and then share, if deemed necessary, with the legal team at your company. When in doubt, communicate anomalies and work jointly with legal to determine if there's anything there that should be reported further.

The challenge here is that many times the security team relies on multiple other technology departments who run operations to be lockstep with security in notification. The biggest hurdle here is to get strong alignment across all tech-teams to first be aware of SEC reporting requirements, and abide by standard incident management protocols for reporting to the security organization for assessment. This is a worthwhile investment of time and something you do not have the luxury to allow for variation and divergence in practices. Focus as much energy as needed to get everyone in line on incident management standard practices, and second only to this is test and retest your SOC to ensure they 1: receive the right alerts and 2: react accordingly to notify their leadership of anomalies. At that point, it's up to security leadership to notify legal and they typically will work with a committee of some sort to assess materiality and address other notifications as needed with your support and consultation.

Take this very seriously, because it can mean bad things for the company and yourself if this is not done well.

1.3 SOLVER OF WORLD HUNGER

So it's scary stuff if you find yourself ill-prepared to deal with the emerging accountability and reporting requirements not just in the United States but globally. The European Union (EU) is, at the time I was writing this book, looking at similar requirements placed in the US by the SEC. the number of data privacy laws springing up everywhere is hard to sometimes keep up with. What's most dangerous to security leaders though is not the growing compliance requirements, nor the growing threat landscape and attack surface. The most dangerous threat to your success is not technology innovation leading to new ways to conduct the same attacks but faster and with greater ease. The threat stems from your corporate culture.

As an insightful leader, you need to see what's beneath the surface and what truly drives decision making at your company. When deciding to work for a company, it's important to feel like you can work with the personalities around you, but when your leadership says they are security-minded, are they really? Do they have realistic expectations of you and your team or do they expect you to solve world hunger without really saying it? Remember, you touch every facet of the organization and so we come back to the topic of where does security report into; is it high enough on the totem pole to effect change? Don't fall for the rhetoric that 'a good leader will find a way to effect change no matter what level they report to. Let's be a bit more realistic about the world... that is true only to an extent.

Even if you have the luxury of reporting to the right level; a strong CFO, CEO or best, The Board; the organization may assume you will resolve every problem with a wave of your magic wand. You can very quickly become inundated with unrealistic expectations for everything and anything that resembles security, so be very careful of the cultural undertones. I've been lucky in that I haven't faced this condition, but I know a few others who have gone through it and it's not a fun place to be in.

More to the cultural danger, the decisions on the future of security will likely be in the hands of leaders who may not completely have the best interests of security, especially if you report more than two levels down in the hierarchy and your voice doesn't carry enough weight on organizational structure. You may be subject to a 're-evaluation' of areas of responsibility and structure because a department may feel security slows them down in the delivery of their services. This very quickly gets into a political battle where the service owner will say security assessments slow them down and it hurts the company's ability to deliver revenue-generating services.

I've seen scenarios where the security team has been championing the 'shift-left' philosophy for years. The leadership team embraces the idea of implementing security at the onset of concept to design but the engineering teams never get the memo. There's a disconnect between what the leader says and what is actually done on the engineering floor. So, the security team compensates for this and builds architecture teams to make up for design misses using brute force methods, but they inevitably dig their own grave because now the engineering team can pass the buck to the security architects saying they are slowing down the development or implementation process. Finger pointing ensues and leadership steps in to resolve the bottleneck, and what happens, the security team comes under fire when in reality, the root of it is that engineering never integrated security by design effectively and we run into failures and critical vulnerabilities downstream that need to be remediated to prevent negative consequences. To be balanced, I have also seen cases where it is the security team's ineffectiveness rather than engineering and security is at the heart of the problem, so be watchful of that case. My hope and recommendation is in both cases, champion incremental improvement rather than big bang changes that result in other problems that cannot be accounted for.

Know who you are working with and understand the nature of how software is designed, technology is deployed and products are manufactured and how integrated security truly is in the lifecycle and if they truly are implemented in design or something that happens after the fact (bolted on). In some cases, this will surface as a 'security bottleneck' that those departments will then lobby to take over security from a central function because the central function is too slow and the security work needs to be closer to the service. Folks, maybe this is true in some cases, but other times this can be a power play to control security in a way that will most likely make security a very distant secondary consideration because it now reports into the very department it is supposed to audit. I've said it before and I'll say it again, security should be an autonomous entity outside of the units it ensures are adhering to security best practices. Ideally, it should report to The Board, but this is not a common practice. The CFO is a good place if not the CEO, but you need to have a good sense of politics as much as personalities and see beyond what is said on the surface. Your success frankly, depends on it. I've known many people who were good CISOs get stifled because they run into similar conditions where they start spending more of their time dealing with justification rather than maturing security. I've also known strong security leaders who worked within the business units who lost their jobs because they identified a significant weakness and when they raised it, they were perceived as blockers within that organization and were eventually relieved of their duties. Keep security separate to allow the team to do the job they were hired to do.

Lastly, I think we can solve world hunger. I believe we can do the impossible given the right circumstances. I've been the beneficiary of being in pretty good conditions because I watch for these red flags and take actions to remove myself from situations that are less about security and more about bureaucracy, posture, and position. However, what I call bureaucracy, you might call normal business; it's really a personal view, perception, tolerance. Good luck!

1.4 THE INSTITUTIONALIZED 'EXPERTS'

At some point all of us have to make room for the next generation of emerging leaders. I gotta say...just retire and move on. Serve as a consultant or something but stop running organizations because emerging generations have completely different views of how the work environment should be, what normal and positive behaviors are comprised of, and frankly what the cultural shift should look like. I left a job because the organization was suffocating due to an 'old guard' who couldn't give up power and were this overbearing group that should have retired more than a decade prior.

All of us get phased out at some point, that is the nature of life. Our beliefs, our philosophies, our values at some point become outdated. Be careful of thinking that just because someone has been around for 50+ years in the industry that they are the source of truth regarding everything. They certainly have a place as a consultant and their experience is always going to be valuable, but be weary of a company who is run by a coalition of 50+years because some of their thoughts around how organizations should behave can be outdated, impacting team morale. You can quickly find your voice becomes silenced because the old guard's inner circle is the only respected source of ideas. If you find yourself in this type of environment, leave.

Institutional experts can get full of themselves and caught up in hearing themselves talk. One Board member from a prior company than the one I am now (as I write this book), carried a potent level of prejudice that 'she' probably wasn't aware of to begin with. She happened to be involved with the institution that is supposed to promote peace and unity around the world and across nations (won't name it but you can figure it out) and felt that affiliation made her something special. She would talk about 'pedigree' and if you weren't a 'Princeton man' or a 'Yale man' (her words, not mine), you really didn't have much value to her. She loved to hear herself talk and prove to herself she was really smart (which was subject). Well I was a State University of New York at Buffalo man so clearly I didn't fit the mold.

Now she was a Board member, and with 50+ years of experience. I was fine with her in that role because Board members serve as advisors to the company, and that is the best place to tap into long tenured industry professionals. The problem was that the management team was also comprised of 50+ years and these conditions stifled the promotion of critical and active thinking because of the authoritative and hierarchical structure that dominated the culture of that organization. Needless to say I didn't stick around and moved on to a progressive organization that was run by a leadership team that promoted a constructive culture and wanted to do the right thing. They could relate to the younger generations and were in synch with emerging industry and cultural trends facing companies.

I share this because you might think you're going in to do a job in security, but make sure the conditions are conducive to make you successful. You have a big role, and a huge surface to protect; make sure the environment allows you to do your job. When assessing an opportunity, profile the leadership and watch for these red flags. You are interviewing them as much as they are interviewing you, so know your worth and set yourself up for success.

1.5 THE UPSIDE-DOWN REPORTING MODEL

I briefly touched on this earlier but let's delve deeper into who should report to whom? That's fundamentally the question being asked here. There are several different models out there and the truth is, it is heavily dependent on the leadership styles, personalities, experience and culture at your organization. I've been lucky enough to have jobs where the culture was constructive and the leadership team genuinely wanted to support security. CISO's can find themselves in a few different reporting structures: reporting to the CIO, reporting to the CFO, the CEO and maybe in some rare situations reporting to a Board subcommittee on security. The one I've seen more often than not is reporting to the CIO. From a hierarchy perspective, you want to be as close to the CEO as possible so as to eliminate layers of reporting.

If the CIO reports directly to the CEO… that's cool. If the CIO reports to a CFO who then reports to the CEO; that can work provided you have an IT organization that has strong credibility and is not in the cycle of cost cutting because top leadership see IT predominantly as a cost center that needs to be trimmed. This can very quickly undermine the security objectives of the organization, because security then gets dragged into the cost cutting exercise as opposed to treating it separately and with a different lens than traditional IT. You'll find that this scenario plays itself out pretty frequently; IT organizations are in transition with the advent of cloud.

Historically, IT owned application development, support, and general administration. Organizations relied on IT to deliver not just commodity services like networking, voice, endpoints, and peripherals, but they also relied on IT to manage and maintain applications. Well, with cloud, you have Software as a Service, Platform as a Service; you have a la carte models and accessibility to applications has become simpler for users to access. Users now have the ability to shop for solutions and sign up for cloud-based services without the need for a traditional in-house IT service team. Development has migrated to the hands of internal teams as well. Because access to applications is readily available, cloud services allow for teams to stand up software development in the business units, which means they no longer need IT for those purposes. The end result of all of this, the value proposition of IT has been eroded over the past decade, and unless you have a strong CIO with strong relationships and credibility who evangelizes value creation and problem solving as the fundamental success criteria of the IT organization, you will find IT being viewed more and more as a utility that needs to be optimized from a cost perspective.

If you are a CISO or are considering a position, make sure you understand very clearly what the reporting structure is and second, make sure you assess the personalities, strength of leadership and culture of the organization, especially if you are 2 or 3 reporting levels away from the CEO. This makes a big impact on administration because CISO's have a large responsibility for reporting, and if you have to go through 3 organization levels every time you need to present to the Board (as one example), it becomes taxing. Second, the more levels means the more possible dilution of your intended message. Each level may edit the messaging based on their vantage point and by the time it gets out of the review cycle, the message can end up far from what you intended. This can undermine your responsibility as a CISO because too many hands have touched the message. Lastly there's the matter of influence. If you are 3 or 4 layers deep, it means you have an uphill battle in championing security across the organization. You as the CISO are accountable for the organizations security but now you have 2 or 3 layers across the organization above you that you need to influence in HR, Legal, Communications, Finance, and all the business units. Your challenge is larger because your hierarchical position is misaligned with the responsibility. Just make sure you set yourself up for success.

So with all that said, I'm going to make a bold statement that the CIO should report to the CISO. From personal experience, I have seen that when this happens, IT is not stifled in any way but makes traditional IT teams conscious of security in everything they do while they carry out their functions in technology. The reverse, where the CISO reports to the CIO is a scenario where there's one team in technology that is security focused and the rest have to be told constantly to apply good security practices. They will always tell you they do and will but when push comes to shove, the first thing that goes is security when tough decisions on cost or architecture or something else has to be made.

When the CIO reports to the CISO, all technology teams under that banner will actively pursue secure solutions, organically. The language of security will not be rhetorical, but rather part of the culture and DNA of the team. I have been in roles where I reported to a CIO, and in ones where I ran security and IT. I can tell you the latter was an interesting case study; I found that every team became super focused on confidentiality, integrity and availability (CIA) and it worked! In my opinion, this is the best model going forward because frankly, the demands placed by companies on the CISO are larger than IT (in many cases), and having this structure empowers the CISO but also gives more credibility to the technology team because while IT teams are losing their value for all the reasons noted earlier, security teams are gaining value due to the ever-growing problem they solve. By tying IT to security and making security the primary, you are reasserting a new value proposition that can help IT grow its credibility and take it out of the cost cutting conversation.

Some of the best models would be the CIO reporting to the CISO who reports directly to the CEO. An alternative would be less frequent but if the CISO was appointed by the Board, then there may be a reporting line to the Security Subcommittee or equivalent Board Committee rather than the CEO but I haven't run across this myself. A third model would be if you have a strong CFO then CEO to CFO to CISO who runs IT as well. Since the CFO is a highly influential leader in organizations, this can work, provided again that you have a strong CFO who empowers security.

1.6 CSO OR CISO?

How many 'C' acronyms can you come up with? So far we've used CEO, CFO, CIO, CISO, and even CIA (no, not the Intelligence Agency). There's CHRO (Human Resources), CPO (Procurement or Product or People Officer), there's

CLO (Legal), CMO (Marketing), CTO (Technology), CDO (Diversity), CPP (People Pleaser...okay I made this one up), I've seen Chief Evangelist, CPA (Certified Public Accountant which has nothing to do with the rest but it's still a 'C' acronym). One I have had in my team is CPSO (Product Security Officer). I think there are as many as you can make up in your head, but for our purposes, let's throw one more into the mix: Chief Security Officer (CSO).

So the question is, if you had a choice, would you accept the role of CSO? I believe this is a preference question more than anything but I'd argue that if given the choice, you should opt for CSO. My personal opinion is that we as security professionals should have a holistic view across all dimensions of security. Physical security uses the same language and many concepts as information security but apply them to physical as opposed to logical controls. Today I was reading the security news of the day and there was an article speaking of bad actors infiltrating companies as employees to steal intellectual property. The forensics for something like this starts with background screening, onboarding, assignment of access rights. It can include camera surveillance, badging in and out, access to systems and information, and behavioral analysis. If you notice, this basic list of things we may look at crosses physical and information. Being able to correlate events across the entire ecosystem allows for a more comprehensive assessment, allowing our teams a higher probability for identifying attacks that can start with a physical breach and lead to data theft.

The opportunity may not present itself in your respective company, but if it does, I would seriously consider consolidating all security under one banner that typically sits under the CSO title. Alternatively, if the opportunity does not exist, then you will need to establish strong relationships with the physical security team so that you share information and some business practices together and maybe even collaborate on using the same correlation engine to capture feeds from their systems (like badging) that can give both teams a stronger ability to identify anomalies and act accordingly.

An example of the close collaboration may be in the investigation of an employee who is reported by their manager as acting suspiciously by accessing secure locations at odd hours of the day and systems they do not have a need to access for their job. This may start as a report to Human Resources who may quickly contact physical security to capture data points on their work hours over the course of a period of time. They may also conduct a check on their employment history at the company to understand how long they have been there, what functions they have performed and if any other anomalies have been reported. At some point, they can decide to pull the infosec team in to see if they can identify folders and files that were accessed and what level of sensitivity is tied to the data.

Working jointly, physical security may confiscate the employee's laptop and other devices so that they and information security can run forensics and determine if the data is on the device, and if there has been any other suspicious transfers from the device to external networks. Enough evidence from both security teams may drive HR and physical security to bring in law enforcement where the involved parties would jointly support any further investigations that can lead to termination of the employee, confiscation of assets, and everything else you would normally assume in this type of scenario.

For those of you who think I'm overly paranoid; I'm not. I have been involved in similar incidents and the continued emergence of nation-state espionage, and IP theft is resulting in more of these types of scenarios than you may think. I close with restating the argument that in my opinion, if you want to have a fast and comprehensive security practice, rolling physical, cyber, information product security under one banner is a good idea.

1.7 DON'T LET THEM FOOL YOU... EVERYONE HAS GAPS

You ever listen to the late great Bob Marley? One of his songs (Could You Be Loved) says:

Don't let them fool ya
Or even try to school ya! Oh, no!
We've got a mind of our own
So go to hell if what you're thinking is not right!...

Channel your inner Bob Marley when it comes to establishing benchmarks for security maturity. Avoid making assumptions that organizations that work in the security industry have it all figured out and are the pillars of perfection in the practice and application of security controls. Some will have you believe they are but the truth is far from it. Every organization has gaps...you better believe it, and some may be alarming when you dig deeper and realize the gaps may be larger than those you have in your own organization.

Side note, if you ever travel to the Caribbean, know that the locals, while they respect Bob Marley, are probably sick and tired of tourists constantly asking for Bob Marley songs. Imagine if day in and day out you have to play the same music to appease tourists who only associate Reggae, the Caribbean and the vibe to Bob Marley. Obviously they will accommodate you, because tourism is a big part of their economy and income but the locals are probably tired of every wide-eyed tourist asking about Bob Marley. That does not take away from the fact that he was an innovator and positive figure in driving social change...but I digress.

Okay, back to it; if you're taking on a role in security leadership, at some point someone will ask you how your practice compares to industry and benchmarks. You can use Gartner to collect some data points around benchmarks but what I'd recommend is at some point in the first year of being there; ideally sooner rather than later, to bring a third party to assess the existing security practice. It's a nonissue if the practice is new and developing; it is important to have an initial baseline against an industry accepted standard like NIST, so that you know where you're starting from. As a newbie, doing an initial assessment doesn't hurt you one bit, but it gives you the ammunition to argue for funding, and the reference point your organization will want as you begin the journey of developing the practice.

Ideally, you assess your practice every three years. Some might say two years but for me, I find that there are enough winds of change that less than three years may not be enough to weather some of the economic or organizational impacts that may limit investment funds, or ability to truly drive the needed changes to maturity. For my money, every three years is a good timeframe to do a third-party assessment. Again you can use any framework that you wish, but many at least in the United States will recognize NIST Cyber Security Framework (CSF) as a respectable basis for maturity.

Maturity is typically measured by a numerical rating from 1 to 5, 1 being no or limited practice in place and 5 being optimizing or something equivalent. When establishing an objective, I recommend that you assign realistic goals that are aligned with your Board and leaderships vision for security. Don't shoot for a 5 because even the best security practices will have a very hard time reaching optimization. If you find yourself in the 1s or 2s, set a target in the 2s or 3s, respectfully for the next cycle of assessment. Similarly if you're in the 3s, set something in the upper 3s or lower 4s (remember, as you get more mature, the ability to advance in maturity gets progressively harder). You will continuously be working to improve your practice, but for what you need to accomplish and the management of risk, you may focus most of your career, if you happen to stay in that job for a long duration, working to a 4 rating and that is likely good enough for what is needed. Whatever your starting point, assign realistic and achievable goals.

1.8 THE UNWINNABLE WAR

The pursuit of maturing your security practice is something that must be done in a systematic fashion. Assess where you are against best practices (take that with a grain of salt), identify an incremental improvement plan based on where you are and recognize that as you get more mature the maturity curve flattens because it gets harder and harder to drive to optimization, and just be aware of that. By establishing a maturity model and measuring your progression; by instituting sound security controls, from basic security hygiene to more sophisticated controls in behavioral analytics, data protection schemas and the like, you will reduce the probability that your company will be marked as a target.

The last point is an important one; there are so many easy targets out there that the bad actors will probe and determine viability and then move on to something that won't require as much effort to infiltrate. Unfortunately for companies, there are ample opportunities out there that with basic attack vectors, a bad actor can infiltrate with relative ease. It's analogous to the story about the two gazelles or whatever animal you choose. A lion is chasing them and one tells the other that he doesn't have to be faster than the lion, he just needs to be faster than the other gazelle. Okay, so I probably screwed the whole analogy up but you get the point. It is actually kind of true here; the bad people are looking for the weak or wounded and won't worry about the one that has decent controls in place unless there is a specific target tied only to that company. So, do what you need in order to strengthen your practice but you don't have to achieve perfection because there's no such thing.

The sad reality is that my messed-up gazelle story is unfortunately the reality of what we are dealing with. The problem security professionals face is growing faster than we can resolve. It's the whac-a-mole problem only the number of holes are getting more and bigger. Think of it this way, the bad actors can do whatever they want without anyone telling them they can't. They have no privacy restrictions, no regulatory controls, no mandatory reporting, no organizational hierarchy (although they are becoming more institutionalized) to decide if their attacks will be funded or not; there's nothing stopping them. You on the other hand will answer to a whole bunch of people and institutions from government to special interest to your own organization. You will build an investment plan, develop a budget request, submit to your boss who probably has multiple other investment plans s/he has to assess and then pass it on to the next level. As more eyes fall on your plan, the level of understanding diminishes until someone other than you, who isn't in security and does not appreciate the problem at large, will determine the pennies you'll get to protect the company.

I have been pretty successful in getting funding in the past because I've been fortunate to have solid leadership above me and our effort to evangelize the need for security investment has been successful. However, I know in many companies the understanding of the problem falls short. Let's say you are the beneficiary, as I have been, to have leadership and Boards that appreciate the problem statement, you still have the overwhelming odds against you where you will always move slower than the attackers. You adhere to GDPR, you adhere to product security controls like the Cyber Resiliency Act, and the California privacy act, and all sorts of others that are emerging. You have to beef up a compliance function just to keep track of all the different regulations and in the United States, all the data privacy controls popping up from State to State.

Let's say you get past this and are really good at building efficient teams and you size them just right. What about the emerging technologies that are making it pathetically easy to attack companies? Let's just talk about what is coming in the next 5 to 10 years; the world of quantum computing. Encryption is a fundamental aspect to securing data both at rest and in transit. There are accepted encryption schemes that have been effective for decades. Well, with the speed of quantum computing, what would take hundreds of years to decrypt, will now take minutes. The data we try to protect will be accessible to anyone who wants it, which means we need to develop new protection schemes. If you don't buy this because quantum computing is still emerging, how about the world of artificial intelligence and neural networks? Just go to any social media platform and you'll see people posting fake (deep fake) videos of prominent figures in video skits and they look absolutely real. It's become pathetically easy for anyone to generate these deep fakes and how long before they become weaponized to trick people to take an action or pay a bill or send data that compromises a company?

We're only touching on very basic scenarios but if you spend time to think about the problem, it is expansive and getting bigger. This is an unwinnable war; the best we can do is establish sound proven solutions that address the top attack vectors. We employ layered security to follow the theme of defense in depth so that if one control is compromised there are others that deter further investment by the bad guys. We continue to invest in research and innovation, and send our architects out to conventions and seminars to learn about emerging attack vectors and tools to circumvent them so they can determine which ones are suited for our environments. We avoid the distraction of marketing, spam, the latest fads and proceed with laser focus to deploy and implement the most effective platforms, regardless of what is being sold as the elixir to save us all…there's no such thing.

Be the fastest gazelle, institute the most proven controls that can be applied across the largest attack surface, avoid falling for the latest craze, become good at evangelizing the importance of security, and be very aware of the biggest threat…your own people. Your people may not want to hurt the company, but their actions and their susceptibility to deception are the highest risk of all. The bad actors are now organized they are their own profit centers; call them organizations of the underbelly of society. However, they have a blank check to do what they want and how they want to without any regulations to slow them down (please don't think I am against regulations, they are there to protect our privacy and rights as consumers, but nevertheless, they slow down security).

1.9 FOREVER REDUCING RISKS

Do yourself a favor and invest heavily in the pursuit of automated practices as much as you can, to reduce risk. The name of the game is risk management. With everything that was said earlier, the question in someone's mind might be 'then how do you prioritize what to invest in if the threat is everywhere?' Very good question whomever asked that. It all comes back to risk. If you try to boil the ocean, well that won't work so while you are maturing your practice against a maturity model, you also make your investment a function of risk. The good news is the same standards bodies that you are using for a security framework are likely to also include a risk framework as well. NIST certainly does. You can use the NIST RMF (risk management framework) along with the NIST CSF (Cybersecurity Framework) hand-in-hand to help you in determining your prioritization of work.

If you want to get your Board of Directors (if you have one) or your top leadership to support your recommendations, you really should talk about organizational risk, making sure you clearly articulate in laymen's terms, how it will affect the company and frankly their jobs (an unsaid part of the messaging) if the company ignores the associated risks. If you go in with a balanced view of how to address this, highlighting the need to tackle critical and high risks first, they will appreciate your sensibility and be more apt to trust your judgment as opposed it if you go in and try to again, paint the sky green (I didn't want to use the boil ocean analogy twice in one section).

Risks come in all forms that fall under three general categories: people, process, and technology. Your people tend to be the hardest one to crack because they are unpredictable. They are susceptible to phishing, smishing and all the other 'shings' out there. Process and technology are more systematic and easier to harden.

You can have risks tied to products, such as legacy products that don't have secure boot capabilities, or communication over unencrypted means, or something else. You can have risks tied to cloud services such as employing devops deployment practices that don't integrate security as part of the development process (i.e. devsecops). You have the age old 'bolt-on' issue versus 'built-in' where security is part of the initiation, and architecture designs from the get-go as opposed to something that is added after the product or software has already been manufactured or deployed. You have vulnerabilities that drive risk in systems, operating systems, databases, and products that generate risks. You also have the merger of physical and information from nation-state compromises that are targeting data theft and intellectual property. The point is, everything security is related to risk management.

As soon as you begin building a risk management practice, you realize trying to mitigate becomes a never-ending task, especially when it comes to system patching. The problem exists in perpetuity, so again do yourself a favor and invest in as much system-based patching, system-based risk reduction and automation as you possibly can. There is such a thing as patch fatigue, where those who are responsible for patching eventually become numb to it because it never stops and they get burned out. Get it out of the hands of humans and systematize it.

Address issues tied to patching, vulnerability management, and end-of-life for systems, OS' and databases. Work closely with the technology owners to establish scripted practices, or introduce toolsets to address on-prem and cloud-based risk reduction capabilities. Work with physical security to establish correlation solutions across the two domains so that you can identify behavioral anomalies quickly so you can drive containment faster.

The most important thing to get out of this is that you as a CISO need to speak risk-talk to the organization and establish a strong assessment practice and reporting schema to that end.

System risk reduction almost always comes back to patching. Products may have to address certain designs and missing security elements but databases, operating systems, and computer are almost always tied to patch management. System-owners will love you for reminding them constantly that they need to patch. They get really excited to hear from their managers that one of your reports out to the leadership or Board pointed to a slowdown in patching in their area because they really want that recognition and spotlight to shine brightly on them. Boy, this is one of the highlights of any system owner, not for the day or week, but in their careers!

To have an opportunity to mimic a hamster on a wheel where you are constantly running but get nowhere; that is the pinnacle of success and the objective of any IT guy or gal. But, unfortunately from a security perspective, it many times means relying on human beings to do the work. It also means there's human error and prioritization that you have to contend with, that can get in the way of the patching effort. There are ways to automate some of this, whether it's in the cloud or on-premise that you should definitely invest some serious cycles towards instituting to take the human element out of the equation as much as possible. There are tools emerging all the time that can aide you and your techie friends (I use that term loosely when it comes to patching) to take the routine of identify, schedule, test and patch, and convert it to a scheduled process.

Patching in of itself is applied to endpoints like laptops, PCs, and mobile devices. It applies to servers, operating systems, and databases. It also applies to products. The latter can be a much more difficult effort then all of the others combined. The reason for this is that products have a wide variety of scenarios that you have to contend with, and a certain focus that is different than all the rest.

The products you manufacture or the software you sell (more so the former) may already be packaged up and sitting on shelves in distribution centers owned by your channel partners. Those running through the production cycle may have already gone through the manufacturing process, only to find out through some late testing (bug bounty, vulnerability assessment, or other) that there is a flaw in the design or software being used that needs to be addressed. This may be easy or virtually impossible, depending on the nature of the product and the work to be done to remedy the issue. Then there is the time function of product delivery; there may be a launch date you can't, as a business miss, but something is uncovered late in the process that puts that in jeopardy. This almost always leads to a negotiation with the product engineering and development teams that again, is not as simple as system-based patching.

Get past all of this, and you still may be dealing with an embedded base of legacy products that are generating revenue and the company doesn't want to touch because they are money makers. Security knows they have vulnerabilities, whether in the product itself or the way it processes data (legacy cloud environments as an example) but because the level of effort and cost to address the issues may be more than the company wants to invest, you can find yourself tough out of luck. The topic of product security is touched on some here, but is large enough where it should be addressed as a topic onto itself.

There are general themes that you always need to pursue: security by design, and shift-left as key principles that essentially say security should be part of the integrated design and the further left you do this (in concept and architecture), the easier it will be to ensure a secure product or software is delivered to your consumer base. What you typically find in manufacturing especially, is that the number of legacy product lines with vulnerabilities is pretty large and the task to reduce them can be monumental for many of the reasons noted above (level of effort, cost to remediate, etc.), so you as a company end up having to put in mitigating controls to ensure you manage your legacy platforms as best you can. The future reality will be though, that governments will not allow this to continue and you're better off dealing with it sooner rather than later, when regulations like the Cyber Resiliency Act (CRA) or Radio Equipment Directive (RED) in the EU or many of the other emerging product regulations force you to do it, and you find yourself having to address an overwhelming issue at a time where you might not be ready to.

1.10 SO WHY FIGHT AN UNWINNABLE WAR?

For the thrill of the chase, for the challenge of insurmountable odds, for the excitement...Need to pay the bills, job security...kind of. Because Sylvester Stallone, or Rocky Balboa gave that awesome inspirational speak about how [it's not how hard you punch but how hard a punch you can take and keep moving forward, because nothing hits harder than life] ...or a security breach in our case. Whatever your motivation, there's something that drives us to enter the ring to battle the bad guys in security. 'Yo CISO...keep moving forward...'

This is a point of reflection and it's different for every individual, but let me share what I have experienced. I started working in 1999 and right away believed I'd probably be running the company I was working at, at that time because I looked around and everyone moved very slowly and they just didn't seem to have the capability or capacity that I, a cocky college grad, felt I had. My mind was sharp, my ambition as large as my delusional perception of my own raw talents, and I had the energy that frankly I didn't see in others. Well fast forward 10 years and when I looked back, nothing of what I had spent the first 10 years of my career survived. The networks I built, the equipment I supported and the work I thought was so important had been wiped out with something different.

This was a turning point for me when I realized, either you're okay with doing a job that in the grander scheme of things is meaningless but at least you get a paycheck, or you re-invent yourself and get into a space where what you do actually has a lasting effect. For me, I didn't and I still don't want to waste time doing something that has no survivability. It's not about legacy or ego, it's simply that if you're going to spend 30 to 40 years of your life working, at least have something that moves the needle even a hair.

Working in the field of information security, more commonly referred to as cybersecurity, is something that can set the example for how organizations can and should behave when it comes to protecting their assets. The entire field is emerging as we speak, between regulatory controls developing in flight, to defensive capabilities that are being proven as we speak to tackling the whole state-sanctioned cybercrime aspect of the field that has implications not only to the company, the employees and to the shareholders, but to the competitive advantage of your country that takes center stage in world politics. It sounds very grandiose, but it's true. I worked in the semiconductor industry and we knew the implications of IP theft; it meant invaluable designs for chips that drove the tech world to those that ran our fighter jets, nuclear submarines, or you name it, could be stolen that can impact national defense.

If you work in any manufacturing industry, the IP or data associated to the latest innovations could be lost in an instant if you don't have proper physical and logical controls in place. Just do some digging and it won't take long for you to uncover case studies of companies being compromised and finding a few years later, the same designs they invented being used by companies sponsored by other nations who were now manufacturing those same designs. What you do today in security has ripple effects in establishing baseline practices, developing critical skill sets, and setting defensive controls to protect the interests of nations, companies, and individuals who stand to lose in the face of the growing threat of cybercrime. For me, the ability to effect change in this climate is a worthwhile endeavor that I can look back and say it moved the needle, however so slightly.

1.11 YOUR VALUE PROPOSITION

Moving the needle gives me that drive to keep moving forward in the area of security. If done right, you can be the leader that makes security part of the value proposition of the organization. This is possible today more than ever before as consumers, regulators, and business customers all want to know that you are providing them products and services that protect their data and privacy and ensure no risk or harm can come to them as a result of what you're selling.

As technologists, our value is twofold: first, protect and secure the organization from the growing threats. Second, become part of the value proposition that drives growth and revenue. In the past, this was hard to do because security was sitting in a backstreet alley playing with indecipherable concepts that the rest of the organization hadn't a clue about. Today, security is in virtually everything we do, from the products we manufacture to the software we design. Consumers see security now as a mainstream topic to consider in their purchases or investment decisions because we are all under constant attack from those who want to steal everything we hold of value.

The world of security has become an integral part of the reputation of our companies to the attractiveness of our products, and the value offered by our software. As a public company, you will get rated on your security posture by third parties who sell this assessment that is in turn used to determine if you are a company that should be invested into or not. The stakes have never been higher and security today must become part of the value stream of any business.

There are so many areas where security can transform itself as an essential part of the company's offerings. If you manufacture products, embedded security to ensure encrypted and secure communications over Bluetooth or Wi-Fi is an example where the security team can help improve the product. If your products have compute elements, injecting secure boot and encrypted key storage is an example of something that can be marketed to demonstrate your commitment to security. Installing a secure software development life cycle (SSDLC) that offers strong authentication capabilities is something on the software side we can give consumers added security benefits.

On the regulatory side, certifications such as ISO or SOC give potential customers or investors a sense of commitment by the company's leadership to security as part of their culture. In fact, by having a certification, you not only give your teams the relief of less audits, but also promote a reputation that can be marketed for future business opportunities. Establishing strong perimeter security is not only important security hygiene but also ensures that when those third-party assessors probe your network to determine strength of controls, they come back with a positive rating that is then shared as part of your public profile.

Your sales and marketing teams can promote your company with many of these security capabilities when showcasing the company to perspective markets and customers. They can talk to the companies certifications, the external audit results of your maturity rating, the commitment to secure product and software development, and adherence to not only comply but to go beyond base regulatory requirements to do right by consumers. Never before have we been able to affect the health of our firms in ways that help us see a direct impact of our actions to the bottom line.

Once you've established the base practices that we work through in the subsequent chapters, see how you can embed yourself into the functional areas of the business to promote security as an offering. It all starts with determining the maturity model you will use as your foundation, building the team that meets the needs of your company, instituting sound execution practices and discipline in delivery of capabilities, capturing the needs of the business leaders and prioritizing them in your pipeline of capabilities development, assessing a baseline maturity level with a third party audit every three years, and putting a huge emphasis on communication and evangelization of security across the company and the Board to name a few areas of focus.

Lastly, you can support your company's community outreach initiatives by volunteering to help small businesses or consumers with education around strong security hygiene and support instituting critical controls that will help them reduce their risk in the most impactful ways. You can support senior citizens with education on what to watch out for in cyber scams so they don't fall victim to theft. There's an entire area of community service that you can support that can make a significant difference in the lives of so many people in ways you may not realize is possible. When I say that security as a profession helps you make a difference and move the needle, it truly is a reality so long as you are willing to see beyond the tactical day-to-day work and see the possibilities to do good for your company and the community.

1.12 IN ALL SERIOUSNESS...PROTECT YOURSELF

Lastly for this chapter, let's spend a little time on how you should protect yourself from becoming the focal point of an investigation that can lead to termination or worse. The starting point is the package you get from your new employer, or for negotiations during a promotion that puts you in charge of the security organization. Ask for a severance package that will give you income protection in the event the company decides to part ways with you. Severance will pay you your income for a negotiated period of time. The minimum, in my opinion, is nine months minimum of pay to allow you the time to find new employment. Obviously the more the better and many times the company has a severance policy they try to hold to, but if you can get twelve months or more then call it a win.

The next big thing to ensure you receive is Directors & Officers liability insurance (D&O Insurance). This is vital for a position like a CISO who may face personal loss as a result of the position they hold. D&O is provided to executives who have liability and are not protected by the corporate veil. These are individuals who can be sued directly as a result of events impacting the company. Make sure you don't take charge of an operation without this coverage.

Moving away from benefits, we need to address your philosophy around security. The simplest way to ensure you don't get in trouble is to follow the rule of law to the tee. Every action, every response, and every operational decision should be strictly made to abide the rules we as security professionals are held accountable for. This means, you need a very strong compliance and governance function in your organization who stays on top of existing and new regulatory requirements, translates them into actionable registries and drives your organization to comply with them, globally. This governance team should also own the development of a robust risk management practice (you can use something like NIST RMF or Risk Management Framework as a starting point). By staying up with regulations and actively managing a strong risk practice that logs decisions, risks, mitigations, and timing, you can help protect your organization and yourself from missed responsibilities.

RMF is one aspect of documentation. Document everything; every decision, every mitigation, every date committed. Here's where you may run into a bit of divergence with legal, depending on how your company views this practice. Remember, as soon as you recognize a risk that is documented, that becomes an auditable artifact that if later is tied to an incident, the auditors can point and say you knew about the weakness and did nothing about it. Now the way to get around it, is to document thoroughly the decision on what to do and the reasoning behind it, such as the organization prioritized other more pressing risks over this and assigned a sequence. This at least speaks to a conscious business decision that can bridge the incident to a logical decision that can be understood.

Another aspect of documentation and logging decisions that drive risk is that many times the final decision to resolve certain risks rests in the hands of the business units. They need to balance revenue-generating activities against security risks. As a business leader, we need to acknowledge that our jobs don't exist if the company isn't making money. We can't suffocate the organization in the name of security but find an acceptable balance. In times when a security risk is accepted, we document the risk and the decision and come back to it the next risk review session.

Above all, when working with your colleagues, executive team, and Board, be transparent and speak plainly. If there's something wrong, raise it in an appropriate manner. The fastest way to gain trust across all these internal stakeholders is to be viewed as someone who speaks the truth regarding the good and the bad but then takes action to remedy the bad stuff in the fastest manner possible. The worst thing to do is avoid a difficult topic because...well... it's difficult and find yourself in a mess later because you sat on it. Raise the topic appropriately, have a conversation across the organization and lead the effort towards a decision that can be driven to execution. This is why you are in the position you are, because you are willing to tackle the hard stuff. Believe me, ignoring, avoiding or hoping it goes away may lead you into a bad spot.

Okay, let's talk about what will make your operation successful from the inside out. Clearly having the right talent and structure are vital; these for me are table stakes. Having good incident management and communication protocols will keep you out of trouble and ensure you get information to the right folks in a timely way. The element I have always spent considerable time developing is project and program oversight. Most if not all security teams are balancing a healthy portfolio of projects against operational activities. Security right now for most companies is in a state of driving maturity, which means, multiple projects running simultaneously. Some functions in the IT space will get to a state where they become dominant in operations and a small set of projects; security tends to have a large percentage of their work tied to projects.

This means, you need to invest into standing up strong project management hygiene, strong oversight, and reporting. You want to standardize the way you run projects, and get your team to a point where all of them, to some limited capacity, can run small to mid-sized projects. Depending on how your organization is structured, you want to have a couple of strong program managers on-hand to run the large initiatives that require committed resources, but you lean on your security team to handle the smaller efforts. Some won't like this approach and will say you should focus operational folks on operations and not require them to run projects… they didn't sign up for that. Well, I agree to an extent. When I worked in traditional IT, this was definitely the case, but in security I go back to my statement earlier that most of security is driving new capabilities and project-based. This means that in my opinion again you can have your own viewpoint, since security deals so much with project-based work that they need to be comfortable running projects along with the rest of the job they are hired to do. Make it part of the job description so you hire folks that understand they will be running small/mid-sized projects.

Look, I'm going to say something because it's a real thing in some cases. In no way am I saying you should expect this to be the case but just be watchful. You will be in a unique roll that can have a major impact on the organization. You will tough every fact of the organization's operation making you a unique figure in the company; very few functions tough every aspect of the business. If you don't belong to an organization that has a strong supporting culture where everyone stands behind each other in tough times, you could find yourself as a scapegoat when things get tough.

I hate to say it, but I've witnessed time and time again how self-preservation becomes a very strong driver for people. How many times have you heard people complain with passion how things are not right or the need for change but when given the opportunity to voice it, they disappear or their rhetoric changes completely? This is the nature of most people, so don't bet on your colleagues standing next to you when things get tough. If you're lucky, you are surrounded by folks with integrity and character who will; if you find that… stay as long as you can because in my sinical perspective, it's rare. The best you can do is expect the worst and hope for the best. People will surprise you from time to time but don't let faith in people sway your judgement and always have your eyes open because the only person who will have your best interest at heart is you.

Chapter 2

Starting points

There are several starting points for security leadership and each of them come with their own benefits and challenges. You can be in a team and through attrition and promotion, you might find yourself earning the role of leader in security. Still another variant might be that you are in the organization working in a different capacity and are asked to take on the security leadership role for various reasons, one of which might be due to your success record and the need to turnaround a challenged security operation. There's the scenario where you are recruited for the role and you inherit an existing operation and one last one we will mention here is recruitment for a startup where the entire technology operation is new.

If we tried to dissect every scenario we would find out that there are more than what is mentioned here and it would result in diminishing returns because many of the considerations converge in a synergistic way. Our primary focus is the scenario where you are new and we speak a bit about both the startup and the inheritance scenarios together. What you'll find is in this chapter there is a palpable difference but as you read on in Chapter 3 and beyond, they really converge into one and the same; you may just have to prioritize some things in a different way. Like any respectable technology community, we need to use special terms for simple concepts to demonstrate our immense sophistication so we will refer to the two conditions as greenfield and brownfield opportunities.

2.1 GREENFIELD VERSUS BROWNFIELD

Greenfield represents something completely new. It's the condition tied to startups where the entire technology team is being stood up from scratch. On the surface, this can be as simple as the company was just formed, but the underlying themes might be tied to innovation or customization. We can postulate that there may be a case where a company wants to inject a new way of thinking and new designs to an already existing operation for the sake of eliminating old and outdated practices with state-of-the-art thinking

DOI: 10.1201/9781003616528-2

and solutions. Maybe there stands an existing poisonous environment that is thought of as hopeless to salvage and the company wants to start from scratch. Maybe the company is moving in a different direction in its business model that requires a new way of thinking and leadership; whatever it is, don't assume greenfield only means startup. Greenfield can mean a rebirth for all sorts of reasons.

In general greenfield can be less complex than brownfield because there's no baggage to carry with you along the way. Now, I'll say that in my career I have been fortunate to inherit highly capable teams that needed a new direction and structure but the foundation was more than solid. In some other cases, you might have personnel concerns and legacy systems that you have to work around that can complicate things in brownfield. Greenfield is a blank tablet with low risk in compatibility matters related to the technology stack. The challenge will be that you'll sometimes find yourself serving roles that you didn't account for, such as working exclusively as a recruiter for a period of time; that's going to be your job until you reach a point where you have a skeleton crew to start asserting an operational practice. You may move from recruiter to trainer and those roles may be the bulk of what you do while trying to address the pressures by the organization to move fast.

Brownfield on the other hand has some exact opposite characteristics. There's less flexibility as you will need to work within an existing set of systems that you may or may not want. This can be good and bad; the good would be that implementation of key changes can be faster since a foundation already exists to build on. The cost of change can be less because of the same reason that a foundation already exists, but you may be limited in driving disruptive changes because of the legacy system constraint. Unless we are working in a startup or some unique situation, we usually find ourselves in some form of a brownfield situation. If we were to summarize the characteristics and compare them, they would look like Table 2.1.

Table 2.1 Comparison of greenfield vs brownfield

Characteristic	*Greenfield*	*Brownfield*
Freedom to Act	Higher	Lower
Cost of Change	Higher	Lower
Change Ready (less barriers)	Higher	Lower
Risk of Disruption (to security operations)	Higher	Lower
Capability Performance	Unproven	Proven
Time to Operational Readiness	Longer	Shorter
Overall Efficiency	Higher	Lower
Adaptability to Future Trends	Higher	Lower
Organizational Resistance to Change	Higher	Lower

Table 2.1 demonstrates that each scenario has its strengths and weaknesses. Ultimately you don't really have a choice other than when you're deciding to accept a job on which scenario applies. What's more important here is to understand the conditions you will face so as you take your first steps that you recognize where you need to be super conscious of potential pitfalls in one or the other. I've worked in both scenarios and my personal experience is that greenfield is a lot more demanding because everything is under time pressure, sometimes extreme ones. The stress of a startup or any greenfield scenario is significantly higher because you start with minimal resources and have to grow your capabilities from nothing into something. Alternatively, when inheriting a team, depending on the conditions, you may simply be replacing someone who retired or taking on a role where your predecessor wasn't the right fit. No matter what the circumstances, you normally find some really good aspects of the old operation that you can rebrand into the vision you set for the future. The predominant conditions will be some variant of a brownfield scenario and we'll work through most (not all) of the content under this umbrella but you can easily translate everything we go through to greenfield with minor modifications.

2.2 PREP WORK BEFORE JOINING

So you're at the point where you've decided to take the job and now you're on deck to start. This is the best time for a new person to assess some key practices with the new company. Security has a part to play in the onboarding process so pay close attention to how paperwork is transmitted and received and how your information is captured and protected from a data privacy perspective. Do you log into a portal to fill out all the necessary forms in a secure way or are forms emailed to you to fill out and you're asked to send them back to Human Resources? If by email, are you expected to submit by email things like social security numbers, and other personal information or by fax, or by password protection?

The protection of personal data is a part of your responsibility and there's no better time than to learn real-time, how that is administered by your new employer. The onboarding process typically includes a hardware and software request and you should pay attention to how this is managed and whether there are standard-issued hardware and software or if there is a lot of opportunity to customize. How are your login credentials conveyed to you? Is it done in a secure fashion and are the initial login credentials abiding by strong standards for password criteria? You are likely joining as a prominent figure in the organization; do they treat you as a VIP and loosen the criteria for system access and assign automatic administrator rights or do they strictly adhere to security best practices? Try to login before your start date; are you able to get in or do they have your account deactivated until you are officially onboarded? Pay attention to the details so that when the right time comes, you have things to share in a way that improves the onboarding process.

Along the way, ask for information about the team, organizational chart, and any strategic documentation the organization has. Ideally they politely tell you 'sorry but you'll have to review these once onboarded'. You might have signed non-disclosure terms so you might be covered there but there's the matter of sending company confidential information to personal email accounts as well. This will tell you how disciplined in data protection the company is, or if there is room for improvement. The operation you are joining is still a black box so the more signals you can get on the health of the practice upfront, the better but be careful about calling out the team on your observations right away because as we'll talk later, there's a lot of anxiety tied to you joining that you don't, in my opinion, want to exacerbate further.

My recommendation is to read up on the profiles of the organizational leadership and any material you can find about the company, its core business and the team. You can learn a lot from the website such as leader profiles, company values, company performance, and products and services. You can also learn a lot about the people you'll be working with through professional social media sites like LinkedIn. The more you know about the people you'll be working with, the better your mindset will be established as you join the company, and the next several sections will go into the plan you want to formalize to get yourself moving swiftly and efficiently from day 1.

2.3 30-DAY PLAN

As a new security leader, you want to take certain actions right away to assert yourself in the company. The theme for the first 30 days is to listen and learn. The worst leaders are those who show up on the job and immediately have an opinion. Look, you may be a prodigy of some sort but if you show up and start making changes or lecturing on how things should be, maybe we need to downgrade your perception of yourself. I'm sorry but that's just the worst thing someone can do and I've been on the receiving end of this scenario where someone comes in thinking they know better and rubbed all the existing folks who have spent time and energy developing a practice and going through the trials and tribulations tied to the company's growth, the wrong way. I actually found myself on the outside looking in once because I refused to feed a certain person's ego and just bend to their wishes and tell them how smart they were and how amazing. Let's just say that a couple of years later, that person didn't survive and was politely told to leave because that type of behavior comes with other baggage that eventually will bite them in the butt.

...But I digress, so let's get back on point. You have a few objectives as you join the company. First and foremost, meet the team as soon as you possibly can. They are going through different levels of anxiety and many of your direct reports are wondering if they will have a job in a few months. Let's be empathetic and get their minds at ease to the extent that it's warranted. Your boss will hopefully do an introduction to your direct reports and then you want to work with them right away to do a session with the full team so that they can see you and hear from you. This is the first step towards stabilizing their nerves and the operation. The longer you wait, the more chance you might even lose some good folks because when left to their own devices, people fill in the gaps in information with the worst possible scenarios. Put their minds at ease.

Your boss may give you some guidance on who you should speak to in the first few weeks to start building relationships. Setup quick meet and greets with those individuals, knowing that on the other side, some may be very interested in meeting you and some are doing it because they have to in order to be good citizens of the company. Let's face it, you're not the most important thing that's happened to them and they have their ongoing work to do so be considerate with their time and setup maybe fifteen-minute quick meets and in that time, get a sense of what their mindset is; are they ecstatic to meet you or are they running through the motions. Act accordingly. For those who are really excited and want to talk more, setup follow up meetings. For those who are not overly interested, circle back to them later as things settle and they have had some time to see you in action and start making connections between what you do and what they need. If you do your job right, they will come around but read the personalities in the room.

Meeting as many people as you can and starting that exercise in building relationships is an absolute must. Whether you're an introvert or extrovert doesn't matter. You need to make this a forcing function because it'll likely be these same people you're going to work with or need support. While you're doing this, setup standing staff meetings and checkpoints with your direct reports to establish a cadence for engagement. You can decide later the frequency of meeting but start with weekly meetings on both and then adjust as needed. This is as much for them as it is for you. In those meetings, you get to ask them more about themselves, and the team. You also need to learn more about key stakeholders you should add to your whirlwind tour to build relationships. During this phase of getting to know one another, you should look for the earliest opportunity to pull your direct reports and those identified by the team as key contributors outside of your direct staff to pull into an in-person strategy session.

Schedule that in-person within the first month of being on the job because it serves a few purposes:

1. In-person, face-to-face accelerates relationship building
2. Best way to profile your team and start understanding the teams composition

3. Get a deep dive into existing strategy and the administration of strategy planning
4. 'They' will gain tremendous value from interacting with you and getting back to 'normal'
5. You'll learn about strengths and weaknesses of the operation
6. You'll gain insights on who are champions, who are retractors to your cause in the organization

These are some of the benefits but there are certainly more to bringing them together right away. The important part to this is to listen more than you speak. In reality this strategic session is not so much to define strategy; if you get to some of that, that's great. The most important reason for bringing them together is to get intel on the team, operation, company and establish relationships. When I've done this, months later when the team gets more comfortable, they point to these session as an important step for them to move from a survival mindset to feeling safe again.

Understanding is the most important aspect of the first thirty days but balance it with capturing your team's input on SWOT: strengths, weaknesses, opportunities, and threats. As much as you want to make them comfortable and build relationships, you also want to assert credibility with your boss that you are fast acting and on point with what you're doing. It doesn't have to be fancy but I'd provide weekly updates to the boss if you don't have weekly checkpoints so that they know your approach and your key objectives for the first thirty days. While you're learning about the organization, you should be assessing the security posture of the organization and out of your strategic session, the team should come away with some key themes surrounding the security practice that can be focal points for the first 6 months.

A little bit about how you enter the strategic conversations. Identify individuals on your team that can help collect feedback from a few sources so that when you get together, you can review what is said about security. If you have access to the executives, get their input on what they see as opportunities and general sentiment. Collect feedback from your future peers that the team should know very well and have them share their thoughts. The most important input is from the team; send out a survey to the team on what they see as opportunities, risks, and investment-worthy efforts for the near and mid-term. In doing this, you are capturing feedback from the collective and it is multi-dimensional. Using this, you and the strategy team can spend time not listening to you but to the voice of the organization and the outcomes will be from the inside out.

By the time you're done, you want to reduce the inputs to a few general themes that drive your strategy going forward and key near-term focuses that you and your team commit to that can be shared with your boss. In that first thirty days, you want to share with your boss your findings and observations on the security posture, how you went about devising those concepts, and the outcomes you want to pursue in the next 6 months to 1 year. This positions you as a fast-acting leader who knows the value of feedback from all aspects of the company and someone who can formulate a plan with precision. What this also does is sets you up as the type of leader your team wants; someone who listens, who elicits their feedback and builds a vision of the future with their contributions being at the heart of that vision. As soon as you leave the strategy meetings, the rest of the team will be itching to hear what came out of it, so craft the message and share with your team in a town hall emphasizing that the near-term activities came from them and the organization and not from you, exclusively.

To summarize, the objectives of the first 30 days are to:

1. Stabilize the nerves of the team and begin developing strong relationships everywhere
2. Assess the current state of security and understand the elements reflected in a SWOT analysis
3. Elicit 360-degree feedback and formulate a near and mid-term strategy
4. Grow your credibility with your boss, stakeholders and your team by being fast acting but balanced in your approach to formulating strategies
5. Give the team a sense of the future and a vision of where you're headed
6. Establish the 'version 1' of a security strategy to get the team moving, knowing it will be refined considerably over time

2.4 60-DAY PLAN

One job I started three weeks before the Board of Directors meeting, and security was a topic on the agenda. I did everything noted in the 30-day plan and used the Board preparation as a catalyst to have deeper discussions with the team to understand what had been presented in the past, how and why content was presented in a specific way and to understand the concepts that were put in front of the Board in the past. We held our strategy meeting the week before the Board meetings so it was a rapid learning exercise for me but one that served the purpose of the first 30 days very well. It not only gave the team a focus for the first few weeks, it also gave me an opportunity to build immediate credibility with the company leadership and Board by coming in prepared and with preliminary observations and data points. The Board didn't expect me to have a formulated plan but by coming in with a view of things and a preliminary vision of what's to come gave them and the leadership team a level of comfort that they picked the right person. These conditions can be stressful but they can serve your purpose well if handled correctly; don't shy away from them.

All of that sets you up for the next 30 days of your planning. There are some themes that will be continually reinforced such as engagement of stakeholders, and developing credibility. You want to elicit feedback from the executive team on security and where you can help them in their efforts. You also want to begin organizing in the next thirty days the way your team will take the near-term objectives defined in the first thirty days and execute. Now you may have lucked out if your team already has an execution discipline and a practice around project oversight. That would be a bonus if there ever was one, but if it doesn't exist, you want to start planting the seeds that 'excellence in execution' is a theme of what you measure your team's success by. Start working with your team to assign and organize the key initiatives and track their progress in a way that will eventually emerge into a practice over time. Expect to see modifications of what will be delivered because you are targeting quick wins but more importantly an alignment of the team towards a common practice and vision that starts now but will take quite a while to get to a refined state.

You want to carry the same approach from the first thirty days, which is listen and learn but during these 30 days, you want to start converting your learning about policies, procedures, practices, and the capabilities of your team into observations and insights. In my opinion, it's still too early to start making changes with what's in place, but if you have identified gaps, you should feel comfortable to talk about the gaps and look internally to see if there's a way to fill those gaps or bring talent from the outside. It's not always a people problem but it's in the first few months that you will have more latitude to bring in talent without going through an intensive justification. During this time, you should take the preliminary results of your initial strategy session and start reinforcing the work of ownership and accountability. Start working with your team to determine what's the best way to track progress and who can lead the facilitation. Along the way, you want to take what you have learned and reconcile the learning with the business objectives so that you can connect what you are continually uncovering as business drivers to the work your team is doing wherever possible.

One thing you want to institute at this time is the establishment of Operational Support Services (OSS). This is called different things but the charter for this function is to do all the cross-domain work that is not part of the core competency of a security team such as financial management, portfolio and project facilitation, procurement coordination, and reporting and presentations to name a few. The development of this function will save you a lot of fires later that need putting out and will establish the business management capabilities of your operations. In fact, in some jobs I've held, this is also referred to as Technology Business Management (TBM).

Identify who is best suited to run OSS and this is a perfect opportunity to tap someone on the shoulder who has been itching to do more and grow their exposure and footprint in the company. I've used this in the past to ask highly capable individuals who have a strong work ethic and aptitude to learn and ask them to partner with me to develop this. The person you select will be someone you will work with closely and will need to be someone you can trust with sensitive information given the type of information they will be exposed to. Once identified, ask them to start organizing bi-weekly reviews of the assigned initiatives from the strategy session. This will get the team into a cadence and routine and also give other members of the team a chance to get exposed to you so they get more comfortable while also getting more exposure. I like to make these types of meetings open to anyone who wants to participate to promote transparency and minimize the typical complaints in teams that there's a disconnect between leadership and execution.

At this time, there hasn't been a conscious focus on mapping compliance requirements to security priorities and business objectives. We've worked on each of these loosely but as you move towards the latter part of this 30-day stint, start having conversations with your leaders around building the connective tissue between compliance, strategy, and business priorities. Some of you will say, Timur, why don't you do this from the beginning to avoid rework? My feeling is that the initial emphasis should be placed on relationships and getting to a new normal. Depending on when you join, you may be marching towards a normal strategy cadence soon enough and the importance upfront is to establish some baselines that can be refined later. However, there's no one way to approach this and ideally if you can get to a systematic approach to connect all of these then do it. I just have found that I don't know enough in the first 30 days to do this effectively, so we do some progressive elaboration as the project managers of the world might say. Ultimately, your objective should be a linkage that can be explicitly identified from organizational priorities all the way to individual goals and objectives.

During this phase, start getting a deeper understanding of the security operations aspect of the team, namely how is incident management handled, how are vulnerabilities addressed, what are the key capabilities in the organization. You're looking for some key things such as:

1. Do you have a security operations team (SOC)?
2. Do you have a published incident management procedure and is it practiced?
3. Do you have a third party that supplements your SOC and if so, whom?
4. How are you structured? Follow-the-sun or a central model?
5. What are the platforms you use and what is the connection between the SOC and IT incident management?
6. Is there a formal incident handling protocol with Legal?
7. Does the operations team run simulations, tabletops, or other scenario-based exercises to keep the team sharp?
8. How do you fit into the incident management protocol; what is the escalation scheme?

These are some of the questions you want to ask and address because I firmly believe that if you don't do operations well, the rest doesn't matter. What is the 'rest'? Architecture, compliance, infrastructure management, and so on. Table stakes are a functional operation, now later I'll talk about what I recommend you focus on if you're coming into a greenfield situation starting in Chapter 3 because it will show the general sequencing but you don't really have an effective security function until you stand up the elements associated with the SOC.

Some will say to start defining how you're going to measure your operation at this time, but I'll say to hold off for now and use what exists for the time being. Let's make sure the patterns we are starting to see stabilize before we put the effort into setting metrics and key performance indicators (KPIs). The work you did initially may change and as you learn more about the environment you have taken on, you might need to adjust priorities and investments, so give it a little more time before setting up measurements. Now there are things like reduction in vulnerabilities or operational metrics like mean time to detect (MTTD) and mean time to respond (MTTR) to incidents, number of major incidents that are universal and you should see if your SOC has these measures, but let's make this a formal exercise a few months in the future.

Speaking of metrics, the most important measure of success for security is how you handle risks and your ability to drive risk reduction. A good security organization associates everything with risk management. It isn't too early to see what your top risks are in the organization and topline vulnerabilities. You should start asking some fundamental questions like:

1. Do we have multifactor authentication (MFA) in place?
2. Depending on where we are, are we implementing Fast Identity Online (FIDO), which is a password-less authentication open standard that improves user experience while promoting stronger authentication
3. Are we providing secure remote access via virtual private networking (VPN)?
4. Do we have a strong single sign-on (SSO) implementation?
5. What kind of network topology do we have, and do we apply a healthy level of segmentation?
6. Are our Internet-facing systems and applications adequately secured?
7. Do we used hardened end point images with end point detection and response?
8. What is the architecture of our network points of entry; are we using firewalls at our ingress/egress points (this should be reflex, but imagine if you weren't)?
9. What kind of authentication scheme do we use and platform for identification (i.e. active directory)?

For me, these are basic concepts that should be in place if the team has already gone past the phase of infrastructure implementation (Functional First as referred to later), but you don't want to assume these are already in place. If you find that any of these are not in place, they would need to immediate be added to the short to mid-term initiatives to shore up baseline security practices. By the end of the 60 days, you should convert assumptions made in the first 30 into confirmed facts that adjust your strategic objectives. Just be careful how you assess and convey the message that there are gaps to the team. This is a time when members are hypersensitive and anything that is perceived as a critique will be extra potent in the impact on each individual. Here's where your emotional IQ comes into play; you will start earning their trust by how you message this and doing it in a way that shows you want to partner with them and give them a chance to make a difference rather than a perceived criticism of their ineptitude, which is never true in the first place if you have willing members who want to do the right thing. Let's make sure they never get that impression, period.

To summarize, the objectives of the second 30 days are to:

1. Reinforce what you learned in the first 30 days
2. Convert assumptions to confirmed facts
3. Double down on getting executive feedback and priorities
4. Install or identify your Operations Support Services team and leader
5. Institute and seed 'excellence in execution' through OSS and the initial strategy initiatives
6. Start probing on the connection between business objectives, compliance, and your teams goals
7. Deep dive into security operations and ensure baseline functions are in place; if they are not, add them to the initiatives you kickstarted
8. Identify how risks are managed and effectiveness of the risk management practice
9. Think about metrics and KPIs, but defer a full-blown exercise to assess and revamp until you normalize your understanding of the landscape
10. Continue to learn about the policies and procedures, including the maturity modeling of the security practice

2.5 90-DAY PLAN

By month three, you're getting a good feel about the operation and starting to know whom outside your team are key players and stakeholders. We already kicked off some initiatives and you want to continue to reinforce the importance and nurture a collaborative approach within your team. They are still uneasy and some get anxious when in the same meeting as you, so make sure the project reviews are positive and supportive. This is imperative as you want your team to feel comfortable sharing the good and the bad in a safe forum. This will take months to develop but you want to start this right away. This is the reason why I start the execution discipline as soon as I can because sometimes it takes quite a bit of time to foster a dynamic where everyone speaks freely and views discussions around their projects as positive as opposed to criticism.

This is probably the right time to dig deeper into your governance and compliance practice. Some things to look for are:

1. Is there an active risk management practice governed by this team?
2. Are risks captured in a governance, risk and compliance (GRC) tool or are they managed in spreadsheets?
3. Is there an ongoing security awareness program that includes phishing campaigns?
4. Do you have a security champions program and is it bottom up, top down, or both?
5. Revisit the standards that are used to drive your operation; do you use NIST, ISO, CMMI, CIS Controls, or something else?
6. What about product security? We don't talk about this much but what standards are used here, if any? Some might be ISO/IEC, NIST, or BSIMM
7. What is the documentation framework for policies, standards procedures, and guidelines?
8. What kind of reporting exists on compliance, risk, and maturity?

Along the way, you want to learn more about the forums that may exist to keep stakeholders informed. These may include a Quarterly leadership review with the CEO and his staff as an example. Does an Enterprise Security Council (ESC) or equivalent exist? The latter isn't required but may be worthwhile for some cultures. We will talk more about this later. The idea behind these questions, especially in the governance space is to determine how a security-conscious culture is nurtured and promoted, and if it isn't yet, how you can begin pushing things towards that end. Don't underestimate the value of training, phishing campaigns and security champions. The sad truth is that you can't be successful on your own, and you need everyone to have a basic understanding of security best practices. The weakest link is not your security team or the systems and controls, but the people in your organization. We need to invest heavily in developing awareness across the company.

A solid security champions program can expand your reach considerably across the organization. This program is very well suited in companies that do software and product development but can be very effective in any industry. The idea is to develop security advocates across the organization outside of the security organization who can then drive security-centric decision making. The program can be run by asking for volunteers or referrals who are interested in learning more about security and its application in their space. This would be a bottoms up approach but another way is to ask executive management to participate in the program so that you can drive a culture from the top down. Both are effective but the most effective would be implementing both models.

Apart from governance and compliance, you've had more time to assess gaps and have solidified an approach to grow personnel internally into new roles to fill those gaps or conduct external hiring if you don't have strong candidates you can develop from within. It's always important to look internally first and offer growth opportunities to the existing team. It shows an investment within and an interest to develop your staff. You do however want to strike a balance between old and new blood. There's an argument to be made that just enough introduction of external staff can reinvigorate an operation, but be careful not to develop a trusted circle of externals who leave the rest of the organization out of key decision making and favor. I've been in teams where a group of externals are hired, all coming from the same source and it wasn't a fun environment to be in.

During this last 30 days of the 90-day plan, you are already starting to think about the next cycle of Board meetings and you want to go in showing what has been achieved, and what you have learned since joining. This next Board session is usually where they will ask you what your opinion is of the organization and the security practice? They'll ask you what you have uncovered as the gaps that need to be corrected. This is your one opportunity to be viewed like an external consultant and really lobby for the right things that have a high probability of being approved. Your credibility is high and based on your newness to the organization. Going forward, this will wear off so take full advantage of it and learn as much as you can about the organization so you can give the Board a fair and transparent assessment that you follow up with a plan to improve. The good news is if you do everything mentioned, you would have already started that activity to improve.

Lastly, Start thinking about the next cycle of strategic planning. Depending on when you joined, it may be coming at you hard and fast or you might have ample time to plan for it, but this go around, you have time and exposure under your belt, so when you go into it, repeat what you did the last time with capturing 360-degree feedback but also add key agenda items like OSS charter, standard Board slides, financial management, and the topic of metrics and KPIs. The next strategic planning in-person should focus on how you measure yourselves from a maturity perspective. Out of this, you will refine your roadmap and update your project portfolio.

To summarize, the objectives of the last 30 days are to:

1. Identification of key stakeholders you need to foster close relationships with
2. Get your execution practice into a routine and promote a safe environment
3. Assess the maturity of your governance and compliance function (if it exists)
4. Determine what practices exist for stakeholder communication
5. Identify personnel gaps and fill internally first and externally if necessary
6. Begin planning the skeleton of the next Board presentation

7. Start structuring the next strategic planning in-person session with a focus on metrics and KPIs
8. Ensure a security awareness program is in place and operational

The first 90 days are vital to assert yourself as the right choice for the job and to stabilize your team and operation. There are things you can do and ways you need to behave. I'm not going to go into a discussion on emotional intelligence because I'm going to assume you have what it takes on that front to get the job done. Make no mistake, the softer side of leadership is what will make you successful. Things like empathy will go a long way. The concept of 'servant leadership', while it has been over advertised, the underlying intent is absolutely key to establishing a strong culture. Your investment in growing trust and safety within your team and honest and transparent relationships externally will be a key pillar to driving the right behaviors and growing credibility.

In these first 3 months, you are going through a crash course of learning who's who in the company, and what is important to the business. You are establishing communication channels internally and with leadership and you are beginning to identify low hanging fruit that you can use to establish 'excellence in execution'. You immediately started defining your strategic vision with the help of a 360-degree feedback model where you were not the dominant driver to the vision but a contributor amongst others, and while doing this, you emphasized the need for the team to be adaptable to developing opportunities missed initially so that you can fold them as they surface into the larger objectives.

Along the way, keep your eyes and ears open to the stories tied to the operation and people you now work with. We have to be conscious of the fact that life at your company did not start when you joined, but it existed long before you arrived. Take the time to learn the story of each person and the trials and tribulations they have gone through. There are reasons why things are the way they are or members behave in certain ways. Spend enough time learning those nuances so you can better plan for the next phase with you at the helm. Be on the lookout for those jaded team members who may feel they were passed over for various things including your job. Work to establish a new normal; one that is positive, and demonstrates you have their best interests at heart. Work to correct any wrongs done within reason, and apply a balanced lens to the needs of the team and the needs of the company.

Let's not judge the practice because of past conditions. Too many times new leaders show up and start questioning why things are the way they are. They don't take time to understand the reasons and by not doing so, they lose the respect of the team. If you are someone who looks for understanding and acknowledges the conditions of the past while establishing corrective actions going forward, you will earn the respect and support of the team. Look, it's more important to get your teams arrows pointing in the same direction as yours because in doing so, there is minimal resistance and everyone is pointing at the same objectives. This reduces organizational friction and multiplies one objective across all the personnel on your team. When things need to be done, they get done fast and accurately because of this. One purpose, one vision. If you get this right, the rest will, frankly, work itself out.

Chapter 3

Roadmap, work packages, and sequencing

We're going to pivot now to talk about the specific elements that make for a successful security practice. These concepts can be started in the 90-day plan but would run across multiple years as you mature your practice. This chapter maps out topics we will discuss for the rest of the book. Structurally, at the top level we speak of roadmap components that are comprised of specific work packages. These work packages are sequenced in a way to allow for a natural maturity with near, mid, and long-term practices being introduced at the appropriate times.

There are six top-level topics that we use to organize the information, which are strategic planning, operational design, a discussion around mindset and collaboration, the management system you want to institute, a section around the SEC, and finally tackling the topic of complacency. These six broad categories capture the strategic and tactical elements as well as the administrative and cultural components that you want to attend to.

For each of the roadmaps, I have constructed a diagram depicting the larger work packages we need to address to drive to a complete model of security. These diagrams can be used as both a view into the key topics to address as you scale your operation, and as a general outline of this book that can be used as spot references you can quickly jump to for specific topics.

3.1 STRATEGIC ROADMAP

> Why did the corporate security team cross the road?
>
> ...
>
> To do a risk assessment, put up a firewall, implement multifactor authentication, and then realize they left the sensitive data on the other side.
>
> (OpenAI. 2024)

You didn't think it was funny? Take it up with ChatGPT. I thought it was on point and what better tool to use than generative AI to make up a sweet joke about security strategy!

DOI: 10.1201/9781003616528-3

Okay, well, we've already covered the elements I associate with strategic planning tied to understanding challenges faced by teams and leaders, as well as understanding the difference between what it means to start up a brand-new operation versus inheriting one. We also talked about how to approach the new role and what your first set of actions should be as you begin your new adventure. These are softer topics, but lay the foundation for building the structure of your security framework. As a leader, you need to understand culture, ensure that your position is stable to build a long-term plan, and have awareness of external forces that can at the very least challenge the way you organize your affairs. With that in mind, let's move forward (Figure 3.1).

3.1.1 What's in scope?

Ever hear people use cybersecurity as the universal catch-all for security? Nowadays the thing to talk about is 'cyber' but security is comprised of 4 distinct dimensions. Cybersecurity deals with protecting electronic and mobile devices against attacks originating from the Internet. Information security deals with protecting the confidentiality, integrity, and availability of information. Product security does just that, it's concerned with the protection of hardware, software or systems from threats. Finally, you have physical security. Most companies keep the first three apart from physical security but if you look closely, the physical and digital spaces kind of use the same language applied to their domain. Physical security talks of boundary layers, access management/access control, identity management and many other familiar terms.

So in my view, these four dimensions of security have to come together to give you a full picture of the state of security in your organization. I said it earlier that the ideal role is as a CSO that covers all, but if you are like most (not all) companies, physical is handled separately from the rest. For the sake of this roadmap, we will speak heavily on information and cyber and some product, but you can easily transplant many of the topics and apply them with slight adjustments, to physical security as well.

In Chapter 4, we will discuss the work packages that we categorize under the broader category of strategic planning and modeling. They address your maturity model, organizational design or structure, and three phases of security implementation referred to as 'Functional First', 'Functional Second' and 'Functional Third'. Spend time in Chapter 4 if you are looking at the overarching model for your security practice and how to kickstart a systematic approach to assessing your maturity and designing your team to support the critical dimensions of security. If you ever find yourself lost in determining where you are and how things apply to your overall sequencing, come back to the diagram presented and go through the thought exercise of mapping where you are across the five dimensions of strategy depicted, and reset yourself. There are a lot of concepts and derivatives of

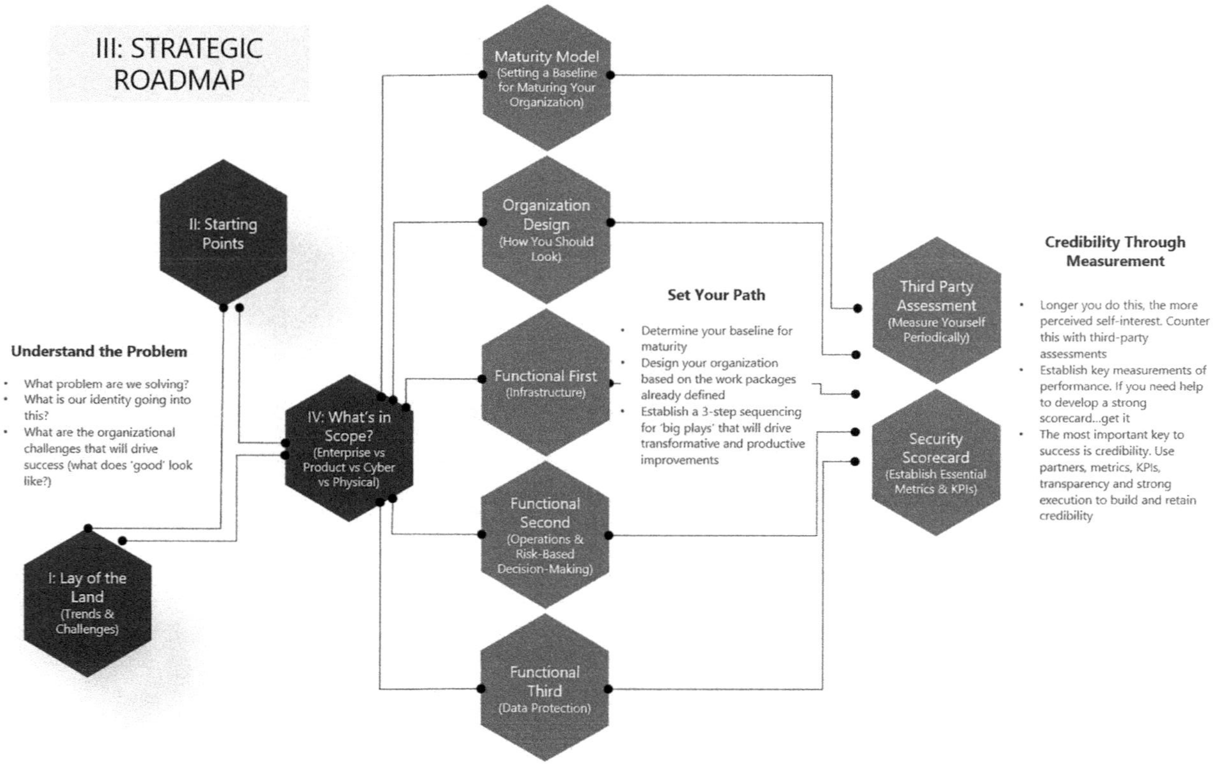

Figure 3.1 Strategic roadmap.

each of the topics, especially when you get into the Functional work packages and if you are unfamiliar, you may find yourself asking where some things fit in the execution strategy. Always keep I mind though that in some cases, you may need to deploy certain things sooner than others; don't find yourself becoming too rigid and allow that elasticity to exist as you merge company needs with security sequencing.

In addressing maturity modeling we can't ignore the National Institute of Standards and Technology (NIST), which is a U.S. federal agency that we use to define the appropriate frameworks for maturing our security practice. NIST is part of the Department of Commerce and among the many standards and other documentation it produces, the ones that are pertinent to us are the cybersecurity framework and the 800 series of publications that we will tap into for establishing a model for our organization.

Chapter 4 will review the NIST publications that are pertinent along with some others that we should be familiar with including ones from the European Telecommunications Standards Institute (ETSI) that apply to operating technology (OT) security, along with cybersecurity. The area of standards and as a close cousin, regulatory publications is a deep area of focus that takes a team to decipher everything that is relevant to your organization, but one that is probably the most vital because if you make a mistake in compliance, it can mean steep penalties and loss of employment. This work package is an important one to start off with and one that should not be skipped. This topic is the basis for really everything else that follows.

Key areas to discuss are the security framework of choice, and then the security controls you adopt for information systems. Other areas of interest include Internet of Things (IOT) (networking of physical objects) requirement sets, security for industrial automation, and a multitude of regulations tied to product security. As of the writing of this book, in Europe, the Cyber Resiliency Act (CRA), Product Security and Telecommunications Infrastructure bill (PSTI) were two that were capturing the attention of product development and security teams, not to mention the emergence of the Radio Equipment Directive (RED); we will do a brief flyby of these but will spend most of our time on the framework and controls that are more generally applicable to an organizations security program.

The cool thing about NIST is that it offers us a wealth of literature that we can use to design a risk program, a maturity model, and even an organizational structure. I caution you to use the references listed here as a guide and not an absolute because each organization is different. The work package on organizational structure speaks to how a security leader can design a successful security department. NIST 800-100 and NIST 800-39 are both good references to aide you in this effort. I can tell you that each time I built security teams, I did not use these references, not that they aren't any good but rather, as you explore the business you're in, you naturally form a concept around structure that is customized to your company's needs, and most times, it will encapsulate elements noted in these references. There is however, no right or wrong approach. Some leaders work heavily with standards and use them to frame their designs. Others feel their way through these topics and build what they sense the company needs. It feels like the right answer is take an approach that makes sense to the environment you're in.

Chapter 4 speaks to what are the big-ticket functions you need to ensure you incorporate into your structure and sequencing them in the right order to address business needs in the short, mid, and long-term. In the case of a greenfield exercise, you will likely start out with the basics of forming an infrastructure operation. I had the opportunity to work for a startup and this was exactly what I did. We didn't have a network, we were introducing applications, and there was no incident management to speak of. It was truly greenfield so what I did was make the operation functional before worrying about overlaying all the other bells and whistles. Functional is a theme that carries over to the subsequent work packages and you'll see three functional groupings that are intended to increase in maturity from the first to the third. For the infrastructure piece, we are talking about Functional First and it includes things like firewalls, and proxies, services like multifactor authentication, virtual private networking (VPN) and the like. We're not talking much about policy and governance, awareness and training, incident management and response; these will organically be derived from the build out of infrastructure, leading to a transition from Functional First to Functional Second.

So bringing this back to the structure, your initial organization will include elements to support infrastructure and it will mature in parallel to your transition from the three maturity stages just described. I have said it before, governance is absolutely essential that typically deals with compliance and audit, training and awareness, policies, and the like, but you need to first establish an operational footprint before overlaying this vital piece of the puzzle. The section on structure is as much a conversation about how you will look, as it will reflect the maturation of your operation, so it will not be a static model but rather, will evolve over time.

Chapter 4 moves from maturity modeling, and organizational structure to support your development, to a three-phase model for deployment of services. So here's the thinking; some will say you have your maturity model defining what you should deploy. That is true, but from experience, I've seen that some privilege is given to a natural development of needs that will drive which parts of your maturity you prioritize first. Intuitively, we can say that without networks and connectivity, you really don't have much to worry about around information and cyber security. Where we start increasing risk is when interconnectivity starts being established and that's when we begin layering security services on top of the transport services.

So with that in mind, what I've observed and sequenced in my own career is the need to initially focus on infrastructure build out to meet the demands of the organization. When you're standing up a new operation, especially in cases of startups, network build outs are vital because you need to establish communication across the growing organization. In other cases where structural IT services are already in place (networks, data centers, applications, cloud services, etc.), you need to assess the condition of the associated security infrastructure that supports and protects these services. Either way, you want to center around the health of these functional elements that I refer to as the first of three considerations that make up the 'Functional First'.

Some of the questions we answer here are tied to how we protect ingress/egress points? The world is moving more to Internet connections and steering away from older and more expensive mesh technologies like MPLS. How are we protecting those points of entry to our network? How do we manage general traffic flow? How do we address access to applications that communicate across these interfaces? What is our security posture around web services specifically? In former times, we built these formal demilitarized zones (DMZ), which were prominent at times when the aforementioned MPLS network topology was more widely used. We had big bulky pipes that then connected to a DMZ where we had a multi-tiered structure that ultimately led to the untrusted Internet. Today, we don' talk as much of DMZs for external connectivity, but rather, we see companies deploying multiple Internet egress points making the architecture more distributed that in turn, requires smaller security builds but more of them. All of these types of considerations fall within the Functional First.

Other areas of interest revolve around intrusion protection/detection, encryption, access control, backup and recovery, remote access services, manufacturing security if you are in that space, lab security if you have research and labs in your company, and similar. The theme here is all the functional stuff we need to put in place to ensure the company operates smoothly at the onset. These are in essence table stakes for security controls to address the biggest and bulkiest risks. This section of Chapter 4 talks about this broad spectrum of activities. I will say that while I have a 3-tiered model for what I term as 'big plays' in maturity, if your company has the resources and your team the capacity to run some of these tiers in parallel, then go for it, but usually what I find is you want to place some level of focus in sequencing to make sure you don't miss any major injections and by miss, I mean all sorts of things like not overworking your team, using finite funding intelligently with the highest impact, stressing your ability to execute in a productive way as opposed to boiling the ocean but ultimately not achieving anything in an effective way.

Assess your organizations tolerance across these and other actors and then make a calculated decision. Don't overlook the importance of assessing your teams ability to execute in all of this. I have literally spent up to two years in almost each position I held in leading teams establishing discipline in execution so that we could grow our ability to run multiple initiatives in parallel and with an acceptable level of precision. This is probably why in every role I have held, I've, in parallel, held some role in developing project management within the greater team I worked in.

> Why did the information security project manager bring a ladder to the data center?
>
> Because they heard the firewall had too many high-level threats!
>
> (OpenAI. 2024)

One word...hilarious! ChatGPT does it again. I gotta tell you, these jokes are the main reason I started interacting with the world of generative AI. What a comedian. To close on the Functional First phase, it typically takes no less than two years to get everything stood up. You will likely start thinking about the next big play (Functional Second) some time in the second year but in my experience, you may not transition to a predominant set of initiatives in the second tier until the third year, as you close out the Functional First efforts. In addition, it doesn't mean that once you transition, you won't have to return to infrastructure efforts; it just becomes tweaking, optimizing, and improving as opposed to full deployment of net new services across the board.

So we now enter the space of security operations and a growing focus on risk-based decision making. This is the general theme around the Functional Second big plays. What I tend to find when I join a new company is that we land somewhere in this phase on a starting point to engage. It's rare to find a company that has zero base infrastructure services in place, but many of them haven't taken the step towards making the invisible, visible. That's a large part of what the second and third phases are intended to accomplish. The first phase is to establish essential controls that are again, table stakes. You have limited visibility into security alerting, correlation, and complex analytics. In the Functional First, you are likely using the same monitoring tools that the rest of an information technology team is using, and probably some localized or platform-specific monitoring tied to your firewalls, IPS/IDS or other.

Functional Second is looking at the introduction of a security operations function, commonly referred to tasks performed by a security operations center (SOC). You are introducing advanced correlation capabilities, and begin to inject logging from assets across the companies technology stack to begin seeing security alerts and anomalies in a new and advanced light. There's a lot that goes into this phase and when speaking of a SOC, you are also introducing all sorts of other capabilities in threat modeling, threat hunting, the injection of threat intelligence, a more formal approach to vulnerability management, and so on. Chapter 4 dives deeper into this area as the mid-tier that starts moving the needle towards risk management and risk reduction efforts. There are other components of your organizational structure that are introduced here as well that we speak to as well; some you frankly can't live without such as those practices tied to governance.

Much of the security organization gets formed during phase 1 and 2. By the time you get to the third, the maturity of your organization is likely getting to a 'managed' state. The Functional Third work package is where you overlay data controls that thus far have been a conversation point, but not a conscious exercise for control. In reality, everything we do is to protect our data but in this stage, you are deploying very specific capabilities that again, make the invisible... visible. The protection of data comes in many forms and at this stage where you have laid the foundation of security with infrastructure and instituted sound operational controls with your SOC, governance, and compliance and maybe even assurance capabilities; you need to redirect a significant focus onto data protection.

In order for us to understand how data protection and security play in the larger scheme of our controls, we should look at what are the general components that make up data governance. Depending on your organizations overall maturity, you may have a data officer of some sort who focuses on the entirety of data management. You want to make sure as you venture into the data protection waters that you are aligned on intent and scope so as not to step into something that leads to a departure from security. Making a clear delineation between data architecture, processing and storage, usage and data quality from data protection and security is important. You are addressing one aspect of data governance, and the rest is something your data management team develop and mature.

Chapter 4 will talk to what our objective is in this space, how we go about it, and what are the outcomes we are trying to achieve. The end game after this intensive exercise in introducing data protection will be a pretty comprehensive security program that dealt with table stakes with infrastructure, the introduction of risk-based modeling in the Functional Second, and an overlay of data protection capabilities in the Functional Third. By the time you're done with these, we would expect your security program's maturity would be extensive. As a practitioner, if you take this sequence and introduce the associated services in the way described, you will have a strong practice. From a timing perspective, you can assume that if you're starting from scratch, this would take no less than 6 years to institute the three phases in a comprehensive way, and that timeframe may be aggressive.

The Functional Third for example can easily take 4 years itself. You may start with a Request for Proposal (RFP) to identify scope and a partner that can help you institute the practice. This is usually followed by a business case approval and financial authorization; all of this can take you a year to get through. The second would be the deployment of services and capabilities. You can probably do this in two or three Quarters. The remaining two years would be tied to change management, tuning, training a team on data protection and the tools, and working through the impact to the organization as you tighten your controls over how data is consumed while in transit and at rest.

Chapter 4 concludes with two additional topics that speak to the role that third party assessments play in your general success and the importance of a security scorecard to promote transparency and drive credibility. On the first topic, it's important to have an initial external assessment done of your security maturity so that you baseline your starting point. My recommendation is to perform one every three years because from my experience, it takes about that amount of time to define actions, secure funding, prioritize and implement. In doing this, you are able to inject an unbiased view of your program that can help in evangelizing your mission. It can be nerve wracking because you never know what they will report, but the good outweighs the not so good.

Second, the development of a security scorecard is a very useful tool in driving security awareness and support. The creation of a scorecard can be frustrating because it needs to be very concise while conveying the health of your entire program. You usually have one page to convey volumes so 'architecting' the scorecard is not an overly dramatic tag we place on this exercise. The last part of Chapter 4 talks about how you can approach the creation of your scorecard and broaches the topic of whether it's a static set of controls or does the scorecard change over time in a dynamic way. Scorecards do not become optimized immediately and many times they can be a bit of a work of art. It takes a few iterations to develop something that meets the needs of your executives and Board. Something what works in one company may not be appropriate for another, but there are some guideposts that can be applied and conceptual approach that can help us.

In summary, Chapter 4 tackles the method to our madness on how we formulate a plan to stand up a successful operation. The skeleton of our practice comes from the above elements and as we step into the subsequent roadmap areas, we start fleshing out that skeleton with operational components, business process and an overall management system to ensure we run things smoothly.

3.2 OPERATIONAL ROADMAP

We are moving away from the strategic overlay of how we approach our security design to the operational elements that will make us successful and keep us out of trouble. Depending on your companies landscape, the elements presented here can show up at different times and stages of your maturity when compared to other companies. The content depicted in the diagram included is captured in Chapter 5. There's a lot to operations but we can catalog the bulk of the activities in a few key work packages, and we start with a conversation around compliance.

As an outline to this book, my recommendation is to spend some time on Chapter 5 that speaks in detail to the work packages presented here. If you are new to security or to the leadership role, a strong practice needs to address all of the elements encapsulated in this operational roadmap. Missing many of these means you will have gaping holes in your security hardening. The information below offers a summary of what we review in depth so that you can determine which topics are important to you for review (Figure 3.2).

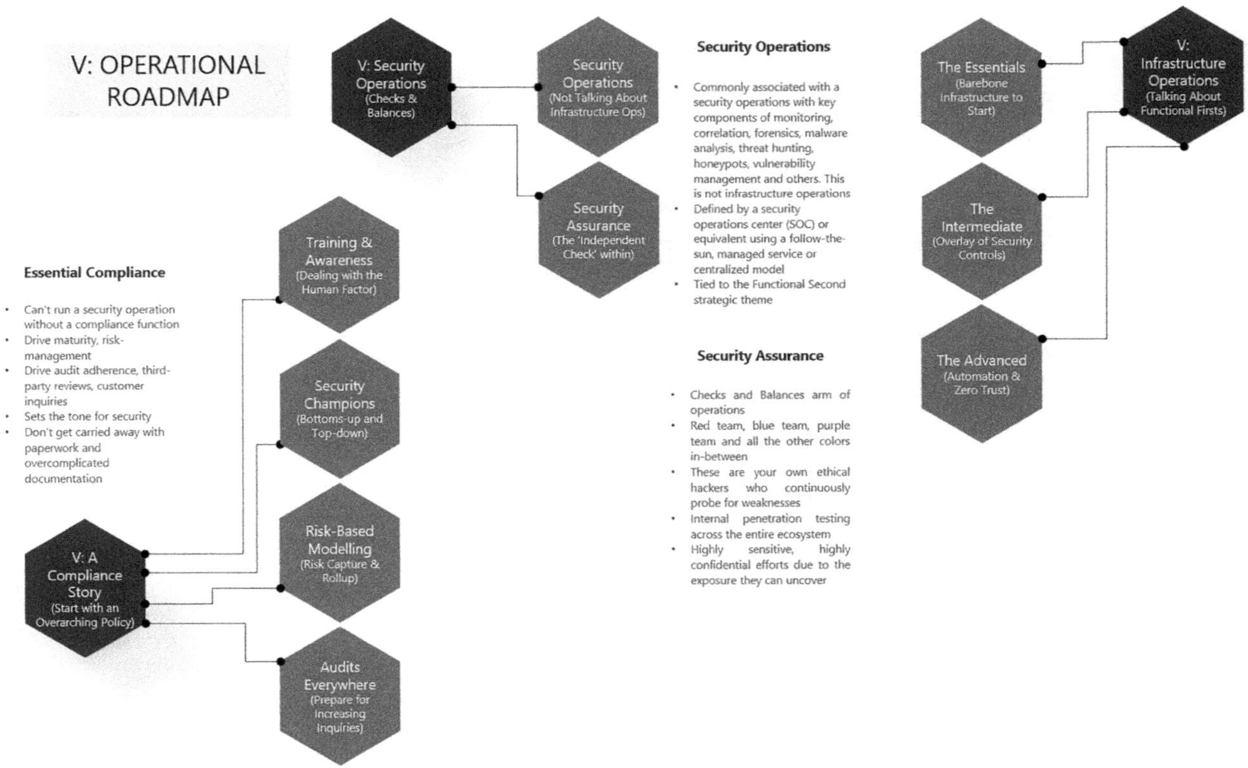

Figure 3.2 Operational roadmap.

3.2.1 A compliance story

As noted earlier in the strategy discussion, governance and compliance are vital to keep us out of trouble but they may surface a bit later than the infrastructure work we do to get things running. It all depends on where you are in maturity. If much of the infrastructure is in place and you're moving more into the Functional Second group of activities then this will definitely be something you will develop. Having said that, depending on the nature of what your company does, you may need some elements earlier.

The world of compliance really starts with what we talked about already; we need to establish a maturity model against which we measure our improvement over time. Now you might say, Timur, if this work package comes later than infrastructure, isn't that backwards? The thought here is that infrastructure build out will happen organically as an organization forms. It's really driven by business demand for baseline capabilities to enable the organization to work. You will be force to do that work with or without a maturity model. When we do identify a path for improving, we will assess what's in place already and formulate an improvement plan to get it lined up with our overall development plan.

So, once we know what our maturity model will look like, we institute some key functions that are typical for the governance of a sound compliance practice. The work packages include training and awareness, the development of a security champion program, risk-based modeling, audit; these are all connected to an underlying policy and documentation framework that provides the guidelines by which the companies security posture and technology will be administered. There are many intricacies tied to this space but for now, these are the elements we will discuss to stand up a compliance practice.

The compliance practice is the brains of your operation. It governs how we move forward in maturing our operation. Compliance drives risk-based decision making which is the cornerstone of any good security practice. The compliance function is the interface with regulators, government, customers and third parties. This team provides oversight to the entire security team and to a broader scale, to the technology teams within your company. The role of the Compliance Officer is not to be overlooked and in fact, is critical to ensure we stay within the lines and adhere to the rules that govern our companies practices and in turn security.

Chapter 5 goes into greater detail around the function of governance and compliance and offers some insights on how to go about developing a strong team, key functions within the team, and the functions you want to ensure are mapped to the work packages noted in the schematic. The role of the Deputy CISO can come from different functions but it's common for that role to emerge from the compliance branch, provided that person has strong awareness of the technical elements tied to the security organization as well.

3.2.2 Infrastructure operations

We talked about infrastructure build as the first strategic step towards your maturity when it comes to new capability deployment. The operational elements tied to this can be further broken into Essentials, Intermediate and Advanced. So to clarify the linkage between these three dimensions and Functional First; Functional First describes a strategic objective that needs to be installed before you go into the subsequent general themes. Within the Functional First, you will have operational elements that need to be deployed that are typically captured in the Essentials work package noted here and some of the others to ensure you have decent coverage. The exercise to deploy and improve infrastructure does not end just because you have met the requirements of the Functional First big plays. You will be deploying and improving continuously but the continued work will be managed within the operation team as part of your continuous improvement, as you move to a focus into the SOC and other elements captured in Functional Second.

Chapter 5 speaks to what are essential infrastructure controls that absolutely should be in place, and then move on to discuss the other levels as they progressively improve your operational posture within infrastructure. You can slice and dice this stuff all sorts of ways but topics like deployment of firewalls, proxies, segmentation, essential access controls, and active directory are all part of Essentials. Discussions surrounding how to handle manufacturing versus labs versus corporate environments are in this space. Conversations around what to do about ingress/egress points are all included.

Intermediate speaks to a few services that improve your posture such as the introduction of virtual private networking for remote access, multifactor authentication, and single sign-on to name a few. In the intermediate space, you want to tackle topics about how you provide endpoint security services, how you establish standard images for endpoints with essential security controls, you address security hygiene in managing your firewalls, and let's not forget the work you need to do in establishing effective security for cloud. Chances are, by this time, development teams are already starting to use AWS, Azure or Google in ways that you're starting to worry about the cloud-sprawl and the lack of technical guardrails and development requirements. All of these need to be addressed, and the delineation between intermediate and advanced is subjective but we want to have a conversation around it to at least categorize things in groups to make organizing efforts a bit easier.

Finally we talk about the advanced topics surrounding infrastructure. Much of this starts talking about the components that make up Zero Trust. Zero Trust at its core, is a philosophy we want to abide by but there are elements that stand out as key practices we should call out. The movement towards least privilege should have showed up at some point earlier and would be more pronounced at this point. The lockdown of access to only assets that are needed for a person's job and the institution of controls to make that happen. These are things we want to address along with some other functionality to further improve the way we harden our infrastructure. The topic of Zero Trust cross infrastructure and enters some of the other topics we talk about including data protection, which is why we raise this a bit further down the maturity model so that it can be a conversation while we are also delving into data protection and privacy. Automation is also a key component in this space, and a topic that we should be starting to invest into more and more to optimize how we work. Chapter 5 will touch on this along with the other aforementioned components tied to infrastructure.

Infrastructure to me, also means an investment into information accuracy. This is where the reach of security must go beyond your direct influences and expand into areas of traditional IT in order to drive maturation. Asset and configuration management are the spaces that can impact your operational efficiency tremendously. In past lives, I've lobbied for direct influence over the development of our configuration management database (CMDB) and asset management database (AMDB).

Both the CMDB and the AMDB are important databases to maintain to grow and mature your organization but if I had to choose which one I start with first, it would be the CMDB that has direct impact on the accuracy of the data surrounding your infrastructure. These records are stored as configuration items (CIs) and elements like network devices, servers, applications, firewalls, and even services will be stored in the CMDB and their association to one another defined in the detailed records. This becomes important when establishing security operations where you want to introduce correlation services, or a comprehensive vulnerability management practice. Without accurate records, you may not deploy monitoring agents across the entire technology footprint or apply key patches to all systems and you can leave your organization vulnerable without knowing it.

The asset management database is something a bit different, it's important but in my view, it enhances your ability to perform lifecycle management on the things that run your organization. You can capture details around contracts, software entitlements, and marry your connection as a security organization with legal, finance, and IT. By having an AMDB, you can ensure you're not violating contractual obligations, that you're not consuming more than you should be on licenses, and you can become better at speaking the language of corporate finance. It's less security but even so, very vital to the maturity of a technology operation.

As we work through the details around infrastructure and Functional Third, we need to address the areas surrounding configuration items and ensuring our records are comprehensive and accurate. If we don't do this, we again, run the risk of having gaps in critical security coverage because we didn't have a full view of our asset base. What's more, our ability to quickly isolate problems, identify asset owners, and work through key upgrades or incident management can be severely impacted. Chapter 5 will tie this back into your maturation as a company and topics around automation apply here as much as other aspects of your practice.

3.2.3 Security operations

Security Operations starts establishing an information footprint in Functional first, but becomes a formal body of work in the Functional Second work package. For the purposes of this discussion, we break operations into two main buckets: the SOC-type work activities and Assurance. Note that in Functional Second, we also embed the development of the compliance function as a parallel set of capabilities that are formalized but for our purposes around operations, we are strictly discussing the elements that are tied to the SOC and security assurance.

The SOC and the associated functions within your operations center are the heart of your rapid response practices. There is a subtle but important transition that happens where you go from having basic visibility into your environment, relying on asset-specific tools that you tape together to give you some views into security health but it's when you start deploying the tools I associate with the SOC that you truly start seeing things in a much more effective way. There's quite a bit you can do with your SOC and every organization will have a slightly different flavor to how it's done, but for me, security incident and event management (SIEM) is the cornerstone of what you need to institute here.

Your SIEM collects logs from all sorts of assets and pulls them into one system, your SIEM, to perform correlation across your entire technology footprint. This gives you a comprehensive view into your general health and will be the primary tool your SOC Analysts will use to see anomalies, and manage risk. You can deploy a SIEM yourself and do all the log review and analytics yourself or you can use a managed security service provider (MSSP) to do the bulk work for you. We will talk about the model I absolutely recommend more, which is a hybrid SOC that uses MSSP services but also builds in-house capabilities as well.

Chapter 5 will discuss the SOC in greater detail, but there are so many things you can do to enhance your security practice; one that you need to install in parallel is vulnerability management. The two most important things you can do here is deploy a SIEM and install your vulnerability management practice, which if you are doing everything inhouse would mean deploying another tool, or you can take advantage of the bundling an MSSP offers to do it in conjunction with your SIEM. Other capabilities you can introduce over time include deployment of endpoint detection and response (EDR), security orchestration, automation, and response (SOAR) which is a complimentary set of capabilities to your SIEM, threat hunting, honey pots, malware analysis, digital forensics and a host of other things that can really blast your security maturity into the stratosphere. We'll go through this topic more in Chapter 5.

The last section that will be covered in Chapter 5 under Security Operations is Security Assurance. This is a function that in my early career as a security professional, I never instituted as a formal practice but as I learned and grew, I realized it's absolutely essential to ensure your security controls are actually doing what they're supposed to. Assurance is the checks and balances to your SOC and IT operation. In a funny way, it's our security paranoia in full force: we don't trust anyone or anything. I don't follow 'trust but verify', I follow 'don't trust and verify continuously'.

Assurance verifies that your controls work, and that your technology footprint doesn't have any holes that can be compromised. In this dimension of operations, you are testing, reviewing designs, supporting audits, running exercises to stress test your operation. Some of the coolest terminology is tied to Assurance such as cyber war games, or red team/blue team/purple team. The fantasy world depicted in movies links back to this space because they in part, are acting as ethical hackers into their own environments, which means they need to have many of the same skill sets as the bad actors.

There are a number of functions that this team will perform and interactions with other departments such as compliance, architecture and business operations like product development that we will discuss in greater detail. Because of what this team does, they are directly linked to product development and engineering in ways that can sometimes introduce new features and functionalities into the products and software being developed in your business. As technology professionals, one of the most important things we need to do over time is to drive value creation. We cannot simply be running systems, networks, and security operations. We need to find ways to inject ourselves into what drives revenue growth and helps the business speed up in its ability to deliver to customers. Assurance can be one of those bridges and therefore becomes an important extension of your strategy.

3.3 MINDSET & COLLABORATION

Now that we have discussed some of the structural elements to what you want to institute, let's discuss a little bit about how you should approach your role within the construct of the greater organization. Sadly, you can do all the things we have already discussed and you can still find yourself on the outside looking in. There is truth to the notion that you can do everything right and still fail. Well, let's address the psychology of a successful security leader and for that matter, anyone trying to run a successful branch of a business. Mindset and collaboration are at the heart of a true success story and there are several key things to keep in mind as you begin your work.

Chapter 6 discusses the Mindset & Collaboration roadmap topic and within it there are several work packages that you want to ensure you cover. The diagram included here identifies the key interfaces that will help you succeed and the way you can grow your credibility and in turn support for your initiatives. Because of the overwhelming scope under a security leader, there are some important things to consider as you develop your team culture that will make you successful no matter what personality type you might have (Figure 3.3).

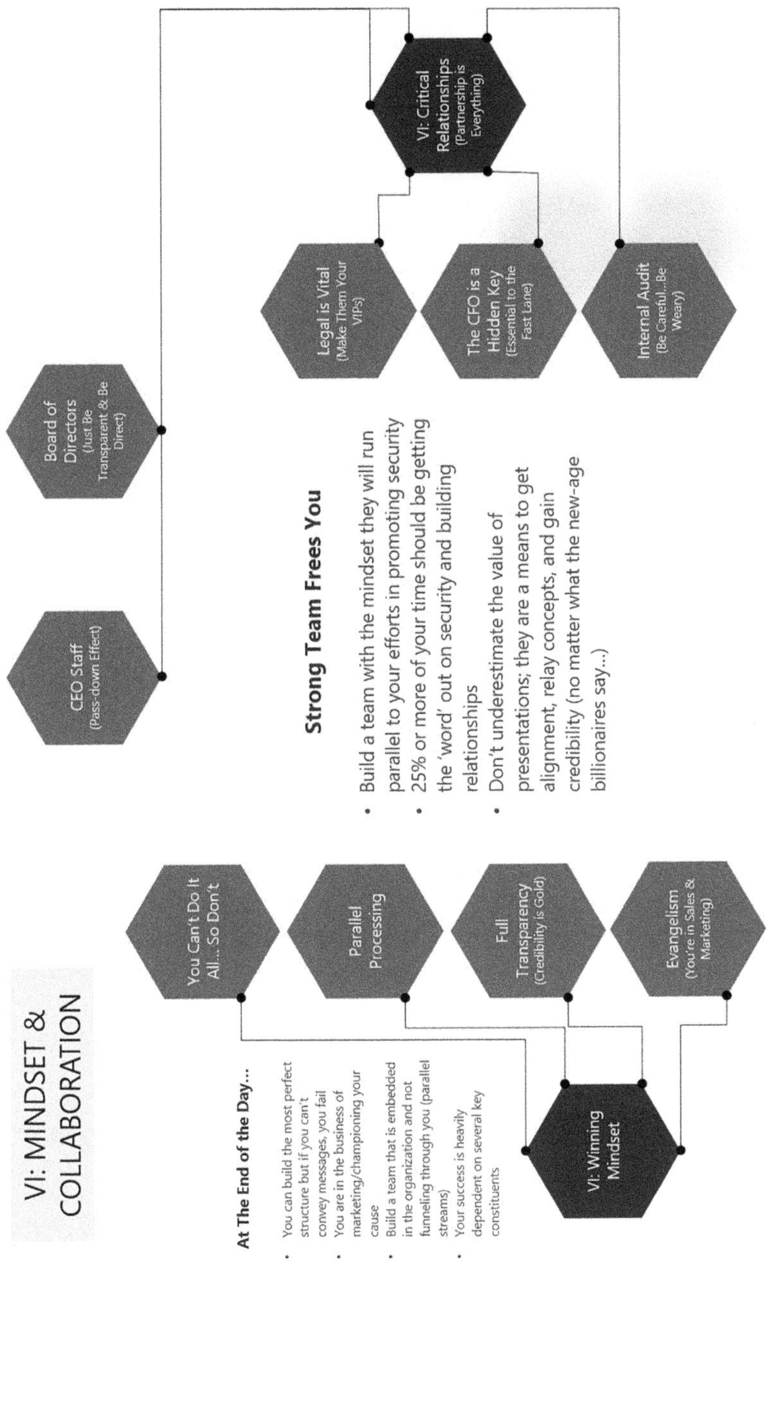

Figure 3.3 Mindset & collaboration.

3.3.1 Winning mindset

Dudes and dudettes, there's a point in your career where you have to concede something to continue to grow. For some it is a natural transition from being an individual contributor who is the subject matter expert on something to relinquishing that expertise to others and becoming more of a generalist. There are some talented technical leaders out there who can do the job of the security leader without any issues but every one of them would say that at some point they had to learn to rely on others to do their jobs and they the leader, had to accept knowing less about topics than members of their team.

You can't do it all so don't try to. Spend whatever time is required to hire the most talented and capable individuals to run the various aspects of your operation. Your job will be to give them challenging work, eliminate barriers, and I hate to say it, but deal with the red tape so that they can focus on their work. It is imperative that topics on finances, procurement, staffing; all the things that are extraneous to the job they do, are kept away from the rest of the team so as not to distract them unnecessarily unless it impacts them directly.

Chapter 6 talks about how to look at your role in relation to the people you interact with. The work package labeled 'parallel processing' speaks to developing your staff to act independently, act with confidence and drive decisions so that it's not just you leading but a cohort of strong contributors who are doing the same in parallel. You set the tempo, you facilitate the strategy and vision with the team and when you align to those, you incubate a culture of active participation and distributed leadership. Frankly, this is the only way you'll be successful in a field that has extreme demands from every single other department in the organization. Moreso than IT, security requires diplomacy and firmness at the same time. You'll be required to work both in a collaborative and authoritative way simultaneously. The sales folks will require things from you, but also Human Resources, and every other team but unlike IT, you will be approached cautiously because while they need your help, they are also weary of the controls you place and the possibility of stifling their access to things they have come to enjoy as freedoms that may not be in the best interest of the company.

Work in a hierarchical organization and promote a flat culture. Run things in parallel and empower (corporate language I know) your team to make decisions. Drive full transparency in the way you work within and outside of your team. The quickest way to give comfort to the organization that you have their best interest at heart is to speak plainly and transparently. When something doesn't work, call it out but then give a plan for how you and your team will fix it. It is absolutely essential to assert your credibility in whatever way you can whether it's being fully transparent, or bringing in third parties every three years to assess the state of security so that you can inject an independent review that can drive investment.

There's an equation for trustworthiness that one of my former CIOs shared with us and has come to be an important marker and reference for me. It states that trust equals the quantity of credibility times reliability times intimacy or safety in relationships, all of this over self-interest. I think this is invaluable to keep in the back of our minds as we engage with others in our journey to make security a highly credible and effective operation.

$$T = (C + R + I) / S \tag{3.1}$$

The interesting thing about this equation is that when you first join a company as the new guy or gal, you have high credibility because you are coming from the outside. It's at that time you want to quickly assess strengths and weaknesses and lobby for specific investments because you will not have the same level of credibility for some time after you've been in the job. As time passes and you are 'institutionalized', you will be viewed as having more self-interest when it comes to the function at hand, and that will go on for a minute until you turn the tides with effective execution, strong operational performance, and the building of strong relationships. Along the way, the use of third-party assessment because a very useful tool because you are infusing credibility from the outside to compensate for the inevitable short-term trend of perceived self-interest.

In your efforts to market a strong and effective team, efficient execution and a source for expertise in everything security, you need to implement these elements and evangelize the story of security in the organization and it's positive impact to your organization. Evangelizing why security is important and making it something felt rather than something known is the trick to getting leadership behind you and supporting your efforts. We will speak to all of this again later in chapter 6 and while the material in other chapters is more concrete, it's these soft topics that actually become the cornerstones of success and you really need to focus on them, sometimes more so than you do on the bits and bytes of the operation.

3.3.2 Critical relationships

Once upon a time, I was a young upstart in a company called Bell Atlantic that soon after joining, went through a merger and was renamed Verizon. Maybe I can use youth as an excuse but I lacked the maturity to realize that hard work and delivering on commitments is not enough to make you successful in corporate America. What truly makes you successful is building relationships and making your colleagues feel they can count on you. Wars are not won through delivering on goals and excelling technically, but in your ability to bring others along with you and negotiate terms that demonstrate one vision and one mission towards a common objective.

Well, I wasn't that, and while I had a strong work ethic, efficiency in what I did, and a capacity to learn quickly and translate that learning into action; it wasn't enough to be picked as a top talent in a proverbial corporate draft if there ever was one. When I was on a team, I was valued but if you had to pick from scratch, I would likely get passed over because I was a little hard to deal with... not a lot, but just enough. This conversation is an extension of what we discussed in a Winning Mindset but our attention is more towards the key relationships you must nurture to advance your security agenda.

Chapter 6 will conclude with talking about those relationships and the reason why they are vital to your success. Among the heavy hitters, Legal is probably the most important of your points of contact because many of the things you do and the controls you institute have a direct line to Legal. Your management of incidents to data protection and privacy to your relationship with external entities for reporting is all tied back to a shared responsibility with Legal. This is why at the very top, you will want to invest into building those close ties and developing plans with the Legal team because you're in it together.

Internal Audit (IA) and the Chief Financial Officer (CFO) are also important relationships to nurture because they have both direct and indirect influences on your success. More on this in Chapter 6 but IA has a unique ability to champion your cause or make you want to leave with a bad taste in your mouth for the organization. Sound dramatic? Well, I've gone through it. Let's just say you can build a strong, powerful security operation that does all the right things but if your IA agenda is not aligned to yours, you can very quickly get bogged down in political red tape that if you don't have the appetite for, can drive you to make a decision on your future with that company. I've been there.

Finally, the obvious ones are the CEO and Board of Directors. In the end you are part of the management team supporting the CEOs strategy for the firm; let's make sure we are doing what we can to make the CEO successful, who is a reflection of the company itself. The Board speaks for itself, you won't go anywhere fast without building strong ties with them and giving them a level of comfort that you know what you're doing and you're not going to conceal (unintentionally of course) the realities of the firms security posture. More on all of this in Chapter 6.

3.4 MANAGEMENT SYSTEM

Let's switch gears now to the topic of how you want to run your operation. When we first arrive on the job, we need to assess the landscape and determine strengths and weaknesses. At some point we need to institute repeatable practices to assert discipline in execution and an active drive towards maturity. That's where your management system comes into play. I've said it before, this is my experience on what makes an effective operation. You can ask someone else and they'll adjust things slightly or maybe even dramatically based on what they've seen but when I look back and assess the various companies and positions I've held, to really do a nice job with conducting the affairs of your organization, you need to have these elements in play. The diagram included captures the various work packages associated with this, and there are a few, so pace yourself as you're building (Figure 3.4).

There are elements in your management system that have to be institutionalized immediately and others that can grow as your team evolves. Things like Board meetings and Quarterly business reviews with the organizations leadership are things you just can't fiddle around with. When getting up to speed, get these two organized right away by determining who will take the lead on content development, collection and how will your team convert into presentations. There are those out there that will say something about how we shouldn't be focused on presenting and consuming all that time on meetings but what's reality and what's an academic principle are sometimes very far apart. Look, reality for most companies is you need to do it, so ... get it done and then you can post on LinkedIn on the utopian world of not spending time on presentations and more on doing the work. In reality the presentations are part of the work.

What I've discovered in my time presenting to multiple Boards is that the exercise of preparation offers a laser-like focus for the team on reassessing what we're doing and how on a Quarterly cadence and is the catalyst for recalibration that is very healthy. Second, by doing this exercise, you progressively get better at presenting material in a way that non-security folks can understand so it aides in our ability to convey information in a straightforward manner while also being a platform to evangelize the importance of security even more. So if you look at it, you're refocusing Quarterly, you're self-evaluating on that same time scale, and you are honing your communication skills and putting the good you're doing in front of the company so that you remain relevant. The side effects are well worth the effort.

The second tier of interfaces can be summed up with what happens with your internal Enterprise Security Council (ESC) or equivalent. I can say that it really depends on how things are run at your organization. In one, we had an ESC that was run by our Chief Legal Officer (CLO) in a very formal way where we brought relevant topics in for conversation and it was really a prelude to the Board presentations. In others we didn't have such a formal structure but rather, our relationships were more informal and we got together to discuss different matters in a variety of settings so there was no structured ESC. However you and your company want to do it, I recommend some aspect of internal content sharing with key stakeholders should be done so that you can ensure your strategy continues to align with the objectives of the rest of the business units.

Alignment is taken even further when you institute a formal risk review. Talk to any seasoned security leader and they'll all tell you in some manner

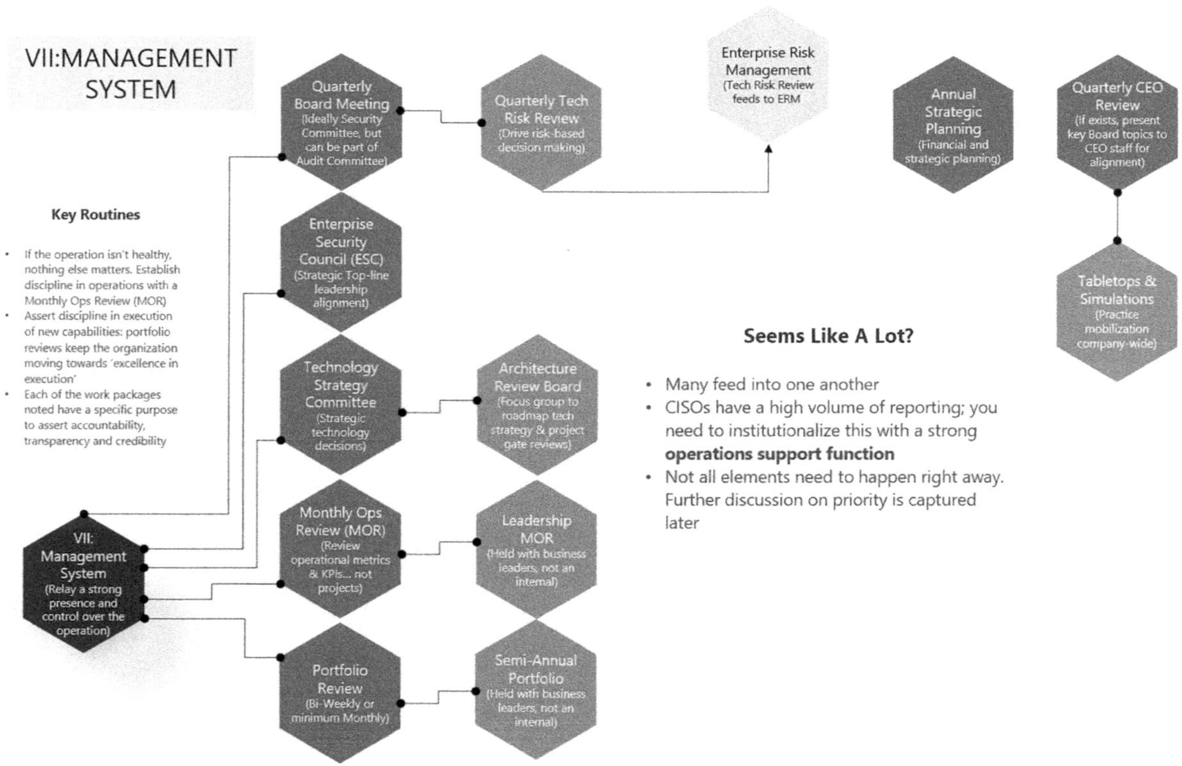

Figure 3.4 Management system.

that our job revolves around risk management. Security is risk management and risk reduction, which means at some point you need to install a formalized technology risk register that is developed under your Compliance function and content and ratings negotiated by the risk owners. Once you have a workable model, you want to start running formal Quarterly risk reviews so that the language everyone uses is risk-focused. As I was structuring this book, I was debating if I should have an entire chapter devoted to risk governance because it's such an important underlying foundation to everything we do in security. Champion, promote, nurture this space because it is your whole underpinning. More on this in Chapter 7.

The remaining work packages will show up in different ways depending on your organizational structure. What I mean by that is if you are running security independent of IT (i.e. you are not in the IT organization), then you'll develop the other components like the monthly operations review (MOR) and the portfolio review within your team. If on the other hand you are inside the IT organization (I do not like this model; let me just say that) then your CIO may already have these in play as part of the larger IT management system. That goes for the technology strategy committee (TSC) and architecture review board (ARB) as well.

What you'll find is each of these tertiary elements is that they evolve over time. For my own sanity, I kickstart the theme of 'excellence in execution' right away and that usually leads to some sort of project management structure that then leads to portfolio oversight. I have a tendency to navigate towards this because I find security in particular is heavily comprised of new capability introduction which means projects. So, we need to be good at running small and mid-sized projects within the ranks and then infuse some professional project managers to run some of the larger engagements. I invest a lot of time and energy in developing this because it will reap rewards in our ability to delivery on our commitments in the long run.

The MOR is key to asserting operational discipline. You'll want to see if something already exists or if you need to build it. If you happened to run security and IT then you probably have a service management team under your wing who would be the right team to develop the MOR and mature it. If you don't have that, then you'll have to target an operational support team of some sort to develop this for your organization. It is important so that everyone remember that without a sound operation, the rest of the stuff we do is meaningless. We need to do the foundational work of operations management well before we dive into all the other so-called bells and whistles.

Quick notes on a few others. Technology strategy committee or some equivalent is built for you to have conversations with your peers on the future state of technology in your company. You may or may not have a climate that requires this, but it's a good thing to have so that there's alignment across technology teams. The ARB is important to ensure the thing we deploy and the 3–5-year technology plan is certified continually. The ARB is also important as an add-on to the portfolio maturity lifecycle that you started building as part of your 'excellence in execution'. There is a point where you will want to have an architectural review of incoming demand in such a way to 1: ensure it's not a duplication of existing capabilities and 2: to ensure the demand meets the strategic objectives of the organization. I will concede to the point that ARB is not an easy thing to install and can go south on you very quickly if a continuous effort is not sustained, but it is important for ongoing improvement.

Lastly, I include tabletop exercises as part of the management system because they are intended to be a routine exercise that you and your team administer on a yearly or semi-annual basis. These are held with the top executives and sometimes even the Board and they are intended to go through readiness exercises for an event that we hope will never occur. You can associate simulations to table tops as well, and depending on the appetite of your organization, you could run a tabletop exercise beginning of the year and a simulated event in the second half to really drive the incident management and response practices to your executives. We discuss more of this later.

3.5 REGULATORY MANDATES

One of the things I stated early in this book is that the good guys/gals are a bit handicapped because they need to adhere to a multitude of regulations to ensure companies are compliant with rules around disclosure, governance, and a slew of other topics. It's not all bad, let me make that point. We need to have minimum baselines so that we ensure the quality of products and services, as well as the protection of privacy is top priority. The grievance I have is that they are springing up in so many spaces that it becomes overwhelming to meet all the different directives. Take the United States for example, As of the end of 2024, almost twenty states had their own data privacy laws and others were developing more. It has reached a boiling point where there is a call for a unified law to simplify the regulatory landscape.

California and New York are known for having more comprehensive cybersecurity laws already that corporations need to design around, and as we speak (or read) more states are beefing up their own regulations. When we expand to the other side of the Atlantic, there are even more regulations to contend with and it's no longer just the General Data Protection Regulation (GDPR) but additional emerging mandates that grow the complexity of this landscape (Figure 3.5).

3.5.1 Securities and Exchange Commission (SEC)

How are others doing it? That's what you'll hear initially when trying to figure out how to address the new requirements (new as of December 2003 that is) placed by the SEC on cybersecurity reporting and transparency.

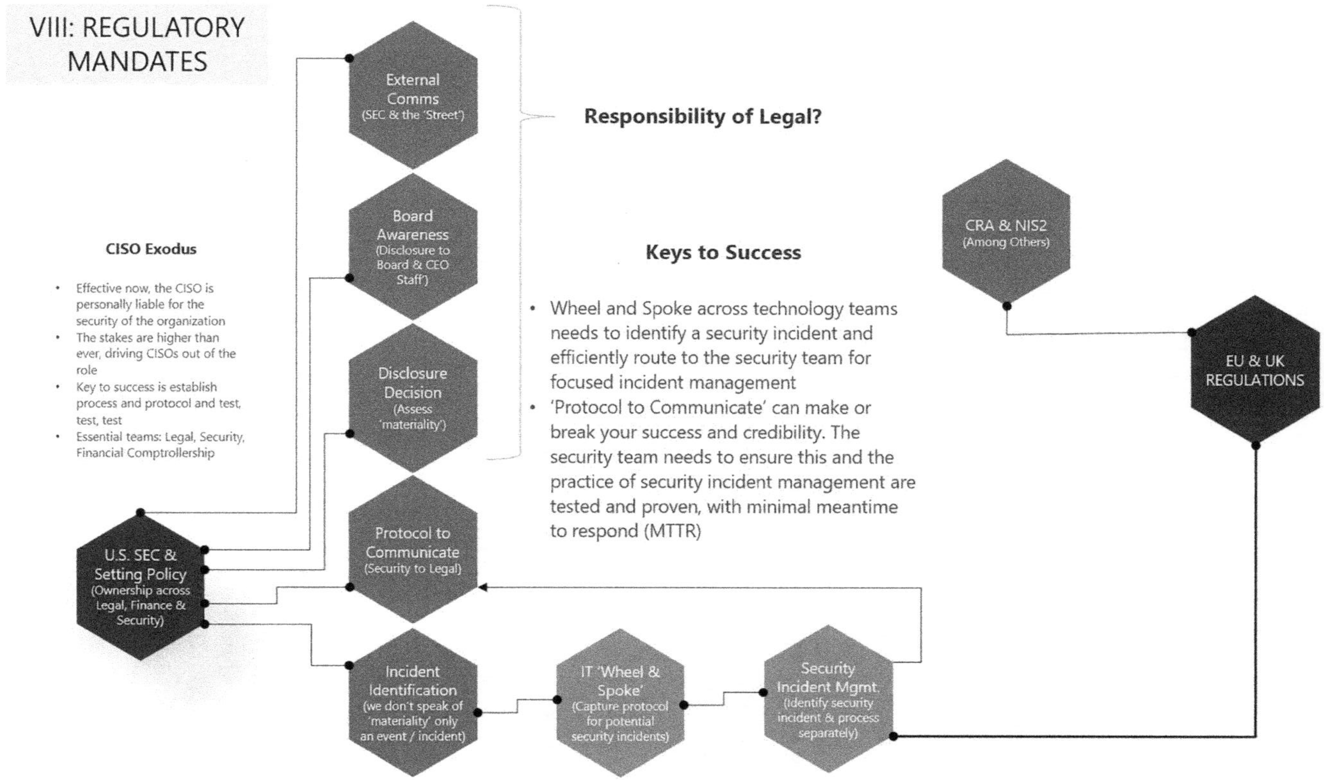

Figure 3.5 Regulatory mandates.

Here's an example where the relationship between Legal and Security is essential. There's a shared responsibility where the security team fields the incident and orchestrates the operational response, while Legal will typically take the incoming communication from the security team and relay it to the internal body of decision makers on what to do with it and whether it is at the threshold of 'materiality'.

The details behind one way you can tackle the requirements of the SEC will be addressed in Chapter 8, so if you want to see an approach to doing that, you can reference that chapter. In that review, we will work through how you can develop a framework for addressing security incident management revisions to communication parameters between security and legal and subsequently to the disclosure and Board representatives that aid in the decision to disclose to the SEC. The work packages captured in the diagram are intended to give you a sequence of things to abide by in order to keep your operation efficient, and your company out of the hot seat for not communicating in a timely manner to the SEC.

3.5.2 Set an SEC policy

The SEC communication and the guidelines your company will abide by for compliance should be captured in a policy that is managed and maintained by Legal in conjunction with Security, and possibly your Controller who is responsible for overseeing your firms compliance with accounting and regulation standards. At a high level, the 'cybersecurity' disclosure requirements apply to public companies aimed at improving the way incidents and security risks are communicated while also promoting more transparency. If you think of the intent, any security leader would welcome this as something U.S. corporations should do to improve overall security readiness. The idea of improving incident disclosure, and releasing annual governance and risk disclosures is not a bad idea, the criteria set by the SEC may be subject for complying to the mandates. Aside from the two areas noted above, there is a third that will be applicable in December 2024 that speaks to how companies will need to communicate cybersecurity information to the SEC. That requirement is called Inline Extensible Business Reporting Language or Inline XBRL.

By the time this book is released, Inline XBRL should be a requirement making the content submitted readable by both humans and machines. The intent of this is to make vast volumes of data submitted by corporations easy to analyze and read for relevant content through data tagging. Without going too much into this, it will add a third requirement to the existing disclosure base but to be honest, I can see why this would be something pursued given the proverbial stacks of reports that would be impossible to sift through without an easily identifiable mechanism to pull relevant content.

3.5.3 SEC incident management handling

In the development of the policy, an overarching approach to the SEC must be developed but this is an odd place to speak about incident management, and yet very relevant given that all the reporting starts with the identification of an incident and the handling from there by the security team. As we expand on this topic in Chapter 8, we need to revisit some of the relevant updates in procedure and practice to ensure we tighten up our ability to triage and communicate events that could be deemed reportable. Because of the aggressive requirements and the repercussions of not meeting SEC expectations, we need to make the process of assessing incidents and acting on them like reflex.

Stepping back from all of this, as a security leader, we need to ensure the practices of general IT incident management are married tightly to security incident handling. We need to ensure appropriate communication protocols are set for key security leads to relay information to Legal at appropriate thresholds. Walking this along, security should not use the word 'material' until Legal reviews it with the right Committee to deem if it's material or not; that entire workflow needs to be in place and tested. The reason we don't use the word 'material' and stick to generic language around incident is because in the case of litigation or an investigation, if you used that word and it turned out not to be 'material' then it becomes a potential messy legal matter. In addition, if you start using 'material' before it's been deemed as such then the clock starts on the requirement to report incidents within 4 business days of determining materiality. You want that determination to be done in a controlled manner.

Beyond everything stated already, we as practitioners need to make sure incident handling, and management involvement in managing risks is in place and clearly understood. If we're running our operation in a mature way, the requirements around incident handling, disclosure, Board involvement, communication and reporting, whether it's in the 6-K,, 8-K or 10-K should be familiar to your company. We will discuss these dimensions and related details later.

3.5.4 EU & UK regulations

For years, security professionals have been working with regulators to ensure GDPR compliance is met, and I can say for myself, I never had a problem with it because as a consumer, I'd rather have precedence set for the protection of my data, and it's good to see on the other side of the pond that there is a heavy focus and mandate to protect personal and other data. Today, the landscape is expanding and you can lose yourself if you try to capture all the regulations that are emerging in the EU but also UK.

Some more known ones include the Network and Information Systems Directive (NIS2) that looks to set security standards for network and information systems, and the Cyber Resilience Act (CRA) that will have a significant impact on hardware and software products. Hopping over the English Channel (or through the tunnel if you prefer), you'll run into other similar efforts to bolster the cybersecurity landscape with the UK pursuing the Cyber Security and Resilience Bill that will impact those industries that are deemed as vital to national security. This space is expansive and we'd need an entire other book to cover everything in detail so for now, we'll refer you to Chapter 8 for additional details.

3.6 COMPLACENCY VS ACTIVE CHANGE

The risk of complacency is everywhere and takes hold when people get comfortable. There's this thought that you need to put yourself in uncomfortable conditions to drive improvement. That seems...uncomfortable; I don't know if I always want to be uncomfortable. It sounds borderline like you like to torture yourself. However, the notion that you need to take risks and challenge yourself from time to time (note: time-to-time...not always), is something I can get behind. In teams, what I've come to see is when people get familiar with one another, there is a tendency to relax. Relaxing is good to reduce stress in high pressure environments but we need to be careful this doesn't lead to stagnation.

Place yourself 2 to 3 years from the day you join and you're now familiar with your team and if you have a good team and culture, you and your team are more than just colleagues. You understand the yearly cycles of goals, performance checkpoints, strategy, and financial planning and have run through it a few times; everything feels under control. The problem is falling into too much of a routine where we naturally lean on a body of achievements that were active and aggressive in the first few years. The question is, how do we maintain that energy but also nurture a growing sense of connection and sense of belonging to the greater community?

The diagram in this section captures several work packages that can help us ensure we don't get complacent. Chapter 9 will cover these move but the broad theme used is the concepts around 'institutional change', and the idea to introduce disruptive thinking into your organization to promote innovation and transformation. There are several ways to do this, and we will touch on the work packages here and further elaborate later (Figure 3.6).

3.6.1 Institutional change

There are several levers we can pull to ensure we are constantly challenging the status quo and stress testing our capabilities to ensure they are relevant

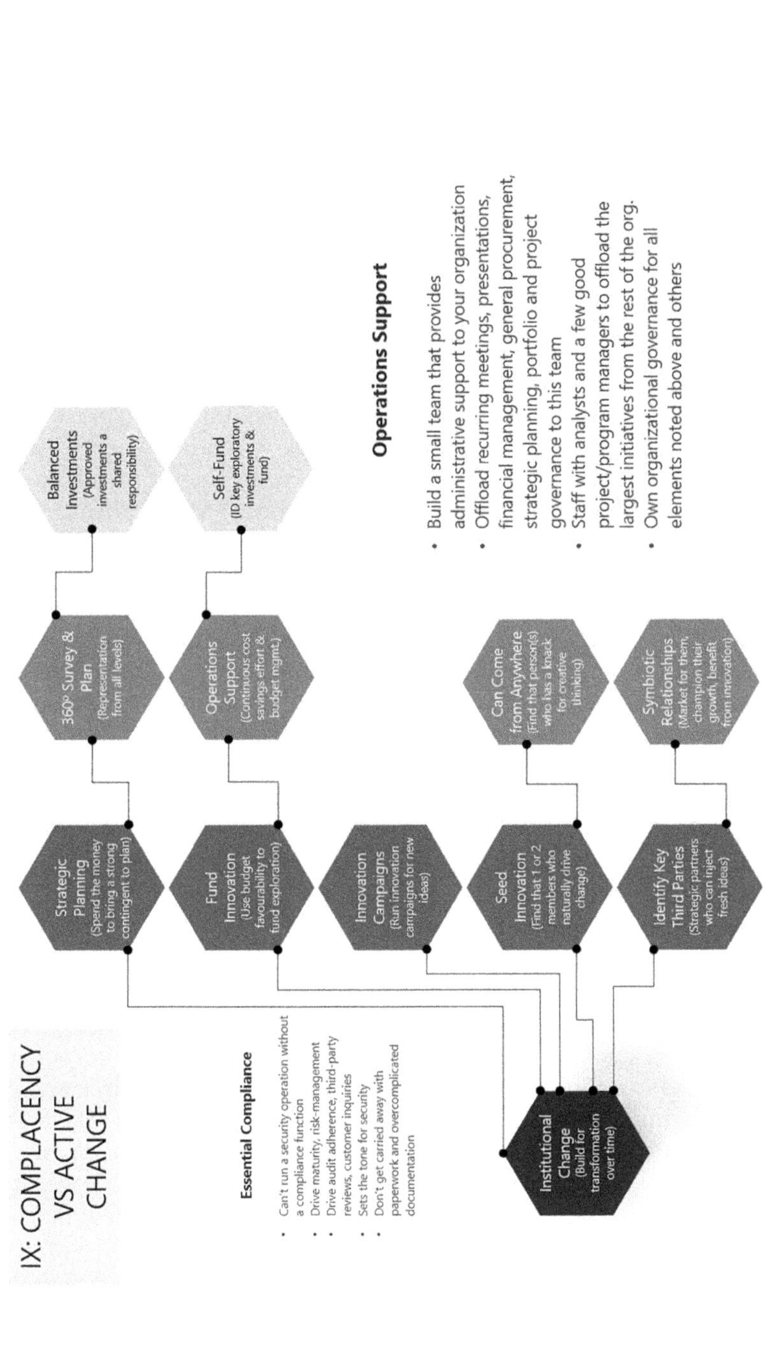

Figure 3.6 Complacency vs. active change.

to addressing the changing threat landscape. Boy doesn't that sound fancy? Well, it's needed, and we have ways to get it done.

> Why did the manager bring a ladder to the security transformation meeting?
>
> ...
>
> Because they wanted to 'scale' their security solutions to new heights!
>
> (OpenAI, 2024)

Okay, enough of that. One of the best ways to inject new energy and ideas is to run a yearly strategic planning meeting that is a focal point of the year and incorporate ideas from all of your stakeholders, including the Board, CEOs staff, your peers, yourself and your direct reports, but most importantly, your team running the day-to-day work activities. The investment in an offsite weeklong planning session where you bring in members from every function within your team and representation that canvasses your entire team is well worth it. The intent is multifold: 1: capture ideas and brainstorm on emerging challenges, 2: plan a strategy that captures representation from all parts of the team, and 3: strengthen team cohesiveness by coming together in person and doing some team development activities. If done right, this exercise will carry you through the rest of the year and the energy will drive proactive strategy, investment and financial planning.

Don't underestimate the importance of sound financial management. If you want support for innovation and investment initiatives, you need to prove you are fiscally responsible so that your CFO is willing to support you because she or he knows you have strong business acumen and can trust your judgment. Operations support services are key to ensuring active improvement of planning and financial control; do yourself a favor and ensure you build this team right away.

Invest in innovation and innovation campaigns. If your company doesn't have a formal innovation program, run one yourself and run innovation tournaments to encourage your team to generate ideas and explore emerging spaces that tie back to what your charter is. By being fiscally responsible, you can set aside an innovation fund to both fund approved ideas and generate rewards to members who do amazing work (HR approval first of course). Innovation tournaments give technical members a way to express themselves and take a chance on something in a controlled environment. By having a good operations support team, the coordination of these activities can be institutionalized so it's not a burden each time you want to do it but rather, part of your culture.

What you should also develop as part of your core is an architecture team that is heavily invested into researching emerging threats and solutions that they bring back and convert into ideas you can pursue. The challenge here is that when you first structure an architecture team, they are fixated on getting their structure in order, and building the practice. After a while, you need to set their mindset to the real purpose, which is to stay on par with developing trends and develop plans for the future. This can be supplemented by taking another step in building strong strategic partnerships with key vendors.

Not all third parties are created equally and just as within your team there are some folks that are ready to think innovatively, the same holds true with your vendor base. Identify those key vendors that can be strategic partners who can supplement your team when it comes to innovative ideas. The best ones are those who know they will get sales by first ensuring they are helping you solve problems. That is an investment on their part but I find it pays off for them in the long run. There are ways to prevent complacency and these are some that I have experience with. There are whole experts on the topic and while this may not be worthy of a Tech Talk, it nevertheless has proven in my world to ensure we stay current and on top of our game.

REFERENCE

OpenAI. (2024). *ChatGPT* [Large language model]. https://chatgpt.com

Chapter 4

Systematic review of work packages

Strategic roadmap

4.1 WHAT'S IN SCOPE?

We briefly went over the topics associated with maturity modeling, organizational structure and design, and several others under the strategy roadmap we introduced in Chapter 3. We will dive deeper into the key areas here to provide insights and recommendations on how to proceed across each of the significant work packages. As always, each company will have a slightly different set of conditions but in general, there's plenty that is common across companies and industries when it comes to the topics at hand. I have worked with the big consulting firms many times over the course of my career and one insight I always tried to extract from them is whether or not what we were doing in that company I was employed at was unique in any way from all the others they worked with? The answer was almost always no. Each time I asked, the answer was the same; you do some things unique to yourselves but as a whole, there's very little variation within industry for sure, and even cross industries. So I take this and suggest to you that what you see is 90-something percent applicable.

4.2 MATURITY MODEL

There are several sources of maturity models we can choose from to baseline our company's security design. In prior chapters we talked about NIST, ISO, CMMI, and CIS Controls as a few that are useful. We are going to focus here on corporate security but you can also expand the conversation to product security that has its own maturity model frameworks to supplement the ones for corporate. A couple of the ones you could consider in product security could be NIST special publication 800-218 titled "Secure Software Development Framework (SSDF)" or Building Security In Maturity Model (BSIMM); each of them have their strengths and focus points and it would not be a bad thing to apply both in a complimentary way because while NIST SSDF offers guidance on secure software development, BSIMM focuses on practices based on real-world execution and observations.

 DOI: 10.1201/9781003616528-4

The approach I would recommend is to have a specific framework for corporate and if you do software development or product security, have an associated one for that dimension of your practice. There is something to be said to stick with the same standard body if doing so because there will be synergies, such as using NIST cybersecurity framework (CSF) for corporate and NIST SSDF for software and product security, however, if you're a global operation, ensure what you design covers your global footprint as well. In addition, you may want to supplement your primary framework with some special publications that deal with specific topics, like the ones noted below:

- ETSI standard for consumer Internet of Things (IoT),
- NIST SP 800-213A for IoT device security,
- NIST SP 800-53 for security and privacy controls for information systems,
- IEC 62443-3-3 for industrial automation and control systems,
- NIST 800-30 for managing risks and risk assessments

All of these publications are available to you online if you choose to review the publications in detail. We will start with NIST CSF as the umbrella framework for our corporate security practice. It is a widely used publication and as close to a best practice as you can find. I have used it as the assessment guide for my security practice in the past and many times when you bring a third party to do an external assessment, they will use this as their measuring stick, especially if your headquartered in the United States.

My recommendation, especially for U.S.-based companies is to use NIST CSF as your overarching framework. NIST CSF first came out in 2014 and was later revised in 2023. The Framework does a good job breaking up the aspects of security into Govern, Identify, Protect, Detect, Respond, and Recover. CSF is flexible enough to be applied to any industry and organizational structure, and offers a way to measure maturity so that the implementation of the controls defined under the categories can be tracked over time as to the progress your company is making in maturing your operation. Using CSF, you can establish practices against its recommended five dimensions. You can then baseline your performance against the tiers of sophistication, and lastly you can easily identify your current versus a target state to set the end goal for your team.

The nice thing about NIST CSF is that it helps us address security risks alongside those of the company as a whole, including those tied to financial, privacy, supply chain and others. As noted, CSF covers the Core catalog of capabilities you want to consider in developing your security practice. It also defines the Profiles and Tiers that will aide you in defining where you are on a maturity scale and where you want to be. The structure makes it really easy to map the functional elements noted earlier to the capabilities and actions that will drive a systematic approach to improvement.

Most assessment firms will take this and develop a radar diagram that shows where you are in the various dimensions versus what your target state is so that you can clearly see what you're good at and what you need to work on (NIST, 2023, p. 20).

In addition to the radar diagram, the mapping is easily understandable, covering topics such as risk management strategy and oversight under Govern, asset management in Identify, data security under Protect, continuous monitoring under Detect, incident management under Respond, and incident recovery plan execution under Recover as a sampling of the types of categories CSF uses in assessing maturity (NIST CSF, 2023, p. 20). The intent here is not to go over the framework but to offer a suggestion on what you can start with to get your practice moving.

The way you can use CSF is to take the categories of capabilities defined in the publication and start defining key roles in your organization to support the capabilities identified. Some of them might sit in the general information technology team and others in your space, but these are great guideposts for development. Second, you can do an assessment of an existing practice and define strengths and weaknesses that will tell you where to prioritize your immediate efforts to improve low maturity areas and low hanging fruit.

Make CSF your overarching framework. Use NIST SP 800-53 as a complimentary Special Publication to further expand your security practice. Where CSF is a general approach to managing security risk, SP 800-53 defines specific technical controls that tie back to the categories defined by CSF. SP 800-53 was developed for U.S. federal agencies and their contractors. It's a mandatory publication that is compliance-focused to adhere to federal laws, and standards such as HIPAA FedRAMP, and others. By combining these two, you get a general risk-based approach in CSF running your maturity and SP 800-53 defining the specific controls that will support CSF and ensure you are meeting the requirements of federal regulations. A quick comparison of the two is provided below in Table 4.1.

Let's add one more: NIST Risk Management Framework (RMF). RMF helps us to identify, assess, and mitigate risks. RMF is very similar to CSF in that it's scalable to any sized organization and industry, but it's focus is on risk management. RMF is a 7-step process that when implemented, will help you establish a risk management program and conduct risk assessments.

Table 4.1 Comparison of NIST CSF & SP 800-53

Characteristic	*CSF*	*SP 800-53*
Directive	Voluntary	Required for U.S. Federal Systems
Model	Risk-Based	Compliance-Based
Specification	Broad	Detailed & Specific
Objective	Framework	Define Specific Controls

As we know, the entire backbone of security is risk management, which means you want to develop your practice around a structured approach that is viewed as a best practice. RMF in the U.S. has become a baseline for many to use in developing their risk practice. As a caveat, Special Publication 800-30 is a Publication used to help you develop the 'assess' part of the RMF. It is a complimentary Publication that offers specifics to this dimension of RMF that is useful to reference as well (NIST RMF, 2018, p. 27).

In summary, use NIST CSF as your overarching Framework, supplement it with SP 800-53 for specific controls. Then combine them with NIST RMF to add a solid practice around risk management; the three of these combined will give you a great foundation for establishing your practice, or assessing an existing one to determine where it stands from a maturity standpoint. This will also help you prioritize your work since we all know that resources including personnel, time, and money are limited so anything that can help us prioritize is invaluable (Figure 4.1).

A note about the European Union (EU) and defining a similar grouping to what I have noted in the U.S. I'm not an expert in the area of compliance and standards but from what I see, and what I can tell you is that there isn't really a single reference that maps to CSF. We do however have a few that work together to provide something equivalent, namely, the EU Cybersecurity Act and the guidelines published by the European Union Agency for Cybersecurity (ENISA).

The EU Cybersecurity Act established ENISA and sets its sights on improving risk management, and cooperation across the EU to establish best practices. ENISA publishes guidelines to improve resilience in the area and defining risk management for what we call critical infrastructure. Beyond these, there are also the Network and Information Systems Directive (NIS Directive), and General Data Protection Regulation (GDPR); the latter protects privacy and data. Finally, I wouldn't be covering enough if I didn't mention the International Standards ISO/IEC 27001 and 27002 that map pretty closely to NIST CSFs approach and establish an information security management system (ISMS). What I have done in practice is to use NIST for my foundation, and then look to get certified in ISO 27001 as a widely recognized, international Standard that provides credibility to the security operation and to the firm as a whole (note that you can get certified for ISO 27001 but not in ISO 27002 as 27002 is a set of guidelines and recommended controls to meet the requirements of 27001).

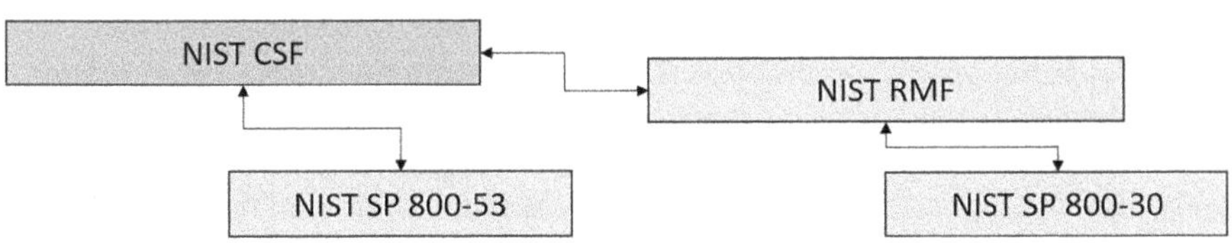

Figure 4.1 Frameworks models.

You can expand your standards portfolio well beyond what I have described here and quickly get lost. As noted in former chapters, you also have the European Telecommunications Standards Institute (ETSI) that publishes references for operating technology (OT) and cybersecurity. You also have other Acts that cover products and communication protocols, but my recommendation is establish the foundation and get agreement with Legal in particular on how you will measure your security operation. Then you can add additional references as needed to deal with specific areas of the company's operation as supplemental. Be careful not to get lost in this, and go back to what we're doing: setting a baseline set of measures to drive a systematic approach to defining our practice and measuring our progress over time. For what I've shared here, anyone, no matter where you're from, can use the sources identified to establish this. Worst case, fine equivalent references in your corner of the world and do the same as described here.

4.3 ORGANIZATION DESIGN

How much of a standards geek are you? Are you one of those that immediately tries to reference a standard or publication for every question asked or do you feel your way through the topic; almost relying on your gut to give you the path forward? I know people who live and die by standards, and I know others who just wing it, although maybe it's not fair to say intuition and instinct-based decision making is synonymous with 'winging it' but the ones I know really do wing it, so I use that phrase loosely. The answer to me to how we approach problems should be somewhere in the middle (isn't that with everything though?). To design your organization, you can reference some of the prior sources like NIST to figure out what to build. You can use NIST 800-100 that talks about key roles and responsibilities, or NIST 800-39 that approaches the same subject from a risk perspective, or even NIST 800-53 that we discussed earlier that talks about key departments that make up security. In the end, you need to understand the dynamics within your firm and design based a little on best practices and the rest from what you observe within the company.

What we discuss here will effectively cover most if not all of the recommendations, especially from NIST 800-53. That is true not because I used the Publication as a reference but rather because in doing this for most of my professional career, what I describe is what works and makes your team effective. What would be awful is if I went through my career building security teams and then later discovered no commonality to what is in the popular standards. That would be a problem, but luckily that's not the case. Let's start this topic by addressing the critical functions that need to be performed and then back into a structure. In this discussion, we'll use SP 800-53 for cross referencing. so here we go.

Let's start with Governance and Compliance. Somewhere in our organization we need to establish and manage policies, standards, processes and guidelines, or whatever terminology your firm uses. To run an effective practice, we need to know what we are measuring ourselves against in the form of a framework as we discussed earlier and then set a security policy that will govern the way we approach security as an organization. Along the way, we need to develop additional documentation in the form of Standards that speak to things like access management and controls, password structure and administration, and several others that define how we work. In addition to this, we need to manage compliance to policies and standards as well as regulatory mandates across the regions our business has a footprint. We may need to comply with GDPR in the EU, or California privacy requirements, or U.S. federal requirements for contractors working for federal agencies. Having a compliance function is vital.

Along the way, we need to establish a risk-based practice and the best place to do this is under a governance function. Training and awareness is absolutely essential to develop an ongoing reinforcement of best practices. There's a whole dimension of audit support we need to manage that comes from customers, regulators and even third parties we need to continually field and support. Depending on your organizations model, you may need to include a data privacy function to coincide with your data protection practice. Needless to say, the area of governance touches quite a bit and is both inwardly and outwardly facing to ensure we meet the needs of the company, our team and external stakeholders. To summarize, we see the function at a bare minimum looking like the list shown in Figure 4.2 below. There are

Function: Governance & Compliance
❑ Document Management & Control
❑ Compliance Management
❑ Government & Regulatory Relations
❑ Maturity Modeling & Tracking
❑ Risk Governance
❑ Audit Support & Remediation
❑ Data Privacy Administration
❑ Data Governance
❑ Business Continuity & Disaster Recovery
❑ Training & Awareness
❑ Security Champion Program Administration
❑ Security Reporting

Figure 4.2 Governance & compliance.

going to be other functions that you might incorporate but this gives you a feel for what this domain covers.

Some additional notes on this; within training and awareness, this team manages any phishing campaigns and associated follow up trainings, including role-specific training. They handle cybersecurity month that normally occurs in October, they also administer the business continuity and disaster recovery function where they work with the system owners to ensure proper resiliency measures are in place. Finally, this team has a larger ownership of reporting than most other teams as they provide oversight across the organization.

Moving along, another vital function is captured under the title of Cyber Fusion. Sounds really fancy and cool but there's a reason why it's named this way. This is not your normal operations team, but rather an integrated approach to running security operations where you are conducting more than monitoring (eyes on glass) and managing vulnerabilities. You are doing incident response, threat hunting, threat modeling, forensics, malware analysis and all sorts of really cool stuff aimed at improving your situational awareness. The name is rooted in the idea behind fusion centers that integrate data and operations to make decision making faster, and more efficient; Cyber Fusion takes this idea and applies it to security.

We already threw out a few things this team does, but fundamentally, they are the ones that are operating in some 24x7 format, whether it's in a follow-the-sun model or central hub. The operational model I used in my career is an insource-outsource hybrid where you partner with a Managed Security Service Provider (MSSP) who does the intensive data capture, assessment, and filtering and you take the verified events and work internally within the company to determine validity, risk, and subsequently remediation. The thinking here is that most companies don't have the bandwidth to do all of this, which also means managing tools and appliances in their infrastructure, so you send this off to someone else to do. By partnering, you are able to do a whole. In fact one of the first things I do when taking on a new operation is to determine how strong this capability is within the organization (second only to infrastructure maturity). If I find we need to install or revamp, it usually takes about 2 years to select, install, tune, and operationalize. A topic for another chapter. To summarize this domain, we consider the below responsibilities in Figure 4.3.

Now something to point out; there are functions noted here (not inclusive by the way) that can be covered under a Security Assurance domain as well, depending on how you want to structure your operation. The importance here is that this is the arm of your operations that owns real-time situational awareness and response. It's the best description I can give it because it is really the front lines to keeping your organization safe on a daily basis. I included SEC administration because the initial signal that something is wrong and the protocol on what to do about it comes from this team, so in my world they are accountable for managing that through escalation to

Function: Cyber Fusion

- ❑ Security Alert & Monitoring
- ❑ Vulnerability Management
- ❑ Risk Reduction (As Opposed To Governance)
- ❑ Threat Intelligence & Awareness
- ❑ Operational Communication
- ❑ Incident Management
- ❑ SEC Incident Administration
- ❑ Policy Enforcement
- ❑ Security Exception Management
- ❑ Forensics & Malware Analysis
- ❑ Recurring Table Top Exercises
- ❑ Data Protection Monitoring & Management

Figure 4.3 Cyber fusion.

both internal security leadership and notification to Legal in a timely manner. Last point on this team, when I refer to table top exercises, I mean both internal and Executive-level. Ideally you are running table tops and simulated events in your organizational twice a year to ensure everyone knows their role and how to respond. This should involve the top leadership of the company and sometimes key Board of Directors members if they are willing to take an active role.

The next one is not something that is always defined but I have found it to be absolutely invaluable as a check and balance to your Cyber Fusion domain. Security Assurance is a team that serves as your internal technical auditors of the technology footprint. Said another way, they ensure your practice across policies, systems, and procedures are working the way they should. They are continually looking to improve your security posture and one way they do this is probing and attempting to hack various services and systems that make up your technology footprint. You've probably heard of penetration testing where company's offer this service to test your hardening; Security Assurance builds this capability in-house, along with many others to conduct ethical hacking from within.

The folks that make up this team are pretty interesting. These are highly technical folks that work in the grey. What I mean by that is they could just as easily be hackers as they are ethical hackers. Be nice to them, always treat them well and just say 'yes you are right', because you don't want to piss them off. They can sometimes cross the lines between Assurance and Fusion but even with that possible conflict, I have found this function is a must. They can perform penetration testing, and code reviews of application code in your software development practice. They can perform configuration validation, and run red-team exercises to hack your environment. They can be a big contributor to your secure software development lifecycle (SSDLC) as they can help integrate security features and drive a shift-left philosophy. There's so much they can do but ultimately they are the team you secretly go to, to test incident management practices, probe networks, and do all the things that fall under stress testing your environment, which usually lead to improvement initiatives that make you that much stronger. You can have this and Cyber Fusion under a single operations function, depending how you are organized but the summary of this domain is show below in Figure 4.4.

There's so much more this team can do including ensuring that the company is meeting regulatory requirements from a technology perspective, and testing internal controls for their effectiveness, but you get the idea. A quick word on the different Team exercises; Red Team is commonly referred to as offensive security, where the team applies tactics, techniques, and procedures (TTP) that the bad actors commonly use. Blue Team is defensive security where they are working to defend against various attack vectors. Purple Team is a combination that looks to run exercises from both vantage points to improve the overall integrity of your operation. This is where war games come into play and you can do some neat things like capture the flag scenarios and others to sharpen your organizations skills.

The next domain I'd like to talk about is Architecture and Planning. This to me has had more variance across the organizations I've worked in than any other function because there's an interpretive element to this space. Something we haven't talked about at all is cloud security up to this point, and the reality is that all the controls you employ on-premise are usually mirrored in the cloud. Depending on your team's skill set, you can house cloud security in a few spots, but I have placed it in the past in this team.

Function: Security Assurance
❑ Red Team, Blue Team, Purple Team Exercises
❑ Penetration Testing
❑ Code Reviews
❑ Secure Software Design
❑ Incident Management Stress Testing
❑ Ethical Hacking
❑ Bug Bounty Program Administration
❑ Threat Modeling
❑ Product & Software Pre-Deployment Testing

Figure 4.4 Security assurance.

There are a few reasons for that, the biggest for me as I stated was that in past jobs I had the capability in my architects to manage this so it just made sense. Aside from this function, your architects are responsible for designing the long-term security framework for your organization. Where security engineers implement and maintain, and security analysts monitor and manage incidents and threats; your architects are designing the future state. Their role is strategic in nature versus tactical and operational. They drive the vision for the future and many times are part of a project management lifecycle as the approvers of new demand because of their strategic vantage point. Ideally this is where you house some of your most experienced thinkers who can promote innovation within the organization and pull in new concepts and emerging technologies to integrate into your technology footprint. The summary looks as depicted below in Figure 4.5.

Note the asterisks. It really depends on what your organization does and the structure. You could find yourself needing a team to support a product engineering and development business unit in which case, this team would help to embed Security By Design principles into that product development lifecycle. We already spoke about the area of cloud and how this team could be an integral part of both designing and administering some key security capabilities. You could alternatively pass this to one of the other teams in operations we already described but it has to sit somewhere and it needs to be a focal point given that so much is moving to cloud (native and otherwise). As a final note, the ARB is something that promotes maturity across your technology practice as an organization; security is one part of the whole. In some cases my team has led the practice and in others, it has been a part of the larger practice. To ensure other technology teams are adhering

Function: Security Architecture & Planning
❑ Research Emerging Concepts & Technology
❑ Technical Consulting to Organization
❑ Technology Roadmap & Business Planning
❑ Idea & Demand Management
❑ Architecture & Solution Design
❑ Architecture Review Board (ARB)
❑ *Cloud Security Architecture
❑ *Cloud Technical Guardrails
❑ *Cloud Access Management
❑ *Product Security Design & Integration
❑ *Product Threat Assessment & Modeling

Figure 4.5 Security architecture & planning.

to security best practices, you want to have some forum to share and review future plans to ensure they meet minimum security requirements.

Beyond the ones I already defined, there are a couple of others that I feel are very important but will depend on where you report into and how your organization has structured security. This also depends on how big your company is, meaning, if you're a massive behemoth that has multiple business units acting independently, maybe some of these don't apply completely but they are at least important to work through for those who have the opportunity or need to address. The first one is what I term as Infrastructure Services. An argument can be made that this should be under IT, but I believe that network infrastructure has a ton of synergies with the security organization.

Call this team what you will, but what I have found is many security projects come out of this team because of what it touches. This team can be responsible for security and network infrastructure, transport services, firewalls and firewall rules, access management, wide area and local area networking (WAN/LAN), and many others. As you can tell not everything is traditional security but there are functions here that work well together, even though this is an infrastructure domain. Sometimes the way your organization is designed, you don't have the opportunity to put this grouping together with the rest of the security organization but if you can, my recommendation is you absolutely should.

Another key security function I have placed in this domain in the past is identity and access management (IAM). Some leaders will make this a standalone function and in very large organizations, that's probably a good idea as a separate domain in security altogether, so consider that as you develop your operation, but in cases where there is concentrated talent and good leadership in this domain, you can plant this here as well. Whichever path you take (separate domain or not), you do want to address IAM and make it part of the security organization. Other security-related functions that can sit here are certificate management, VPN and MFA administration, and data protection engineering. Yes, I know to those who are looking at this and saying it can be done differently… most things can be done differently so I'll again concede that you want to consider your culture and structure in deciding how big or small the scope can really be here.

I've looked at it this way; you need a pure security operations function that is your Cyber Fusion, and we also described Security Assurance. You also want to address the presence of security in traditional infrastructure operations as well in some way. I have opted to handle it in this space, and when I didn't want to have too many direct reports, I placed IAM in here but you could simply carve that out into another grouping. In fact if I were to do this again in the future, maybe I would do just that but when something works, don't go trying to fix it has been my motto in the past. The functions you need to cover in some way look like the following list in Figure 4.6.

The top section is your traditional transport services team. The ones in asterisks are functions you can move into another domain if you don't have

Function: Infrastructure Services
❑ Security & Network Infrastructure
❑ Firewall Rule Management
❑ Tier 2 & 3 Operations & Engineering
❑ WAN/LAN/Wireless
❑ Capacity Management & Planning
❑ Telecom Management (Usually)
❑ 24x7 Network Operations Center (NOC)
❑ *Active Directory Administration
❑ *Identity & Access Management (IAM)
❑ *Certificates Management
❑ *VPN & MFA Management
❑ *Email Security & Engineering
❑ *Single Sign-On Administration
❑ *Endpoint Security

Figure 4.6 Infrastructure services.

the alignment within a single team. You have to balance size of team against the desire to reduce the number of domains. So far we have talked about five domains including this one. We have another one or possibly two to discuss so if you do decide to break this up, just know you will then have eight teams under you. That may be okay but make a decision based on your own capacity to manage eight direct reports while also meeting the demands of working with the rest of the organization on evangelizing security.

You have to have the mindset that you're running a business and with that, you need to have a team that helps you manage it as such. There are things you need to care for like financial management, procurement services, and strategy. In most companies, there are finance and procurement teams, but you need to maintain the interface points to these departments that represent your interests and drive your own internal improvement. Don't go out and try to build your own finance team; that's simply not our mission in security, but develop the practice of managing your finances in a way that keeps you and your team under budget and acting responsibly. The same thing holds for contract and procurement management. You have specific contractors that provide key services. You want to ensure you are managing them effectively and partnering with the Procurement Organization to manage them effectively. If done right, this team should take the burden of administrative responsibilities away from your core security teams and allow them to focus on their core competency. Another way to say it is this team reduces the noise and allows for focus, while establishing a center of excellence to continually improve those practices that make your organization efficient and effective.

A few other areas this team touches include managing your strategic planning practice, managing internal and external reporting and communications, and portfolio and project governance. As a security leader, you have a lot of reporting responsibilities; this team can help manage timelines for reporting, facilitate the creation of repeatable presentations like Board presentations, and also drive process improvement efforts. At first when introduction this function in an existing team, the other domains may question the value of this team and come along reluctantly but if you have the right leadership running it, this can quickly become that domain that the others didn't realize they needed all this time. A summary of some of the functions you can include is captured in Figure 4.7.

In most organizations, this would be the last domain I'd define but since we are not just an information and cyber security organization and we include product security as part of our case study, we should address one more domain to cover that aspect of our operation. Now what you'll probably end up doing is distributing the support of product security much like you have done with the other aspects of your operation. Within your compliance team you also govern product-related regulations. In your architecture team, you manage design responsibilities for products, and develop threat models as part of the product development lifecycle.

Your entire team would be connected to the product and software development lifecycles and within them, you're driving secure-by-design and shift-left into those practices. If you are responsible for data privacy, you are also driving privacy by design and conducting privacy impact assessments and ensuring that all the requirements are met prior to signing off for deployment.

Function: Operations Support Services
❑ Internal & External Communications
❑ Financial Management
❑ Procurement Support
❑ Vendor & Contract Management
❑ General Learning & Development
❑ Reporting & Analytics
❑ Portfolio & Project Governance
❑ Resource Management
❑ Process Controls & Improvement

Figure 4.7 Operations support services.

So, product security support should be engrained into the domains already defined, but with that there are still very specific things that need to be done in order to support your product engineering and development functions.

Everything tied to product development runs in parallel with what you do in enterprise but at the same time has a unique component to it as well. We speak a lot about secure-by-design because it's in this space where we are developing products and software that having security as an integrated part of the design process will improve your security posture tremendously. The alternative is bolt-on security which for me, isn't really a practice approach but what happens when security isn't a serious consideration of your product development cycle and ends up being amended because it was missed. Secure-by-design gives us the opportunity to connect our security architects along with the rest of our security experts to the development teams so that we can help our company produce secure products as a functional part of engineering.

When you apply secure-by-design and shift-left, you are providing security requirements to product designs as enhancements and sometimes features to the product itself. Your team is performing threat modeling for products throughout the lifecycle of product development that identifies possible risks to the design. With software, you are providing tools and practices to develop secure code and capabilities to test that code for vulnerabilities or flaws in design so that you can correct it real-time as opposed to at the end of the development cycle. Code reviews are a big part of what you do in companies where you develop products in-house. Alternatively if you outsource your product development then you are making it a requirement for your third party to conduct code reviews or injecting an audit of products to ensure the code is robust and stable.

Code reviews can come in various forms, and they can be automated or manual, and apply static and dynamic analysis. Note that your Security Assurance Team and Architecture Team will have a big part to play here in support of the Product Security domain. Security Assurance may be helping with penetration testing and they'll be providing services like Bug Bounty to find weaknesses in the platforms being produced by third party ethical hackers. Within the domain, you are providing product security incident response services that compliment what's done on the enterprise side. Naturally you'll want incident response to be handled in a consistent fashion but the tier 2 or 3 support may come from the Product Security domain.

In your continuous integration and continuous deployment pipeline (CI/CD) that enables fast software development, this domain may be performing checks on the software to ensure secure development is applied. There are multiple touchpoints on software but leadership and direction to the rest of the security teams will come from this domain. Guidance on emerging product threats is something this team will do, as they are expected to continuously be researching this specialized area and are the 'experts' within your team. There is a specific role that I've learned in my time leading security teams that you want to consider defining in this domain called the Product Security Lead or PSL. You can call this whatever you want; I happen to know it as this but they serve as your top personnel who are highly proficient in the area of product security and are able to serve as your relationship managers to the development and engineering teams. They work under the guidance of the Product Security Leader that is your direct report and are key drivers for best practices and compliance in this space.

PSLs can be carved out as a separate unit or folded into your compliance operation, because they spend quite a bit of their time working with product-related regulations, serving as liaisons to the product teams, and serving as gatekeepers for product and software launches. They work to ensure privacy and protection is built in and work exclusively to reduce product and software risks. They manage product vulnerabilities and work closely with the other teams to capture them across software, mobile applications, and products. They manage the product risk profile, and systematically work to reduce the risk exposure. Your Product Security Leader who works with the PSLs will be part of the product engineering team's extended team and will work closely with them to develop scorecards and help facilitate the seamless delivery process with security as an enabler. As you can see there are a lot of things that get concentrated in this one team that run parallels in others but we need to have a center of excellence focused on product security because this area touches the areas that drive revenue and it demands a dedicated set of relationship managers. As with before, a summary of the types of responsibilities you can include is captured below in Figure 4.8:

Function: Product Security

- ❑ Issue Product Security Requirements
- ❑ Conduct Threat Modeling
- ❑ Conduct Code Reviews
- ❑ Tier 2 & 3 Product Incident Response
- ❑ Software Testing Guidance
- ❑ Consult on Emerging Product Threats
- ❑ Product Security Regulatory Guidance
- ❑ Research and Innovation in Product Security
- ❑ Relationship Management with Product Teams
- ❑ Product Vulnerability Management
- ❑ Product Risk Management
- ❑ Executive Reporting & Scorecards

Figure 4.8 Product security.

This list doesn't specifically call out the PSLs but you can assume they are involved in all the activities noted. The team isn't very big. It depends on the size of your product engineering and development teams and if you have multiple business units but normally you have a small unit of PSLs that work under the Leader. These PSLs then rely on the other aspects of your organization to provide services as needed. There's always the debate of whether product security should sit in the product engineering teams, and my view is no. There are a few reasons for this, first, if you were to build this in the business units, you would have to replicate a lot of the other structure that we talked about in your organization in that business unit. This is not an efficient model where you have multiple security teams doing similar things, unless there are regulatory reasons for it. Second, you want to maintain independent governance so that your team is not influenced by the engineering teams and pressured to make decisions that are inconsistent with their objectives in security. When push comes to shove, engineering teams will usually roll out products at the expense of security for obvious reasons; you need to maintain independence so you can voice the risks and then allow the business to determine the best course of action. We all know that without products and services there is no company to secure so we have to have a balanced and reasonable approach to security, but at the same time, we need to ensure we have an independent voice that is heard and not silenced.

The last point will be around the role of the CISO. If you have separate security teams in an organization where there's no regulatory reason for separation then you've effectively eliminated the CISO role. Maybe folks have an opinion on this but the CISO is supposed to represent all security interests, and by splitting security she or he no longer has the full authority over security. This can be a messy scenario because nowadays governments and regulators are moving towards single liability and accountability for security. The discussions on the SEC and the requirements speak to how security is led. Ultimately who becomes accountable for security if the function is distributed? I think the answer is security then rolls up to the CEO, and I'm not sure if she or he wants to field all the responsibilities of security. I can say that for me, if I don't have authority over the development of secure practices then I'd prefer to relinquish the title of CISO because that title carries with it personal liability, and now you're liable for something you don't even control. There is always a debate around this and others will have different renditions, and that's fine but this is my perspective that you can consider in whichever way makes sense to you.

One other point to make on organizational structure, you'd probably be wise to identify a person who is your second-in-command that can serve as your Deputy CISO (dCISO). We cover a lot of ground in the work we do and if you try to do it all, it becomes very challenging. In addition, we are critical leaders in the organization for the work we do so you should be thinking about being a responsible member of the organization and have a possible succession plan in the event you win the lottery or get abducted by aliens; the latter is more probable. Make the dCISO as a growth opportunity for someone who has emerging leadership capabilities and experience in the spaces you manage. They need to have good relationships across the organization and viewed as constructive members of your organization. As you lift off in the alien ship, you want to know that your organization will survive, although that's probably not going to be the first thing on your mind.

So if we summarize all the talk about organizational structure we come up with a rough organizational chart that looks something like what's below. Depending on your size and your company you may also have executive support or you may not. The dCISO may be an individual contributor but many times I assign that title to someone who is performing a functional role. This can be good and bad; the juries out on that, but it appears that extracting them from the operational responsibilities and assigning them a couple of analysts to help make sense of the overall function may make sense so that they can truly assist you in managing security in the company. This really depends on what you have already in place and the personalities. In one case I had a separate dCISO who had one or two direct reports and that's all that existed in their organization. In another case I had them run a function but what happens is they can get into operational conflicts with other domain Leads that can drag them into more tactical matters. You should consider both approaches and determine what fits for your organization. A sample organizational chart is depicted in Figure 4.9, and you can use it as a way to organize your own team structure with whatever variations make sense.

As a final note on the topic of organizational design, if you refer back to SP 800-53, you'll see most if not all of the recommendations made here, captured there as well. The recommendations made here are based on experience and they have worked for me in my career. Sometimes though, we want to check to see what the standards folks recommend, and I can say we're pretty much in line with them with some variations. Hopefully you have what you need to build a solid team and well-rounded organization.

4.4 FUNCTIONAL FIRST

The conversation around organizational structure and modeling ended with at least seven domains and up to nine (Product Security, and IAM). Depending on where you start, the Infrastructure Services could be your primary focal point if in a greenfield scenario for at least a couple of years. Alternatively, if your scenario is a brownfield, it will still be your focal point at first to ensure the core services are in place as a baseline of practices in the company, but here you may run this assessment in parallel to the security operations aspect of the practice that is captured under Functional Second.

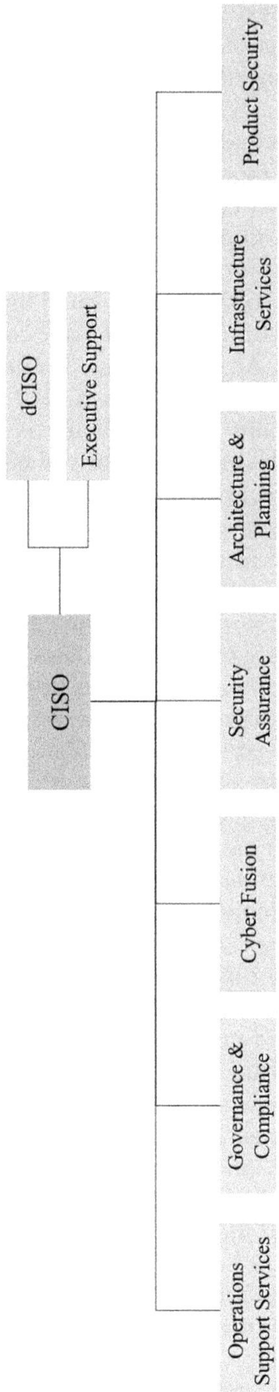

Figure 4.9 Organization chart.

Whatever the scenario may be, you want to immediately do an assessment of core infrastructure services to ensure the foundation is there.

Functional First is a set of controls we want to ensure are in place or being developed to offer the baseline security for the company. I normally associate them with infrastructure activities, and so if you were mapping the work activities to the domains, it would be tied back to Infrastructure Services. In a greenfield scenario where there's no IT or security to speak of, you are likely spending most of your time building the capabilities to get the company moving towards becoming productive; that typically means base IT services and in our case transport and network build outs. Within this, you are also working in parallel to secure that build and lay the foundation to harden this very quickly as you don't want your company to be vulnerable at the onset of its operation. As noted before, in brownfield, you just want to check to see if these controls are in place and at a healthy state or if you need to invest further. The reality is your job here is never finished and you'll be improving them or introducing others for some time.

Let's start with network security. You want to have strong security controls for local and remote users. Today, the workforce is mixed in this regard and no matter what the current return to work movement in some companies tells trend analysts, remote work is here to stay. So with that, you want to make sure on the inside, you have a segmented network architecture. Compartmentalizing your network prevents lateral movement and can box in any potential attack to minimize impact. Segmentation usually means some form of firewall infrastructure that serves as gateways between segments but also control points at your ingress/egress points to your network. Review the architecture of the network, how it's segmented and how your company controls traffic flow in and out of the company and within it, with next generation firewalls that can perform deep packet inspection.

In conjunction with segmentation and firewalls, you want to understand exactly how network access control (NAC) is administered. NAC manages authorization to network resources by people and devices and ensures the connecting device is compliant with certain base standards. Some of the elements that make up NAC are username and password combinations but also certificates or tokens and multifactor authentication (MFA). There's a lot more to NAC but you want to understand at a high level, how access control is administered in your infrastructure. What I'm describing here is part of the popular Zero Trust strategy you want to deploy. Now I keep hearing zero trust everywhere and frankly it gets pretty annoying. However, putting aside my viewpoints, as security professionals, we have been applying zero trust all our careers, and as a philosophy, it is essential to how we think about security our operation.

Okay, enough of that. Zero Trust Network Administration (ZTNA) verifies user and device access to network resources and NAC is a component of this general principle. ZTNA verifies identity of users and devices and maps rights to policies for accessing applications and other resources.

ZTNA takes away the notion of implied trust and forces a mapping of user/device to service on a least privilege model, using 'never trust, always verify' as a principle. You can expect your network to be segmented, you can expect firewalls being present and hopefully specific firewall rules in place to itemize traffic flow. You can even expect some sort of access control to be present but you may find that some of this ZTNA implementation might be loosely defined. That's okay, but add it to your initial set of initiatives to strengthen.

Other things to look for on the network side is if your company has implemented any type of intrusion detection and/or prevention systems. This starts getting into more security-type operations but sometimes these do get deployed as a part of the initial infrastructure build out. They allow for monitoring and threat prevention in your network so as an initial part of the rollout, these would be very useful for a security engineer.

Look for how you encrypt data at rest and in transit. Even at the onset of build-outs, you don't want to be relaying data unencrypted. Check to ensure all data communication has some sort of encryption built in. I don't speak too much about application security here, but at the very least ensure your applications, databases, operating systems have vulnerability scanning and patching in place and for web applications, you want to ensure they are adequately protected with some fort of web application firewall (WAF). A WAF protects web applications from threats and it blocks malicious HTTP and HTTPS traffic. WAF protects from attacks such as DDoS, and file inclusion among others. You want to ensure your company does something to protect Internet-facing applications and WAF is one tool that is a best practice. When external assessors come to determine your maturity as a security operation, many times, they will look to see if you use WAF in your environment.

Some quick-hit security best practices to look for are the use of Virtual Private Networking (VPN) for remote access to company networks, where you create an encrypted connection from the user's device to your company network. You want to also ensure multifactor authentication (MFA) is in place. MFA confirms identity using two of three factors which are something you know, something you have and something you are. It has been a best practice in authentication for some time, so you want to make sure at a minimum you have this in place. To overachieve, you can push for Fast Identity Online (FIDO), an open standard-based authentication method that is more user friendly and more secure. FIDO supports passwordless authentication and uses cryptographic authentication techniques. If your infrastructure includes FIDO then you know someone has been staying on top of emerging authentication trends. Now, remember, this is 2024 I'm writing this so if you're a few years in the future, then it should probably be assumed a mandatory implementation at that time.

Additional quick hits include the use of Single Sign-On (SSO) as foundational to a strong security practice. You would be surprised how large companies might have missed this one and you need to jump on this right away to prevent data loss and account information leaking into the dark web that can then be used to access your network in the simplest of ways. Address this right away if you find your company does not have a comprehensive SSO implementation. I'm mostly focused on network-related security here but check to see if on the mobile side your company is using mobile device management (MDM) and on the device-side, some sort of device encryption is being used. In Windows-based devices, BitLocker is a popular disk encryption tool that prevents unauthorized access to data on the device in the case the device is lost or stolen. I'm not endorsing BitLocker or Windows in any way, but reality is most of us are using Microsoft tools and this is a highly probably scenario. The endpoints deployed at your company should have antivirus software installed. If you use endpoint detection and response (EDR) then it may come with a built-in antivirus. If your EDR doesn't come with it or you don't have EDR (which would really suck), then you can use Microsoft Defender in the case of Windows-based devices, that comes with antivirus.

Now let's circle back and ensure we're not just ticking off a whole bunch of controls without some structured approach. In maturity modeling, we talked about NIST SP 800-53 as the set of controls that compliment NIST CSF. If you look at that Publication, you will see key controls identified that fall into the categories of Access Control, Systems and Communications Protection, Identification and Authentication, Media Protection, System and Information Integrity, and a few others. In those categories, NIST speaks of access enforcement and remote access management. The Publication talks to the need for boundary protections in the form of firewalls or demilitarized zones (DMZs) that were referenced in Chapter 3. Cryptography is noted as a control to protect data and the need to protect data at rest and in transit. If you look at the things I ticked off in the prior sections, they map out pretty well with key controls listed in 800-53 (NIST SP 800-53, 2020a, p. 16). If you're new to security, lean on your standards to help guide you but speak to your security and infrastructure architects to come up with a solid set of base controls that compliment NIST. There are going to be technical gurus out there that will call out all sorts of other elements that should be included and maybe describe some of the items discussed differently, but the important point here is to ensure this is the first place you address to make sure your foundation is rock solid.

If you notice, in the space of infrastructure there's a lot of security. This is why I have always been a proponent of having network services as part of the security organization. In fact, you'll find that a large percentage of your initiatives in security are driven by this team; I feel the alignment warrants folding this within the security family if at all possible. All of this falls under the Functional First work package because you want to ensure these are in place to enable the rest of your expansion. This doesn't mean you have to run this in serial to Functional Second, but consider these as essential.

4.5 FUNCTIONAL SECOND

In Chapter 3 we introduced the work package associated with establishing security operations and compliance into your practice, and we labeled as the Functional Second set of activities you want to pursue. As you mature your practice, you want to begin gaining deeper visibility into the ins and outs of your organization and that means you need to begin looking at collecting logs, managing alerts and mapping various signals into correlated events. You want to begin capturing data from as many sources as you can, including physical security systems, and performing analytics to determine health and security of your environment.

Earlier we talked about the useful value of Cyber Fusion and Security Assurance teams, the types of capabilities you want to introduce in the initiatives you set in Functional Second from an operations standpoint will likely be driven by a Request For Proposal (RFP) that you issue to multiple providers of managed security. Conditions will vary over time, but an example of the types of capabilities you are looking for are depicted in the requirements definitions below.

The fundamental premise behind why you use a Managed Security Service Provider (MSSP) to supplement your team is that most organizations are not equipped to handle the amount of raw log data analysis. Many organizations will install fancy security event and incident management (SEIM) platforms only to realize they sit idle not being used because the tuning, filtering, analysis is something they are unable to tackle. The answer to this problem is a hybrid staffing model between insourced personnel and managed security services. Unless you are a security organization that delivers security services as your core competency, you will likely never catch up to the volume of data that needs to be analyzed to adequately protect your organization. The number of endpoint devices are growing, the barrier between the public network and your private network has been erased with the movement to cloud, and the Internet of Things (IoT) has made our job as security professionals even more complicated.

Select a strong and stable managed service provider to supplement your SOC for log analysis, and event management. Let them do the correlation work and setup the tools needed to collect and analyze so you don't have to waste cycles deploying more infrastructure and maintaining it while you have other more important things to do like driving down organizational risk. There is so much analysis that needs to happen that allowing the MSSP to do it saves your team a lot of time and effort. What is typical is that out of the total number of alerts, a very small few convert into incidents requiring your team's intervention. The rest of the alerts will be eliminated because they are false positives, not actionable, inconclusive, auto-mitigated, or even authorized activities that showed up as an alert. Logs are being collected from servers, infrastructure (switches, routers, proxies, firewalls, etc.), endpoints and many more sources. Within these logs, we will uncover that the bulk of the events are perfectly acceptable. That determination then leaves the true events that your internal team can then take action on, which means they're performing meaningful work and not spending it doing data analysis.

Several major players exist in the security managed service space, and many more are entering because of the growth opportunity with security. Some of the notable ones include SecureWorks, Verizon, Forcepoint, and Rapid7 but there are many more that offer MSSP services. You want to explicitly mandate the collection of logs from as many sources as possible so that correlation of events can be more focused and accurate. Use the following requirements in Table 4.2 as an example and sampling of the platforms you want to include but make sure you factor in your specific environmental elements, and recognize that over time some of these disappear and others appear.

The threat landscape has expanded to become more complicated than ever before. With the growth in cloud, the expanded use cases for Internet of Things (IoT) and the emergence of generative AI, machine learning, augmented reality, virtual reality, digital twins, and so on, our jurisdiction seems to have expanded in ways we couldn't imagine 10 years ago. Critical to our defense posture is to capture a comprehensive source of monitoring and

Table 4.2 Requirements Set 1 for MSSP RFP

REQ001	MSSP must support collection of feeds from all critical company platforms. The following list is an example of the logging that must be compatible with MSSP solution: • Firewalls & Remote Access Solutions – Palo Alto, Cisco and similar • Proxies, Intrusion Detection, and Prevention Systems – including but not limited to Blue Coat ProxySG, Zscaler, HAProxy, Snort IDS, Zeek, Palo Alto IPS, Cisco Secure IPS, and/or any others you run in your organization • Network Load Balancers like F5 BIG-IP, or software load balancers you might use like Microsoft Application Request Routing (ARR) • Antivirus and Antimalware software • Access control platforms like – Okta, Microsoft Azure Active Directory, Ping Identity or other • All Windows environments including legacy • Linux platforms – like Linux Mint, Ubuntu, Fedora, etc. • Unix platforms • DNS services • Vulnerability platforms – those that you may have in place such as Tenable Nessus or Rapid7, however, use the MSSP to reduce complexity and remove unnecessary platforms • Endpoint security platforms – CrowdStrike Falcon, SentinelOne Singularity, Microsoft Defender, Carbon black as examples • Mobile Device Management feeds • Cloud PaaS, IaaS or other • Flexibility in onboarding logs from new systems – net flow, syslog, APIs, etc.

Table 4.3 Requirements Set 2 for MSSP RFP

REQ002	MSSP must filter the bulk of the logs and perform active analysis that reduces the threat landscape to the few events that pose a risk. • Monitor all ingress/egress points in the network for malicious activity • Correlate all logs from REQ001 sources to provide comprehensive detection of security events • DLP event monitoring with integration into the popular DLP products • Alert ingestion from cloud access security broker(s) (CASB) • Filter out false positives and improve accuracy over time as trends develop • Monitor and track failed login attempts to high protection systems • Maintain 12 months of logging • Deliver 24x7x365 monitoring services • Correlation of anomalies to external sources and feeds to corroborate the findings

control across all technology aspects of our business as well as all our ingress/egress points. You want to call out the monitoring specifications you want from your MSSP and Table 4.3 above is an example of some items you want to call out.

Everything up to this point has been foundational to service delivery and incident response services. If done correctly, you have all the devices needed being logged and correlated, and you have all the critical environments covered to ensure the solution is comprehensive. Now the fun begins. We develop the service contract that will compliment your internal team's set of responsibilities that is focused on risk reduction and remediation. Within this, there are several key elements that you need to ensure the provider supplies. For one, they need to be a 24x7x365 operation. They need to deliver a non-tiered service response plan that does not stratify between junior and senior expertise. Service Level Agreements and assignment of severity must be agreed to so that there is no variation between what you deem as a severity one event and what your MSSP views the same.

Very important in the solution is to have a retainer setup that provides you flexibility in getting advanced support. As you begin collecting more logs, and start correlation, your incidents will grow and the more you look under the hood, the more things you will uncover. Do not skimp out on the retainer hours; get as much as you can afford. The first year, you might feel like this was a wasted expense, but as soon as the first forensics event happens that consumes 1 to 2 of your analyst's time, you will see how quickly those hours are consumed.

Usually forensics comes in multiples. As soon as you get one, it opens a path for more help. What seems to be a spontaneous need manifests itself into new investigations that require time. You will be ill-prepared for this unless you have already invested into a forensics lab and discipline. Many times, this happens as a result of other things, and it's okay if that's the case because you are making the invisible visible, and this is natural. When this does happen though, have some hours so you can get help while you sort out how to handle this. A forensics lab doesn't have to be some fancy setup like the movies; it needs to simply be functional. If you can't see it in-house yet, plan for the service with your MSSP.

One final note on this section, retain the flexibility to identify where your services come from. If you are a U.S. company involved in military contracts or part of the power infrastructure, you may be regulated by controls that require U.S. person or U.S. soil or both; the same holds true for the European Union in that you need data analysis and response from someone on European soil to meet data privacy regulations. Even if you aren't required to do so today, you may be tomorrow, which is why defining the parameters of SOC support is essential. Within this, explicitly call out that wherever you obtain support from, they have the ability to meet aggressive response times, meaning, in less than 30 minutes someone is assigned on their side to work the problem with you. Many providers will have a multi-hour threshold before assigning someone; insist on a 30-minute response for high severity incidents. Table 4.4 briefly highlights some of the considerations you want to capture in your requirements set.

Table 4.4 Requirements Set 3 for MSSP RFP

REQ003	MSSP must provide professional services tied to incident response and support • 24x7x365 SOC operations • Use of company SLAs and severity ratings to coincide with our service management framework • Dedicated members who are familiar with firm's environment • Available on-site support for severity 1 incidents as part of service plan • Non-tiered support structure: i.e. top incident responders work with us on cases • Incident response support as part of the comprehensive service offering • 120 hours per year of advanced services to be used for forensics, malware analysis, training or onsite support • Compliance reporting for audits as needed to demonstrate the controls in place. Examples of compliance standards may come from NIST, ISO, Common Criteria • Provide Executive-level reporting to summarize performance and controls • Explicitly defined service level agreements (SLAs) with categorized response times assigned to severity levels • Explicitly defined penalties for not meeting SLAs that demonstrate strength of service offering • Flexible usage of retainers with option to use for training, consultation, design or other if the hours are not entirely consumed in the year • Forensic and malware service support as needed • Company-defined location of SOC if required • Less than a 30-minute response on high severity incidents

In our world of cyber security, our adversaries evolve very quickly and while it's important to know what the current threats, vulnerabilities, techniques and processes are that adversaries use, we need to be on top of emerging trends. Your MSSP needs to provide both dimensions with thoughtful analysis and recommendations. The data on existing makes sure you develop good detect and protect controls but the data on emerging tells you what your strategic vision needs to be for the future.

Vulnerability management and internally-facing intelligence is the other aspect that needs to be captured. By the time you and your MSSP have completed deployment of the loggers and agents and collectors, they will have a heavy dosage of information that tells them all about your exploitable areas. The money you pay for the MSSP has a large percentage of value in this intelligence. The type of information that can be shared includes:

- Event statistics
- Device event trends
- Asset tracking data
- Configuration change data
- Top talkers on your network
- Vulnerabilities against existing software and hardware
- Non-optimized data flows

There is a lot more you can get and your investment into this relationship needs to give you full access to all the information and intelligence through a customized portal that you can request specific information that is pertinent to you. The information can help you with asset management, configuration management, identifying priority for vulnerability remediation. As you can probably tell, once the logs start getting captured and become information, your internal security team will start looking like it has a lot of holes because all of this needs to be consumed and acted on otherwise it is meaningless. Make sure your leadership is ready to invest into the growth of your team. You will start with a core group and then it will need to expand due to all the new capabilities that emerge. Threat intelligence is critical to your development of those vital services to keep your organization safe. Some associated requirements are noted in the Table 4.5.

Now that we have gone through the main solution, you need to make sure the relationship has all the blessings of a good marriage but all the protections in case of a divorce. In most cases, companies have a procurement function within their organizations with specialists who focus on this space. Please make use of this and don't try to create your own contract; that may not be your strength. Some of the key parts to the contract are listed in this requirement.

Everything should be developed by your procurement team. If you don't have one, then your lawyer or legal office should help you develop the components that will become the contract. Use your existing service

Table 4.5 Requirements Set 4 for MSSP RFP

REQ004	MSSP must provide active feeds for emerging threats that can compromise the organizations security protections. This includes emerging threats in the wild, vulnerability assessments, as well as internal assessments of the firms posture that poses a security risk that are captured as improvement opportunities. • Leverage your client base to provide comprehensive threat intelligence • Share intelligence around evolving adversary tactics, and existing threat infrastructure • All threat intelligence must be customized to our environment and relevant • Remediation must be accompanied by the threat actors' tactics and our vulnerabilities • Explicit vulnerability analysis is part of this service set • Active consultation with companies security team is required on a routine basis • Additional intelligence feeds for consumption are required for security team access • Use of knowledge about our firm's domain and IP space to identify targeted threats

management SLAs and have your prospective MSSP use those same ones, along with the mapping to incident severity. Build into the contract reference to these with an expected 30 minute or late response time.

The payment plan should not have any upfront charges. You will be deploying their solution for the next year, which means the first year should not see you paying a full payment for services that do not exist. Make sure a graduated payment plan is negotiated so that while ramping up, you only pay for what has been deployed. With the payment plan, every company has their own payment term; find out what it is and have the MSSP adhere to that payment term. The last thing you want is Finance coming back and saying they cannot honor the agreement and you need to rework the contract.

Liability will be important and terms for a mutually agreed contract termination should be defined so that there is an exit plan. For liability, several factors need to be considered, some of which are:

- Intellectual property infringement
- Noncompliance to laws and regulations
- Environmental damage
- Material breach to contract
- MSSP survivability

A word on the last one of these, survivability. We have gone through selection of such a partner several times and there is a point when you have all the data you can possibly collect, and yet there is still a leap of faith. There was a specific case when we had two very credible MSSP providers who were

Table 4.6 Requirements Set 5 for MSSP RFP

REQ005	MSSP must provide professional services tied to incident response and support • Explicitly defined service level agreements (SLAs) with categorized response times assigned to severity levels • Explicitly defined penalties for not meeting SLAs • Service sunsetting strategy and transition approach • Conditions around mutually agreeable premature service termination • Penalty structure for delayed service integration • Defined contract term • Payment plan with zero payment due upfront • Graduated payment plan mapped against service deployment progress • Standard payment terms (45 or 60 days based on your own terms) • Clear plan for dispute resolution • Evidence of liability insurance • Definition of liabilities for loss or damages • Fixed pricing tied to service packages within the offering • Rate card for professional services such as the retainer packages • Freedom to multi-source by your company for any part of the package • Contract end and transition plan

receiving accolades from everywhere, including Gartner, and so the choice was a difficult one. It almost felt like we should flip a coin and see who wins the contract. There was more to it than that, and ultimately, we chose to go with the team that acted less like sales people and more like engineers: it was the right choice. Soon after the other party, who again was a strong player in this space, was bought out and their future in this arena went on pause until the new owner figured out what to keep and what to purge. The moral of the story is to have a survivability clause and terms to allow you to exit from the contract with compensation in this type of scenario.

The prior guidelines are meant to be only that, guidelines to get you going on what to look for in that RFP you issue. Nowadays, solid MSSP providers can offer you a suite of services that you will grow into overtime. Some of those include:

- Log management and correlation (SIEM)
- Security orchestration and automation (SOAR)
- Incident response
- Incident retainers for professional services
- Table top support and simulations
- Penetration testing

- Vulnerability management
- Red/blue/purple team exercises and simulations
- Endpoint detection and response (EDR)
- Forensics and malware analysis
- Threat intelligence
- Threat hunting
- Web application scanning

As you can see, there's a lot that you can gain from having a partner. When you couple this to your internal analyst team, you can become a very capable operation, spread across Cyber Fusion and Security Assurance. The intent of Functional Second is to inject these types of capabilities into your operation. In addition, you are also beginning to introduce Governance and Compliance as a domain (if it isn't there already) because you are now entering the world of risk management and the demands for audit support, and regulatory compliance will soon overwhelm you if you haven't already done this. Hire a Compliance Officer during this time to begin building out the functions noted below:

- Audit and assessment support
- Contract assessment and review
- Government relations and regulatory compliance (if applicable)
- Document management
- Third party risk assessment
- Training and awareness
- Risk management
- Strategic planning
- Security oversight
- Stakeholder engagement
- Dispute resolution (related to compliance issues)

4.6 FUNCTIONAL THIRD

So by now you know how to measure your team, you have a structure for a team that you're building out as you inject new capabilities. By now you have built a decent infrastructure foundation and you're continuing to strengthen it over time. The last thing you did was to overlay the foundation with some serious security capabilities that make the health of the operation visible while also adding a strong compliance branch to your function that ensures you are governing your operation the right way and meeting legal, regulatory and strategic needs. You should be well on your way, but there's something missing.

What's missing is the next evolution of your visibility into your organizations health. We could get all philosophical here and start stretching into how in life our vision of what's around us expands and you strip away the veils of reality one at a time as your awareness grows. Yeah, we're not going to do that, BUT, there's some truth to it here. We have visibility into a lot but we are blind to how our data is moving in our network; we are blind to how users are consuming that data and we really don't have a robust data management and protection schema that is worth noting. It's time to install those capabilities in the Functional Third set of initiatives to bring this security maturity thing full circle. A quick note on your organization structure at this time. You should have the Infrastructure Services Team in place. You now have your Cyber Fusion and Security Assurance domains built as you pursue the Functional Second capabilities, and you also have Governance and Compliance being built as well. I'd recommend that the operation has grown enough to warrant the Operation Support Services to be built in conjunction with the others defined at Functional Second, and the same holds true for your Security Architecture Team.

By the time Functional Second is complete, the full structure should have been formed. As you move into Functional Third, you are amending to the existing team to support new capabilities in data protection, and this can mean adding a couple more analysts to your SOC, an architect who has specialized expertise in data management and protection (if you don't have that already) and a data protection engineer to name a few viable pieces to the puzzle. Having said that, you might find you have existing talent on your team that can absorb this but make sure you have the bandwidth to support what is going to be built here.

The controls introduced as a result of data protection capabilities will change the way your company works. There is a huge change management component to this that you need to be fully aware of and before you embark on this journey, you must get support from the executive team to pursue this. This is both a transformative and change-intensive exercise and you and the organization need to be ready to do this and be all-in. As noted in previous chapters, the Functional Third is a journey and can take up to four to five years to completely institute. You should start with a Request for Proposal (RFP) to identify scope and the right partner(s) to carry out your vision, but only after you get the buy-in from the executive team.

The first leg of your journey is to determine what you want and seek out candidates to partner with, most likely by way of a Request For Information (RFI) that leads to an RFP. That will take the first year to gather support, structure the team to pursue the RFI/RFP, define requirements, go through the issuance, Q&A, and multiple rounds to down-select viable candidates. If you start this in the beginning of the year, you should have all the pieces you need by August (assuming a January start) to then formulate a business case and present it for approval and funding. If you're efficient, you can get approval in September and then use the remaining few months to clean up how you will run the program and address any lingering things like implementation plan, budget capture for the next year, and working through the staffing model and approvals for year-end. The intent should be that by year two, you are ready to begin implementation.

Year two will be all about deployment of capabilities. You are conducting detailed planning sessions and finalizing design. Nowadays this part is easier because much of the solution is likely cloud-based so not as much on-premise setup and configuration to worry about like years ago. You want to prioritize the delivery of capabilities and map it to user expectations and risk. Today, most partners will say this phase will take less than a year to get everything deployed but don't get fooled in thinking that's the end of it; it's only the beginning. Along the way you need to complete your hiring of technical staff to support the platform and get them integrated into the program and finalize the deployment.

Year three will be tuning and optimizing the way the platform works, and integrating into your operation. It's at this time the real work begins to, in a careful way, begin instituting the controls with the support of leadership, Legal and Human Resources. At some point in the beginning of year two, you should have already presented this to the Workers Councils in the EU to ensure you get support; now you are looking to begin locking down and managing that change across the enterprise. I keep pointing to the sensitivity of this because you are essentially taking away freedoms that company personnel have enjoyed. Cloud Access Security Brokers (CASB) lockdown the ability to interact with cloud platforms and the free-for-all goes away... people don't like that. Eliminating the ability for users to send attachments to their personal email accounts will go away (you could do this prior but maybe you waited). Your buddies wills soon view you as an evildoer. You're going to start enforcing classification of content and data and labeling. In doing this, you are restricting how that data can be used based on the criteria for that tag. Your buddies who are now not very fond of you, may start getting calls or emails from the data protection folks saying, in a polite way of course, that an anomaly in behavior was noted and we need to investigate this. Now for sure you are bringing on the 'big brother is watching you' condition. So, please be conscious of this and proceed with caution; as much as you can say it's for the security and protection of the company, if you completely stifle the operation then you'll be on the outs before you know it. Year five is a catchall to stabilize things and get to a steady state. If you reach this point without losing your job, then you are something else! Maybe now you see, from my vantage point, why we left this for last, because you need a fairly mature operation to do this right.

A little about the capabilities you are deploying here. You can categorize them in five buckets. The obvious is data protection and you may have some of this already. You are introducing data loss prevention (DLP) in your network and your endpoints. This capability alerts on anomalies and is used to drive investigations on data exfiltration from your environment or any other anomalous activities. DLP is now going to be prominent for files and emails as well, and while you may have had some aspects of this in place, you would be expanding into a comprehensive DLP solution.

DLP doesn't work without information classification and tagging. At the onset of this whole program you will introduce a data classification policy that defines the categories, whether they are publicly available, internal, internal confidential, or some other variation. You need this as a first step so that you know what behaviors are appropriate for the respective data sets. Ideally the promises that third parties are making to help automate labeling are actually true and they can help you with this, otherwise if you leave this up to the employees at your company, it will become difficult to put it mildly.

You're also introducing enhancements to identity management and access management through this program. You are introducing or strengthening risk-based conditional access controls, and shoring you your entitlement management. This is also the time that you are doubling down on insider risk management. One of the most ignored threat vectors is insider threat. The introduction of user and entity and behavior analytics (UEBA) and information barriers will give you the ability to ensure your IP and other crown jewels are not compromised. As a whole, you are really strengthening your ability to enforce sound data protection schemas and as a side effect, you are also instituting the exact controls that can help you enforce policies tied to generative AI. In a time when genAI impact is still being discovered, this is the balance you need to enable usage while being able to control consumption as well.

A last note on Functional Third. I didn't craft a similar set of general requirements like I did for Functional Second because I find what you need here will vary from company to company. The requirements really depend on your current state. There are some universal things like requirements around classification and tagging, data protection and associated controls including cloud DLP, but you can then get into things like encryption, and capabilities to combat advanced persistent threats (APTs) and even reporting that you may or may not need or your needs are specific. The good news is that by the time you get to Functional Third, you have the maturity as a team to define these well enough to get going and your candidate's feedback will help you evolve your requirements from the time you close out your RFI to the time you make your final down selection in the RFP.

4.7 THIRD PARTY ASSESSMENT

A quick section about third party assessments. This was noted as a work package in the Strategic Roadmap to callout the value it offers to asserting your credibility. The premise here is, the longer you are in your role, the more bias you will be perceived to have in favor of your operation. Consequently, it's a good practice every three years, to have a third party to come in and assess your maturity. Since we are transparent and confident in our ability to run a structured organization, we should have no issues with doing this, especially if we have the same assessing body come in and do this each time. They will likely use NIST CSF as the basis for the assessment and you have been using that to develop your own practice so between the first time they came when you started to three years later, you should see a pretty decent jump in maturity.

This helps you in multiple ways; yes it helps with credibility, but it also gives you support for the investments you need to make for the company. When that report comes out and it's reviewed with the executives and possibly the Board, it will show the prioritized set of investments mapped to risk (hopefully) and that can drive funding for initiatives. This obviously depends on the health of the organization and the economy as a whole, but it supports your position in a positive way. Measure yourself continuously and in a systematic fashion. Develop a program to drive maturity by linking your framework to the investments and initiatives. Then, when you bring the assessors in, you can check to see if you're being too liberal or conservative in your efforts, and get an injection of support from your leadership.

4.8 SECURITY SCORECARD

The last topic under the Strategy Roadmap is around your security scorecard. It's one thing to do all the right things but you need to measure this and report your progress to maintain support. Here the word systematic becomes very important as you need to demonstrate the connection between your framework(s) to the categories that make up those frameworks to the measurements you use for those categories. You may use more than NIST CSF here depending on what is important in your organization. For example, in past lives, we used CSF but we also used measure specifically for perimeter security and product security to foster a more holistic view of our organization. Now you could say perimeter security should be encapsulated in CSF and you shouldn't need to call it out but in our case, it made sense given that nowadays, third parties assess your security rating by the strength of your perimeter hardening that they can probe and then report that to creditors. We felt this was an important enough consideration to include at least one measure of perimeter health. Product security can easily have its own scorecard but if you are dealing with product vulnerabilities or legacy systems, you may want to incorporate a measure of how you are reducing your vulnerability exposure in your product portfolio.

If I were to be prescriptive, I'd say use the categories in NIST: Identify, Protect, Detect, Respond, and Recover, and map key measures against those categories. Under Detect for example, you would map mean time to detect an incident (MTTD). Under Respond you would map mean time to respond (MTTR). Under Protect you would measure patching progress against your measured service level agreement (SLA). NIST SP 800-55 lists a number of measures that can be used; not all of them are useful (in my opinion) but Measure 4 on awareness and training can be used that measures percent of employees that received security training (NIST SP 800-55. 2020b, p. 54).

You can measure things like percent of end of life (EOL) systems, percent of employees that are phish-prone as a result of your phishing campaigns, number of major incidents in a given quarter (hopefully this is zero). You could even go into asset management measures because we know that if you don't have accurate inventory of your assets, you can't really know for sure if you have full coverage in monitoring and patching. You can create a measure on percent of environments inventoried in your configuration management database (CMDB). This could be in the Identify category. The point here is you want to determine what's important in your environment and then map it upwards. Downstream from this, you want to then associate the measures to specific initiatives that you're running.

So let's say you are trying to improve MTTD and MTTR, you moved your SOC from 24x5 to 24x7 to eliminate callouts for support thus improving your response time. You are tuning your system and running simulations to stress test your operation on detection of anomalies, working with your Security Assurance Team. You want to demonstrate from the things you're doing to the measures you value to the mapping to your framework on how you are progressing. Lastly, the measures you pick should prioritize the biggest deficiencies in your operation. That is, there's only so much you can report before it becomes overwhelming. You want to report on the heavy hitters, so when you have your assessment of maturity, identify the biggest deficiencies in operations or capabilities, and try to report on those with the associated mapping. That way it's always in front of you that the things you're doing will guarantee improvement in your overall capabilities and maturity. As those items go from red to green, you can cycle them out with other measures that are next in line so this way, you have a dynamic scorecard that evolves over time as you address gaps so that you're continually improving your operation and the measurement adapts with it.

The last, last word here is that if you take the approach this chapter has defined, you will have a structured approach to going from startup to mature with a repeatable process that will continue to improve your security posture. The rest of the chapters will double down on the nuances tied to making this effort successful. As I have said several times, cater this to your specific needs and conditions, but the general concepts are sound and they have worked for me many times. I will share an observation that I've made that differentiates successful leaders from average ones. I've noticed that the best leaders are those who can take a vision and convert it into a strategy and then execute the heck out of it. You'd be surprised how many can't bridge the gap from strategy to execution and they faulter for whatever reason. If you can take this approach and then implement it, you will find yourself being perceived as a very effective leader. You have all the tools and functions you need to make that happen, now it's a matter of sharing your vision and approach and getting all the arrows to align in your organization so everyone is working as one.

REFERENCES

National Institute of Standards and Technology. (2018). *Risk management framework for information systems and organizations: A system life cycle approach for security and privacy* (NIST Special Publication 800-37 Rev. 2). U.S. Department of Commerce. Retrieved from https://doi.org/10.6028/NIST.SP.800-37r2

National Institute of Standards and Technology. (2020a). *Security and privacy controls for information systems and organizations* (NIST Special Publication 800-53 Rev. 5). U.S. Department of Commerce. Retrieved from https://doi.org/10.6028/NIST.SP.800-53r5

National Institute of Standards and Technology. (2020b). *Performance measurement guide for information security* (NIST Special Publication 800-55 Rev. 1). U.S. Department of Commerce. Retrieved from https://doi.org/10.6028/NIST.SP.800-55r1

National Institute of Standards and Technology. (2023). *The NIST Cybersecurity Framework (CSF) 2.0*. U.S. Department of Commerce. Retrieved from https://www.nist.gov/cyberframework

Chapter 5

Systematic review of work packages

Operational roadmap

Let's expand on some of the topics we spoke to in Chapter 4. Strategically, we know we have five work packages that speak to how we baseline our practice, how we structure our team, and the key phases of implementation depicted in Functional sequences. We understand the underlying thought process for developing our security organization and here we dive a little more into the specifics in each of the teams we identified. Between Chapters 4 and 5, you should have a clear understanding of structure and roles and responsibilities within your team. As you move into Chapter 6 and beyond, we expand the conversation to how you interact with the rest of the company and what practices both internal and outward facing, will help you be successful in doing so.

5.1 A COMPLIANCE STORY

There once was a time when passwords were easy; you could use Password1 and all was good. Then that pesky security team came around and told you this isn't good enough and you need to strengthen your password. Security gave you guidelines to make it more robust, saying you need at least one capital letter, one special character and one numeric character with a 10-character minimum length. By following these guidelines, you would certainly make yourself less susceptible to credential theft. So, having understood the criteria, you created the password P@ssword12. Now you are way more secure than before!

Well, now we're on a roll; your security is getting stronger by the minute. Then things changed, that pesky security team came around again and argued the weakest link in security are employees. Because of this, they need to make security training mandatory. From this point on, you the employees of this fine company, will need to take no less than 2 security training classes per year to meet our requirements. Man, what an annoying team they are. They're worse than HR, you think to yourself! So, you get assigned training, but you sit on it for as long as you can before you start getting hate mail,

DOI: 10.1201/9781003616528-5

reminding you that you are delinquent. What do you do? Like any rational individual, you keep ignoring it. Then finally your boss gets escalation notices and at this point, you need to stop what you're doing and deal with this nonsense! Luckily, you notice you can fast forward the video and slides and all of a sudden, what was going to take 30 minutes will only take you 5; this is perfect! You fast forward to the quiz at the end. First time you fail the quiz, but you jot down the corrected answers. You then run through the content again, skipping to the end. This time, you know the answers, and you plug them in and poof, you got a 90% (still got 1 wrong), but you met the minimum requirements. Awesome, now you can get back to work.

There's a difference between being compliant and being committed. Being compliant simply means we checked all the boxes but our aim should be to make the objective of security so obvious that we get commitment by stakeholders to support and champion the cause. The essence behind a security champion is that they understand the underlying value of security and have bought into it, and we need to strive for that, otherwise, it'll be like the password and training scenarios above; on paper it'll look great but the reality will be something completely different. We will look at some of the functions in Governance and Compliance a bit closer from an operational lens to reinforce value and approach as you work to establish a management operating system (MOS).

5.1.1 Training & awareness

One of the most important operational elements to install is a training and awareness program, namely because so long as our workforce is not comprised of robots, we will have to address the human element of the threat equation. This aspect of Governance and Compliance has the objective of educating all personnel who interact with our company in security risk, policies, and best practices. This will include employees, contractors and any other stakeholders that do business with us. Our objective are threefold:

1. Expose personnel to the real and present threat tied to security
2. Expand our combined knowledge base around risks, policies, and practices in security
3. Make security part of our culture and something everyone commits to supporting

The big risk topics should revolve around how bad actors target personnel in social engineering and phishing tactics for gaining a foothold into our company. We drive awareness of the ways we are targeted and the mechanisms used especially in phishing attacks to compromise our systems, such as inserting links to fake websites that harvest credentials, attaching malicious executable files that the victim unknowingly clicks on, the use of scripts embedded in documents that trigger exploits, the use of impersonation, and fake requests for sensitive data. The number of ways we can be targeted is growing so it's important to ensure everyone has a trained eye for identifying questionable elements.

We develop our training and awareness through first determining gaps in awareness. We can do this in several ways, including through incident root cause analysis, captured risks and their prevalence, and surveys to name a few. We want to marry compliance requirements and prevalent risks to the training topics we define. Once we know where our people stand related to knowledge gaps, we can develop a few different types of training. We want to have general security training that is applicable to everyone but we also want to have some specialized content, especially for those who touch sensitive systems like administrators, and those who hold sensitive positions like finance team members. The good news is we don't need to craft the content by ourselves and there are several good partners we can use to delivery professional content on various subjects associated with security and data privacy. They do very well on general security topics and some of them do really well on role-based training as well.

Delivery can take many forms, including lunch and learns where we present content in an interactive way. We can develop e-learning modules that can be embedded in our company learning platform (if one exists). Sometimes the use of in-person training may be warranted but as teams are distributed more nowadays this may not be as practical to reach the largest audience. We can also use recurring phishing campaigns that are very effective because they can run on a monthly cadence, targeting various business units and allow you to collect trending data on click rates on specific topics that then give you further analytics on which topics our people are strong at and which ones they just suck at. This can make its way back into the scorecard as a percent phish prone-type of metric under Identify. If done right, phishing campaigns can become a talking point where you'll hear folks say 'you almost got me', or 'that was so easy', as it becomes a bit of a game, and on the other side, those who click will speak to their woes of having to take security training because they fell for it.

Lastly, there are some key topics you want to touch on in your training that can give you the biggest back for the buck. Training on how to get a hold of your security team is probably something you should start with, but right on its heels, you want to hit on topics around password hygiene and the importance of using strong passwords and changing them periodically. You also want to give the topic of social engineering enough air time because this is where people get hit with quite a bit both at work and home. The sophistication of the bad actors in information mining and crafting believable scams is alarming and we need our people to be aware for their own sake as much as the company's sake. The types of exploits is important to know about, and the importance of protecting data are all good topics to hit on in a repeatable cycle. At some point, you want to reinforce the importance of these campaigns with the executive staff and ensure they understand the reasons why these campaigns are imperative to a strong security practice so that you get full buy-in from the organization.

5.1.2 Security champions

Another very effective method of driving security into the organization is to stand up a security champions program. What this intends to do is train individuals outside of the security team, in security, so that we can plant seeds in development, engineering and common practices across the organization in all departments. The reality is that security is a hard thing to control and there's never enough personnel to do all the work needed. By having champions, we can make those folks an extension of the security team. The objectives of a security champion program are:

1. Increase collaboration with non-security departments
2. Increase awareness of security and drive a pro-security culture
3. Engrain security into the development activities of the company, promoting a shift-left mindset
4. Expand the reach and execution of security without having to hire an unsustainable number of personnel
5. Reduce resistance and friction to security initiatives that may stress the perception of freedom in the company

When developing a champions program, you want to clearly define the investment you are asking from the prospective candidates. Clearly define the scope of work such as their participation in training, awareness initiatives, and even technical activities like security reviews and policy administration. Always remember that participation is optional and therefore you want to be sensitive to their 'day jobs' and ensure you give as much as you receive, meaning, they should come away with new skills, more knowledge, and exposure to things they wouldn't normally be privy to. There's a whole topic of incentivizing the champions through recognition and other that you want to develop thoughtfully to encourage participation and growth of the champion pool. With all the smart people I have worked with, in some cases the strategy was bottoms up and in other cases it was top down. Both have their strengths and weaknesses so why not do both? Build a program that executives are willing to sing up for to set the example for the organization. Build something that also encourages the rest of the organization to participate because it is meaningful and has value to them. In doing so, you drive adoption in a multi-dimensional approach.

Pair your champions with senior security leads so that they can get the support they need in the development and learning process. Eventually you might supplement the security leads with tenured security champions from the last cohort, but at first, make an investment by committing mentors from your team to the champions. For those in the development or engineering functions, give them tools to perform vulnerability scanning, and conduct structured risk assessments. Coach them if they are part of the software development lifecycle so that they integrate security as far to the left as possible (shift-left), and promote integrating security as part of the design and not later in the production (secure-by-design versus bolted-on). If you really want to beef up this program, you can offer financial support in obtaining industry recognized certifications like CISM, CISA, and CISSP or others like OSCP or whatever four-letter acronym certification in security they want, but make sure it's four-letters, not three. Build a friendly competitive program that keeps track of accomplishment by way of leaderboards and issues badges for measured accomplishments. The sky is the limit, and the more robust you make it, the more prominent this will become and prestigious, attracting even more participants.

If you do choose to gamify the program, then you need to establish metrics and key performance indicators (KPIs) for various milestones and accomplishments so that you can track outcomes. This helps measure the friendly competition but also demonstrates the success of the program. Say for example you measure patching percentage in their specific domains, or number of vulnerabilities remediated; you could really make this a measurable program that you can promote as a key success in your organization.

5.1.3 Risk governance (risk-based modelling)

Training and awareness, and a security champion program are important tools to spread the word about security. Without having a culture that's security-focused, you are going to be overwhelmed when you try to stay ahead of all the challenges that will face you. Having said that, the fundamental truth in security is that everything revolves around risks and risk management. An effective security team talks about risk all the time and frankly, should be pretty annoying because you can't get through a single meeting without hearing the word 'risk', but that means they're doing their jobs. You need to have a dedicated staff that administers the risk practice and it is governed out of the Governance and Compliance Team. Here's where NIST RMF is applicable. As you start up the practice, have your team use this reference to develop a structured approach.

There are several steps to take in the risk-management practice and it starts with establishing the boundaries and definitions for your company. RMF recommends to first identify the company's risk tolerances along with the roles and responsibilities of those who govern and manage risk. Along the way, you need to understand what you define as the environment you will measure, and begin inventorying the assets and categorizing them to develop the basis for assessment. This is where your service management team in IT becomes very important. The IT service management team (ITSM) is responsible for asset inventory and uses both their configuration management database (CMDB) and asset management database (ASDB) to manage the asset base in the organization. If your company is mature, you will have a reasonably accurate CMDB that will identify and capture characteristics of your asset base that can then be used in your risk management program.

Let's take a detour and talk a little bit about the value of a CMDB. Without a true catalog of assets, you never know if you're risk program is comprehensive or not. Apart from Compliance, you don't have a reference to onboard and monitor security alerts that rely on an inventory of assets to cover. Without a solid CMDB or AMDB, you don't have a clue about license entitlement and are open to true ups or litigation because you are consuming more licenses than you are allotted, or you are using software that is not authorized for your use. Take this as a marker for triggering a discovery initiative so that you can strengthen your CMDB in particular. If you don't know what's out there, how can you protect it?

Okay, back to the topic of risk, once you have established the boundaries of your risk operation under Prepare in RMF, you then assign an impact level of Low, Moderate or High mapped against the age-old acronym in security: confidentiality, integrity, and availability (CIA). This falls under Categorize in RMF. From here, you're going to identify the controls you need to install for that asset plus impact criteria from NIST SP 800-53 that is appropriately matched and then you measure the effectiveness of those controls through the standard tools security uses: audit, testing, vulnerability scanning. If you find the results are not where you want them, then apply additional or more stringent controls. If you take a look at RMF (in the references), you'll find reference to the seven-step lifecycle that NIST recommends (NIST SP 800-37r2, 2018, p. 27). Remember, RMF is a framework that tells you how you can manage security risk across the organization. If you want to hone in on specific threats then you want to use some other complimentary references briefly described next.

You'll want to develop a risk register that identifies the risk, the risk owner, a description, impact and likelihood of the risk being realized, mitigating controls and timelines for action. There are various threat assessment models you can use such as DREAD that is a qualitative approach that measures five factors for scoring and prioritization of specific threats. You can go mathematical with something like Factor Analysis of Information Risk (FAIR) that is a more quantitative risk assessment approach and assigns measures in terms of financial and operational terms. DREAD and FAIR are used for different purposes; where DREAD is a quick way to rank and prioritize, FAIR is more comprehensive and defines risks in business terms. The use of one or the other, or even none of these will have to do with how your company and leadership wants to view risks in the organization. Do they want you to apply judgment across subject matter experts and come to a mutually agreed upon score and prioritization? In that case, you apply subjective measures. Do they want you to have some sort of general measurement approach for risks and get to an answer with relative simplicity? Go with DREAD. If you're dealing with detail-oriented, engineering types who want precision damn it, and nothing short of that will do? Go with FAIR and DREAD and every other means you have at your disposal... or use some other framework that I haven't referred to here.

I joke a bit about FAIR, but you may be hard-pressed to convert risk into financial measures. Now my word of advice, don't overcomplicate your risk management approach if you're a new operation. Stand up something to get things going and then get better and more precise over time. It's okay to start with a subjective approach that directionally assesses risks through agreement across stakeholders but eventually you'll want to move to a light structured model. The key is to start somewhere and mature as you go.

Recognize the relationship of cause and effect and measure current risk with existing controls (or lack of them) and then demonstrate what the residual risk will be as a result of implementing mitigating controls. Have an active exercise of evaluating and re-evaluating risks on your risk register and establish timelines for mitigation and hold the owners accountable for the actions. Hold functional risk reviews and Quarterly reviews with organizational leadership and risk owners to assess risk landscape and changes to that landscape. As a security organization, you are required to assess the company's technology health through risk management and will be asked by regulating bodies about your practice in the event you are audited for whatever reasons, so make sure you have a solid practice and an approach to track decisions and efforts in risk management.

5.1.4 Audits everywhere

Speaking of audits, this is something you can quickly find is bogging you down if you don't get your hands wrapped around it relatively fast. It's one thing to self-initiate an audit of your security operation, it's another to participate in internal corporate audits and external audits by third parties, regulators, and customers. The latter can grow in volume as your practice matures and it's peculiar but a reality I experienced that the more controls you institute, the more interest to audit you there is by parties outside your team. Let me say this about an Internal Audit (IA) Team at your company, in my personal experience, it's been a love-hate relationship. I've always had good ties and found the folks I worked with to be friendly but things can go south very quickly. If you have a mature internal audit team, they will work with you and apply a fair assessment to your practice, but if you find yourself in a situation where IA is establishing its operation, then watch out, they may target you as the platform to build their brand upon. No need to go into details but just be mindful that this can happen.

Let's start with how you can develop a practice in auditing to aide your team in assessment, and prepare you for those externals that you'll undoubtedly need to support. The objective of an audit team is to systematically assess your systems, policies, procedures, and applied controls to determine effectiveness, and identify any gaps that misalign to any of the four areas noted here that can drive a weakness in your security posture. In that assessment, you are looking at regulatory requirements and internal requirements that drive compliance. Everything goes back to what you measure yourself against in terms of a framework when doing an internal assessment. Use NIST CSF to create a checklist for compliance, map the appropriate controls to meet the maturity modeling, which you should have already done as spoken to in Chapter 4. Take inventory of assets that include databases, assets, endpoints, network and security appliances, applications, and operating systems to name a few, and begin taking samples to map against the required controls and how they map to the preset criteria.

Part of a good audit will review access controls. In most technology audits, you identify the systems that manage access, and the different permission levels and roles. In the technical assessment, you are looking at how the teams are assigning access rights, if there are any idle accounts, and the processing of offboarding and how user accounts are deactivated and in what timeframe. As we know, compromised accounts are a primary way to infiltrate a company's defenses so it is a vital part of any audit to ensure access management practices are effective.

Another dimension of audits is reviewing your documentation (policies, standards, procedures, guidelines) and (1) if they are updated and when the last review was conducted and (2) if they are being followed. Incident response plans are a favorite to review because it touches such an important part of your operation so an audit will look at whether the incident procedure is updated and being used as a part of the operations teams normal routines. As you build the capability to support audits and to run internal ones, you want to get one or two of your compliance team members certified in auditing and have them run these types of scenarios to harden the organizations applied practice against what is written and expected in the documentation.

Beyond documentation and process reviews, an audit can conduct technical assessments as part of the exercise. Penetration testing is a fairly well-known tool used where the auditors will simulate an attack to determine weaknesses and whether they can infiltrate the network or specific services. Another popular approach is to conduct vulnerability scanning and see what kind of vulnerabilities might sit in the environment but here you'd want to be careful on what you scan and how because certain environments like those in manufacturing may not be resilient enough to withstand an active scan. Other types of technical scans can be an audit of configurations of key appliances like firewalls or routers or critical systems and whether they are patched or have a hardened build consistent with documented practices. They will also test to see how access is managed to those systems; are there shared accounts or user-specific accounts and cycled passwords over a set period of time?

Now, as a team that is responsible for supporting an audit function, conduct these whether fully or as a table top exercise and work to systematically automate as much of the data gathering as possible. The last thing your technical teams need are continuous requests for evidence. Spend the time to automate data collection because what you'll find is 90% of the data you need for one audit can be used for all of them. Automate the collection of that 90% so that you don't need to tie up the team. From those audits, you will trigger additional initiatives to automate, fix, improve practices that are found to be weak. This is yet another method to add to what Security Assurance does to improve your security posture. If you go through a certification of your security practice, they will go over these things, and expand it to things like training practices in the company, skill development through mentoring, and every aspect of your practice so taking the time to learn and improve from this function will move you forward nicely.

From a development standpoint, you can offer your auditing subject matter experts some certification opportunities. I'll say that in general, I believe any education is good but I don't put a lot of weight on certifications alone. Many out there will make a certification a requirement in a job posting but I find making it a 'nice to have' is better suited for my needs. I say that simply because I've hired a lot of people over the course of my career and in several cases, a person who had a whole bunch of four-letter acronyms after their name proved to be less effective than someone who has none. There are people wo are cert-collectors. They are great at taking tests and studying but when it comes to practical application, they are weak. I do believe that combining certifications with proven practical knowledge and experience goes really well. That's probably common sense right? Well, I can't tell you how many times I've seen positions posted where there was this major emphasis on certifications; I knew just by the job posting, these people are amateurs. I get the right to judge because I'm the one writing and there's literally no room for debate!

Having said that, offer them the chance to get their Certified information Systems Auditor (CISA) Cert offered by ISACA. This is focused on IT processes, governance, risk management, among other spaces. It is a widely popular and recognized certification that can give them the credentials they may be looking for in their career. Another one to think about is Certified Internal Auditor (CIA) that is offered by The Institute of Internal Auditors (IIA). This is more of a formal IA function but it includes security and risk processes in its scope. Both of these are very good for promoting learning and development within your team.

5.1.5 Data privacy & governance

It really depends on how your firm organizes the responsibilities associated to data privacy, and sometimes this responsibility falls under Legal, but in others it sits in Security, under Governance and Compliance. Data privacy is focused on protecting personal information in a way that secures the confidentiality of that data. Data privacy is interested in how such sensitive information is managed from collection all the way to its protection. There are several key components to data privacy, they include: protection, consent, rights management, and compliance.

Data protection refers to ensuring personal data such as personally identifiable information (PII) is secure and protected, which means installing processes and controls to ensure that data is not readily accessible and the systems that house them are secured. Consent refers to certifying that the individuals whose data is being collected are informed as to the purpose, and methods for safeguarding that data. It also points to approval by those individuals to collect their data. In the same light, rights management means the individual must explicitly provide authorization for you to manage their data, whether it's to store, access or port the data for specific purposes. In general, data privacy works to ensure only essential data is provided and works to minimize collection and use for very specific purposes.

There are regulatory requirements and laws that are set to protect personal data, including one we have spoken to before that is commonly referred to in security, the General Data Protection Regulation (GDPR), and in recent times the California Consumer Privacy Act (CCPA) has gained a lot of interest and focus by security teams doing business in California. There are many more emerging across the United States, and in all parts of the globe as a sensitivity to data theft and violation of personal data rights takes center stage. We want to ensure this area has focus if we are responsible for it because for one, as an individual, I want my rights protected as much as the next person, and two, it's our responsibility to protect and we need to take it seriously in a time when all our data is being leaked out daily and companies keep saying 'sorry' but no comprehensive solution is in place. Have you noticed how almost every week; some new company is announcing a major data leak? It's become almost impossible to safeguard our data, unless we go completely off grid, which seems very difficult to do, and I'm not sure exactly what that truly means.

The operation of data privacy has many similar components that other aspects of your operation embodies. You need to have policies and standards that define the rules tied to data. An assignment of responsibility must be set on who will ensure compliance and administer the program. There's a technical component to this that ties to data architecture; this can be an entire practice within IT that does this and many times data architects are expensive and worth their weight in gold. Data architects are not just tied to privacy but work to manage company data in the most efficient ways so as to allow consumption for driving business decisions, and offering key analytics on industry trends and other key insights. You will want to have a data privacy owner in your team but you can't be successful if you don't have a technical data architecture lead or team in IT to help you. Some companies are putting in Chief Data Privacy Officers because of the importance of this space, and you'd plug your lead into their overall objectives. Beyond architecting the way data flows, is stored, and consumed, you have an element of quality management that ensures accuracy. On the tail end, you have the compliance aspect and then the measurements to ensure the controls put in place are meeting the needs of regulators and company privacy directives.

The mix of roles noted above are split between your data privacy lead and the data management team in IT. You handle policies, standards, compliance, risk management, and measurements. The data team handles architecture, quality, and consumption. Extending this, you also handle data protection, which is driven by the Functional Third set of initiatives. A subtlety that should be understood; you manage data privacy, but data governance covers all of the responsibilities noted above. You are working as a subset of the larger governance practice and you are not the driver for Governance in this space. Governance looks at structures and processes to address all organizational data; you are focused on the privacy and protection aspect of this. The reason some companies put data privacy in the hands of Legal is that it's such a large and important function that under Legal, they can assign that Chief Data Privacy Officer and that person can reach into the organization to ensure compliance to privacy laws, and oversee and monitor the practice through the lens of the Legal Team. Whichever approach you take, this is a set of responsibilities that absolutely need to be cared for.

5.1.6 Business continuity & disaster recovery

A quick word on business continuity and DR. As part of your responsibilities, you may be tasked to provide oversight to this space as part of organizational resilience. The question sometimes is asked as to why is Security responsible for driving this? Well, as part of our security framework, whether it's NIST or ISO/IEC, business continuity, contingency planning and incident response are included as crucial elements. We talk a lot about confidentiality, integrity, and availability (CIA) as the basis for security; BC/DR is tied directly to CIA and therefore we are the obvious choice to govern the activities surrounding this and general resilience of our technology. Taking it a little further, you can see BC/DR specifically called out in ISO/IEC 27001, and NIST SP 800-53. You also see this in GDPR as a requirement for compliance. Even HIPAA has statutes that make contingency planning mandatory.

Out of CIA, availability is directly connected to this topic. The concept of availability is resiliency. Integrity is not that far off, and the underlying premise of integrity which means maintaining data integrity, is tied back to continuity and recovery. The tie-in of incident response is how quickly you react and recover normal operations? If you look across IT, there isn't another team that can really cover this space other than security and more specifically the governance and compliance team. We then take this and fit it into the corporate crisis management planning to define the larger business continuity practice.

You can stand up a practice by using some basic guidelines. First, figure out what kinds of risks can truly impact your operation. Things like cyberattacks, power grid failures, natural disasters, aliens attacking, and Armageddon could all be part of the equation including things like hardware failures. Once you've come up with the sources of risks, figure out how those related threats can affect your business. Do they impact operations, do they move you out of compliance with regulatory bodies, how about impacting revenue or reputation damage? Do they have physical plant impacts like shutting down a manufacturing facility, is their loss of life (life and health safety)? Spend some time categorizing the impacts and map them accordingly. Once you've done this map all the critical systems to recovery parameters for each system and their connection to specific business requirements. It's always important to understand how the risks or threats rank against one another in criticality and what are the minimum thresholds for recovery. You've already defined impact, but you want to be prescriptive with the business functions affected so you can itemize the recovery planning. What we commonly term this whole exercise is a business impact analysis (BIA).

Next you want to assess how long you can go before it becomes a problem for each of the systems in your inventory, also called a recovery time objective (RTO). You also want to consider the acceptable amount of data loss in an event. How far back can you go in data loss before it becomes a problem? This is called your recovery point objective (RPO). These two parameters give you the design criteria for building your recover and DR plans. You might be asking 'what's the difference between business continuity and disaster recover'? Great question! Business continuity plans are intended to define how you will keep the ship afloat in the wake of a major issue. It talks of essential operations that need to be upheld during an event and during recovery. Disaster recovery plans define how you will re-establish operations after a disaster. Do you have redundant systems like a mirrored data center in an offsite geographically diverse site that has full redundancy, or do you have data backups stored somewhere offsite? Do you employ high availability (HA), and how do you utilize the cloud for recovery objectives? So once you build your BIA, you then develop your business continuity plan (BCP) to do that very thing, define how your specific systems will recover.

You're going to want to do this for systems and applications alike. Once the BCP is defined, you identify the gaps in achieving the parameters set, and then look to implement the changes you have described to achieve the objectives. You then run DR tests to check if the system works as intended. In fact you should be doing DR testing yearly to ensure your most critical systems are working properly. Obviously there's a financial component to all of this and if you do go for an HA model with mirrored active/active data centers, that's going to cost you. Your company has to figure out what's the right mix of resilience and cost. When you've defined all of this, you need to document your BC/DR approach as third party auditors will ask for these when assessing your maturity and your compliance to say ISO, SOC 2 or other. Even the

Sarbanes-Oxley Act (SOX) indirectly asks about BC/DC by asking about the integrity of the systems that deliver financial reporting. They don't explicitly call out this function but they do indirectly in speaking about availability of financial systems (Sarbanes-Oxley Act, 2002). Identify the system owners, identify the business owners of a service, build the BIA and BCP and start systematically addressing gaps in your DR infrastructure. It's important for the business and compliance.

5.2 INFRASTRUCTURE OPERATIONS

Well then, that's it for now on Governance and Compliance and just in time for us to jump to operations. We talked a bit about the types of capabilities you want to introduce in infrastructure in Chapter 4, so here we'll spend a little bit of time speaking about how to structure the operation to support the capabilities and go into some additional details on some specific points. We also double click on the Functional First capabilities and attempt to further organize and catalog them on what you can prioritize in three tiers: Essential, Intermediate and Advanced capabilities. Please remember, there are multiple ways to do this, but I'm sharing what has worked and this is not intended to be a comprehensive infrastructure conversation, but a general overview of what to install in support of your general build out of security.

5.2.1 The essentials

Looking at this from a greenfield perspective is probably the simplest way to approach the topic. Assume you are tasked with building a new operation for a startup and within your scope is network and security. Your goal is generic and there's no talk of fancy assurance components or orchestration capabilities or anything of the sort, but rather, your task is to get things moving fast and enable the business to get to a steady state operation fast. So what do you do? Well, you don't focus on security frankly and you spend your time building transport services. Now diehard and purists in security will be up in arms around that, but I go back to a fundamental philosophical belief of mine, first it's the business operation that needs to be working so that you can stand up security to support it. If the business can't run then you don't have a security operation, period. So, if you're supporting a startup, help it get on its feet and then very quickly wrap security around it before people get used to the openness and freedom of the first days of operation.

What does that mean? Get your wide area network (WAN) stood up, get your Internet connections built, define what voice services you'll use and the architecture and start getting those in place. Design your office, retail, distribution, manufacturing models and begin building out the local area networks (LAN) to connect up to the WAN for interconnectivity. Depending on what your company does, get your wireless network up and ensure essential business sites and services are immediately connected such as manufacturing tools or network segments that support critical applications and the like. In order to do this, you need staff; your immediate job is to hire critical network and voice architects to start designing and implementing. You likely will need to supplement your team because you probably don't have one, so look for a third-party implementation partner that can help you kickstart this while you are in the recruitment process.

Your first job is effectively a recruiter because until you get to a point where you have the people, the rest doesn't matter, but along the way you need to work closely with your third-party implementer to get moving. There are cycle times for getting orders for equipment in, circuit orders and installs, delivery and installation of hardware, as well as testing. If your company is constructing new facilities then you need to tie into the schedule set for construction in order to get transport services up and running. At this time, there's no talk of information security, it's strictly high-pressure efforts to get the business operation up. You are not generating revenue at this point so focus on that.

Your first hire should be a strong and seasoned network architect/engineer. This person is a unicorn in that she or he can design a network and implement it, and also support it. Your second hire is a voice architect/engineer. This person is the same, only in the voice space. Your third and fourth are network engineers who can implement the design and work on deployment and business support. If you have a manufacturing function, you need personnel to help with tool deployment and hookup; these are the folks that do that. By the fifth, you can start thinking about a security architect/engineer to join the infrastructure team. This person will start in infrastructure but eventually may be moved out in Functional Second into a security architecture function, depending on the conditions and circumstances. This person will start designing the baseline controls to secure your systems, applications, transport, and network services. The next hire is a security engineer, so long as the network folks are able to stay afloat if not, you should bring another network engineer. At this time, the security folks are looking at introducing firewalls at your ingress/egress points, and segmenting the network for administration, production, and maybe a facilities network if deemed necessary; the exact initial segments are dependent on what you do, but you are investing in firewalls, and beginning to install some baseline security. In the ingress/egress points, they are deciding what kind of security is needed; if you have retail sites, you will need some lightweight but secure solutions that are low cost so that you can deploy a bunch of them across the countless retail facilities you own. This space changes constantly and today appliances like Cisco Meraki is popular on the network side for delivering scalable, easy to deploy and secure networking. Palo Alto Prisma SD-WAN Instant-On Network (ION) are also very popular in deployments nowadays but who knows, by the time you read this, the technology might have changed, so let's stay away from the talk on appliances and simply say, because nowadays we use dedicated Internet connections in sites and on the backend the connect to WAN technology like MPLS, your architects will have to design standards to enable them for rapid deployment and easy support remotely. Let's leave the details to the experts who you hire.

The point here is that your network and security architects are now working in unison to overlay security controls at your points of entry and exit, as well as your internal segments; these are the essential and emerging security controls. Alongside this, the faster you get to defining firewall rules, the better off you'll be because it's a painful exercise to come back to this and eliminate any-any rules later. Between the segments, start identifying traffic flows; validate legitimate business flows, and start writing specific rules and descriptions. The other security build you want to start tackling right away relates to how you manage externally-facing services. The use of demilitarized zones or DMZs still has useful purpose and aside from securing ingress/egress points, and segmenting, you want to absolutely address isolating externally-facing systems by employing some form of DMZ. Now things have gotten a lot more complicated than the days when cloud didn't exist. Today you not only have to build traditional DMZs for on-premise systems like maybe web servers, DNS, and email servers if you use them, you also need to address your cloud environments. Again, I'm not a technical expert, but you'll likely use virtual Private Clouds (VPCs) and security groups to secure your cloud environments. Depending on how far you take segmentation on the initial build, you could employ micro-segmentation that is more granular than described earlier where you are creating separate zones for specific systems and applications, thus reducing the attack surface. The point is, these are the three areas you want to focus on, along with working with your endpoint team to ensure at the very minimum, devices have disabled USB interfaces, and anti-virus installed so that while you're looking outward in the network, someone doesn't infiltrate with a stolen laptop or something and steal whatever IP you have already. There is so much more you can and will do, but prioritize getting the business up and running, and then begin introducing security controls. The most important thing out of all of this is the people. Bring in good people at the right time so that you can have highly talented folks making the right decisions on the company's behalf.

A couple of additional points. Initially no one is thinking about appliance security or change control because you are standing up services and in build-out, but soon you need to turn your attention to locking down access to your infrastructure so that they can't be compromised. Ideally you do this right away, but the fourth thing you do want to do is start managing accounts for all your infrastructure and establishing individual accounts rather than shared accounts. Try to avoid direct access to devices, and use some sort of jump server instead so that in the event accounts are compromised, you have an intermediary that can add to your defense in depth approach. So absolutely eliminate shared accounts and move to jump servers for access. Also, most technical folks will want a secondary/backdoor to the equipment in the event of a network failure so they can remotely access systems to reboot or troubleshoot. Make sure those backdoors or support network is locked down the same way. Sometimes we forget to ensure proper security controls on them and they end up being the path for access and infiltration.

One other point, and this is strictly operational in nature, determine when your build-out is stabilizing and introduce change control. Your internal customers will love you for building fast but very quickly, if the network is bouncing, they will become your biggest critics. As soon as you see things stabilizing, lock things down and institute change control so that you can assert discipline in how you run your operation. Ideally a service management team is being stood up simultaneously so that they can own the change management process, but if not, implement one for yourself while they are getting that space stood up in your organization. One last thing, as with everything, new patches come out to address vulnerabilities in security and network system as much as operating systems and databases. Build the discipline prior to moving to the Intermediate work to assess infrastructure vulnerabilities, and determine which patches will be applied and which ones will be ignored. Yes, sometimes you will ignore some patches because they may not apply to your environment or their impact after assessment is potentially more damaging than not having them. Build the practice to assess, track, and capture decisions so that if something happens later, you can refer back to this for root cause analysis or explaining the rationale.

5.2.2 The intermediate

> Why did the intermediate firewall start meditating?
>
> Because it wanted to reduce traffic congestion and achieve inner packet peace!
>
> (OpenAI, 2024)

You know, the first time I read that, I wasn't smart enough to get it, but then I found 'inner packet peace' to be hilarious. That's one for those IT-types. Okay, let's get back to business, you now have the following initial controls in place and it's time to expand:

- Security at your ingress/egress points
- Segmentation and maybe even some micro-segmentation
- DMZs to protect your network from externally-facing systems that are prone to attack
- Cloud DMZ solutions like VPCs and security groups or some other solution to protect cloud infrastructure

- Individual accounts for accessing the systems on the network
- Jump servers to remove direct access to network and security appliances
- Disabled USB ports on endpoints
- Anti-virus and anti-malware on endpoints
- Security measures in place for your out-of-band operations network for backdoor access
- Change control to mitigate service disruption
- A practice for assessing and implementing relevant patches to your infrastructure to reduce vulnerabilities and risk of infiltration

By now your operation is developing and the business is running. You have ups and downs in IT infrastructure and you get called out now and then, and have to report on root cause and do all sorts of permanent corrective actions, but this is par for the course. High pressure is now medium pressure as your blood pressure begins to come down to close to normal. It's time to start thinking about additional security controls. You want to begin paying attention to all the ways users gain access to the network, so remote access management becomes a topic of interest if it hasn't already. You want to make sure the tools we noted in Chapter 4 are in place like VPN and MFA at this time. You also want to expand access controls into a formal practice so that users and devices are verified and authorized for specific services. Certificate management has likely showed up already and depending on what's going on when you are reading this book, FIDO may be a default service for authentication and the move to passwordless environments.

In the network, you should be considering intrusion detection and/or protection systems (IDS/IPS) to start identifying anomalies and ideally reacting to them with an IPS. Threat prevention becomes increasingly important as your business takes form and a natural evolution of the infrastructure services deployed. At this time you should have standard templates for infrastructure builds, and when I say infrastructure, it applies to software-based appliances as well (like software-based firewalls). Those templates should be hardened and certified by the security team. Verify all your data transport is encrypted; it's not abnormal that years into the build of a company that you uncover some group somewhere has unencrypted communications of some sort. If we're running a solid network operation, this should be captured immediately but just do a check to make sure all data is encrypted.

Again, technical folks will run circles around me but generally, these are some of the key capabilities you want to develop if you haven't already done so. You want to ensure your operation is developing the discipline needed, and your controls are emerging. You may not be in a position to bash what we're describing against a maturity framework or controls that we discussed but intuitively, we know that these are the types of things we need to install to protect our environment. NIST SP 800-53 talks about access controls, logging of events in the network, and monitoring among other things but frankly, you should at first rely on the experience of your network and security architects to formulate the right security measures at the right time, until things stabilize.

After the Intermediate set of activities you should have a pretty decent setup but obviously you can do a lot more. The things you have implemented by now between the Essentials and Intermediate are:

- Security at your ingress/egress points
- Segmentation
- Micro-segmentation where it makes sense
- DMZ build out
- Cloud DMZ with VPCs and security groups or other
- Individual accounts, not shared or group accounts
- Jump servers
- Disabled USB ports on endpoints
- Anti-virus and anti-malware on endpoints
- Security measures in place for your out-of-band
- Operational change control
- Patch management
- VPN for secure remote access for remote users
- MFA for authentication to use company resources
- FIDO as an enhancement to MFA for passwordless authentication
- Certificates and certificate management (part of public key infrastructure or PKI)
- Encryption everywhere (at rest and in transit for data)
- Hardened templates for key infrastructure appliances

You can amend to this as much as you like, but these are the types of capabilities you want to ensure are being introduced as your infrastructure buildout matures. I'm sure if I took a poll, folks would add more but it goes back to what your company needs and when; that can be different for different firms. You could add SSO for example to the Intermediate or wait for Advanced but at some point you need to ensure your company applications are protected by single sign-on and frankly, the sooner the better. Another one you could add is web application firewalls (WAF) that we spoke about and these are important because they protect Internet-facing applications like webservers. Now that you have a DMZ, you should really think about getting this in place to add that extra layer of protection because the Internet is dirty and the source for practically all attacks. You can't have enough layers of protection, and WAFs are considered best practice in blocking malicious traffic.

5.2.3 The advanced

By now, you are on the tail end of the Functional First and moving in parallel to developing Functional Second that includes a compliance function.

Whether on your own or through a maturity modeling exercise, you'll begin introducing more infrastructure-related capabilities to shore up your defenses even more. Your operation is expanding and you're starting to form a recognizable security operation with Governance and Compliance, Cyber Fusion, Security Assurance and others. Sticking to infrastructure, you want to start talking about ZTNA and itemizing the access to resources by mapping user to service based on business need. Up to now, you may have an environment where once you authenticate and the device and user are validated that they have access to any network resources they know how to get access to. With ZTNA you start locking down to least privilege and the philosophy of 'never trust, always verify'. Somewhere along the way, if you have had a third-party audit, they have probably told you that Privileged Access Management (PAM) should be something you should pursue. PAM is a derivative of access management but it hones in on administrators, sensitive information and critical systems that we talked about earlier under BC/DR. This can be an expensive solution to implement which is why some teams push this out, but nowadays you can explore cloud PAM and that may reduce the cost of implementation. PAM does a few things, once you identify all the applicable accounts, you store the credentials in an encrypted vault. You also apply stringent password polices because the users who are targeted support the most sensitive systems. PAM requires you to implement a concept called Just-in-Time (JIT) access, meaning you are implementing role-based access and you're limiting the use of these privileged accounts to specific tasks and the rest of the time, you are using your normal accounts that are not elevated in privilege.

At the time of my writing this, the concept of Secure Access Service Edge (SASE) was becoming popular because of the advent of more complex scenarios due to cloud and on-premise needing to coexist. SASE is a framework in of itself that looks to simplify the combination of networking and security services. SASE is comprised of numerous topics we have already discussed, and ones that are covered in Functional Third such as data loss prevention (DLP), cloud access security broker (CASB), ZTNA and several others. That's pretty cool but why do we need to make up yet another acronym if we're going to implement all of these anyway? Good question, there are services that sit on top of these capabilities that lead people to identify SASE as unique, namely, the introduction of dynamic policy enforcement where your network and access policies adapt. Access control becomes even more robust than we described in the last two phases because you're determining access based on multiple variables: device, user, location, and risk level (Cisco, n.d., December 6th, 2024). There's a lot to SASE, but the point is in Advanced, you are looking at intelligent controls that go beyond appliances. You are establishing dynamic solutions that can adapt to your user base and risks. By the time you get here, you may be running a DLP initiative and rolling these types of toolset in to move towards a very robust security posture.

So the summary of controls gets a bit ambiguous as you go into Advanced because you're not putting in spot solutions but looking at security from a higher level. You will absolutely want to continue to strengthen your various segments based on what they support and value. You will continue to improve your infrastructure but as you go through Advanced, you want to marry your efforts to the rest of the development of your security program, as SASE for example illustrates. Summarized controls across the three levels are:

- Security at your ingress/egress points
- Segmentation & Micro-segmentation where it makes sense
- DMZ & Cloud DMZ with VPCs and security groups or other
- Individual accounts, not shared or group accounts
- Jump servers
- Disabled USB ports & anti-virus and anti-malware on endpoints
- Security measures in place for your out-of-band
- Operational change control
- Patch management
- VPN, MFA & FIDO
- Certificates and certificate management (part of public key infrastructure or PKI)
- Encryption everywhere (at rest and in transit for data)
- Hardened templates for key infrastructure appliances
- PAM
- SASE and all the underlying controls tied to this framework, including ZTNA

5.3 SECURITY OPERATIONS

The emergence of Cyber Fusion and Security Assurance drive the distinction I make here between infrastructure operations and security operations. In parallel, you are building these teams, the Governance and Compliance Team, and you are carving out your architecture function to stand as a center of excellence to drive technology strategy. You want to be careful you don't take your architects out of operations completely because as soon as you do, they become increasingly ineffective so have one foot in operation and one foot in planning. Here we'll talk a little bit about some characteristics of the two functions under operations to supplement what was said in Chapter 4.

5.3.1 Security operations

Cyber Fusion is the name of this team, and they are the first step to making the invisible, visible. You've got elements that have shown up prior to their arrival and during infrastructure build but in truth, it's when you start building out this team that you are truly starting to grow your security operation. In every job I've had, this is a 24x7 support team, so you need to figure out what model works best for you. My favorite is follow-the sun for many reasons, 1: you have a fresh team that is working their day hours to support the operation, and you get the best out of them because they're not tired, 2: they are working with others during their normal day as opposed to being the third shift and no one is around; it makes a difference, and 3: typically there's less turnover because most people don't like to work evening and overnight. I'm not going to speak about differential, which is the added cost for night-shifts because if they're going to give up their evening and night then they should be getting paid more. Okay so I ended up talking about it anyway; that's number 4 reason then.

Working in a normal work schedule and then having an on-call rotation can be something done but for a tier 1, front line team, I don't like this because 1: mean time to respond (MTTR) will be slower, 2: accessibility can be an issue when trying to reach the person on-call and they're not responding, and 3: just the nature of administering it. If you're running a critical function as security operations then put in a model where staff is active and you have guaranteed access to them, and plus when there are no alerts, they can continuously be chasing down risks, vulnerabilities, or analyzing data tied to other aspects of your operation. The one I want to explore more is automated SOC services. With the advent of artificial intelligence, in particular the generative stuff, we now have the potential of building self-healing systems. There are companies that are marketing platforms based on gen AI that monitor, identify, assess, remediate, and notify without any human intervention. The value would be 1: very fast, almost immediate response times, 2: no fatigue, and 3: always on. What this does is allow you to raise your SOC staff into higher dimensions of your operation to start doubling down on risk reduction, vulnerabilities, forensics, malware, threat hunting, and all the things the Cyber Fusion team wants to do but doesn't get to as much as they should. This would be a win-win for everyone; you get an automated SOC while your SOC analysts become SOC engineers, doing a lot more sophisticated things as part of the operations cycle. Now be careful not to rely fully on AI because it can get things wrong sometimes. AI can have hallucinations where it presents wrong statistics or inconsistencies in reasoning that can lead to a mistake that can in turn take down a system in the extreme. My expectation is this will be resolved over time as technology matures but for now, be aware that this is a real thing.

To run a follow-the sun model, you need a minimum of 12 individuals. I'm not going to assume anything regarding your philosophy on hiring, but in industries far and wide that are global, you will typically find a concentrated hiring in India followed by Eastern Europe and Latin America. These emerging markets are attractive because the talent pool is growing and they are relatively low cost when compared to Western Europe and the United States. You'll want to distribute your hiring as 4x4x4 ideally to cover things like sick time, vacation, redundancy in coverage, and supporting all the other things you do beyond eyes-on-glass (i.e., monitoring). Latin America, especially Costa Rica and Mexico as examples, have come into play because they are in the same time zones as the U.S. Whatever your philosophy, make sure you distribute your hiring across the globe and if you're not global, then you'll need to have a localized call center that runs the three shifts with handoffs. Bare in mind that as you start the Functional Third activities, you'll need to hire in that region, meaning, if you do business in North America then you want to have someone on that soil due to data privacy rules, and this is absolutely the case in Europe. Regulations mandate that sensitive data and personal information must be handled by employees in that region.

When you're first standing up this team, you're really taking on a lot because on one hand you are going through hiring and all the frustrations tied to that process during and after hiring, and second you are issuing an RFP to find a suitable MSSP to work with you and provide all the tools your team will be using. We talked about the RFP and some general requirements but my fundamental belief is to minimize the number of tools this team supports so that they can concentrate on actual risk reduction in the business. Don't tie your people up in maintaining, tuning, and general administration because that's not the point of your team. The reason you want to do this simultaneously is because as your team members onboard, you want them to be on the ground floor of the platform you're developing. You want your team to support the rollout and tuning while you are standing up your operation and establishing incident management practices. I've tried to run everything in-house in the past and it failed miserably and I had to move to this hybrid model. We were patting ourselves on the back for maintaining systems and installing redundancy and high availability but we never got to the essence of why we have the tools, to secure the organization! Needless to say very quickly in those early years, I realized I need to get rid of system administration in this space.

I'm not going to repeat what was said in Chapter 4 but you want to split the capabilities between your Fusion and Assurance Teams and institute a checks and balance model where the Assurance Team is acting as the technical auditor who probes process and controls to identify gaps that you can then close. Over time, you'll see all the loopholes being locked down and your security posture strengthening because of this feedback loop. So the tools and capabilities you want to house in your Fusion Team are, wouldn't you know, focused on threat detection, and incident management. They serve a key role in reducing technology risk and staying on top of what's happening in the wild, and instituting new practices and controls to combat emerging threats. Logging, alerting, and correlation are at the core of what they do through a SIEM that we spoke about prior. Incident response is at the heart of Cyber Fusion. The deployment of a vulnerability management tool is a good coupling given that this team should be also responsible for oversight of vulnerabilities. There are all sorts of services that should be run out of this team, as a recap, things like threat intelligence, threat hunting, the use of honeypots that are used to understand attack methods by the bad actors. Forensic and malware services are all part of this space, and usually an MSSP will provide some sort of endpoint detection and response (EDR) or if you go the extra step, extended detection and response (XDR) that extends beyond endpoints and incorporates networks, servers, and cloud for example, to get a wider view of threats and the response to those threats.

Another aspect of Cyber Fusion is the responsibility to run table top exercises and simulations. One of the important exercises you can do with your team and then with the executives is to ensure they have practice addressing security incidents that rise to a crisis level. Table tops consider a scenario and you talk through how you would approach the response as an organization that includes identification, containment, remediation, communication, and recovery as some of the aspects discussed. These exercises can include your Board given some of the communication will be to the Board if the issue is significant enough. Simulations are when you step into an incident and you're following a crisis plan as if it's going on real-time. Both are very useful to ensure your organization is ready to address situations that nowadays are more common than we'd like to believe.

Along the way, you need to establish some protocols on how your operation functions. How will you manage incidents, how will you coordinate activities, how will you manage root cause? These topics are all captured in your incident management procedure where you identify all the components that make up your operation. In most established companies, you have some sort of ticketing system that IT uses that you can piggy back on and establish a secure and confidential queue for security. I've used ServiceNow in several scenarios and while I don't sponsor this platform, it has proven itself to be very versatile and you can customize it to meet IT needs and also security. ServiceNow is an expensive platform but has so much to it that if you are ready to invest into the maturity of your technology practice, it's a good choice, but you can go with something cheaper. One other capability your MSSP might provide is security orchestration, automation, and response (SOAR). SOAR automates repetitive tasks, connects your suite of tools in a way that you can improve your intelligence around events. SOAR improves your response time while making your overall operation more efficient. You may not want to implement SOAR right away but once your operation is stabilizing and the team knows what they're doing, you should start looking into this as a very powerful tool to improve your capacity and optimize your incident handling. One service you don't want to wait on is an incident response retainer. Get that setup right away so that in the event something happens, you have your MSSP on standby ready to support you.

Quick hit responsibilities, this team is focused on risk reduction, and they are heavily involved in communication management within the technology teams, during incidents and to stakeholders like Legal. This team does a lot with document management between maintaining procedures for operations to handling all the documentation tied to service delivery. Cyber Fusion plays a big part in audits because they run a function that customers and regulators want to ensure are in place and effective. This team ties directly to the reputation of your company to shareholders because the outside world can measure your weaknesses in your perimeter by probing your network and assigning a rating to your company. Cyber Fusion is where I've placed the responsibility of perimeter security and a continual effort to drive weaknesses down by using tools like BitSight or something equivalent.

I hope I've conveyed the value of this team and the need to set it up correctly. There is so much that happens here, and you'll find that once you set this team up, the attention on what you do increases. For some reason, as soon as you stand up elements of this team is as soon as your internal audit team decides to audit your maturity in running security operations. This has annoyed me more than you can imagine in the past. They don't call it out as a gap when you don't have it, but as soon as you build it, all of a sudden the back seat driver, Monday-morning quarterback (U.S. phrase) shows up who tells you all the things you're doing wrong, as opposed to all the things you did right in filling a gap that you and your team identified. It's the most unnerving thing that happens, but it does happen and you find yourself defending your operation for all the wrong reasons and spending your time justifying the decisions you made as opposed to focusing your energy on continuing to improve your practice... but I digress. Hopefully you have a good IA team that works with you every step of the way and if you do, then the two departments can work cooperatively and build together.

5.3.2 Security assurance

I'm going to just take a moment to talk about the things in operations that you can plant in your Assurance Team. You want to arm this team with strong hacker-type good guys and gals who will be probing your environment for weaknesses. This is where your in-house penetration testing can happen. This is where your Red Team exercises are run, but they can also coordinate war-game activities across the organization. This team can be heavily involved in vulnerability management by maintaining special tools for mobile applications, open-source code, containers, and other specialized spaces that you capture information about weakness in your operation. They might have tools for performing web application scanning, or introduce tools for software code reviews or software integrity scanning offered by fuzzing tools.

This team is highly technical and is involved in everything that has to do with assessing the integrity of your operation. If your organization does any software development, fuzzing tools are valuable, but a bug bounty program can be pretty powerful to add to your arsenal for ensuring what your company develops is secure. What should be obvious is that this team really adds that element of quality check to everything you do, including software and product development, process assessment, and capability testing. You use Assurance as a counterbalance to Fusion, in that your Assurance team makes sure the operation works, is tested and goes through a continuous improvement exercise.

REFERENCES

Cisco. (n.d.). What is SASE (Secure Access Service Edge)? Cisco. Retrieved December 6, 2024, from https://www.cisco.com/c/en/us/products/security/what-is-sase-secure-access-service-edge.html#:~:text=Secure%20access%20service%20edge%20(SASE)%20is%20an%20architecture%20that%20delivers,and%20zero%2Dtrust%20network%20access

National Institute of Standards and Technology. (2018). *Risk management framework for information systems and organizations: A system life cycle approach for security and privacy* (NIST Special Publication 800-37 Rev. 2). U.S. Department of Commerce. https://doi.org/10.6028/NIST.SP.800-37r2

OpenAI. (2024). *ChatGPT* [Large language model]. https://chatgpt.com

Sarbanes-Oxley Act of 2002, 15 U.S.C. § 7201 (2002).

Chapter 6

Mindset and collaboration

Keys to success

The last two chapters got into some of the elements that make up the team you are building. Chapter 4 spoke to maturity modeling, organization structure and how to sequence the three functional categories that will get you to a mature operation. Chapter 5 looked a little deeper into the operational aspects of your team and what you should consider to establish, and when. Let's now talk about the softer elements that are just as important. Mindset and approach will influence your success more than you know, and we want to make sure we are approaching our jobs in the right state of mind. In addition, there are very critical relationships you need to establish so that you ensure you are getting the right information out, and you are getting support for the initiatives you will have to champion.

6.1 WINNING MINDSET

If I were to develop security leaders, and maybe this applies to more than just security, then I would have the following guidance to give. Look, I'm not really into telling folks how to be or behave; there's enough of that going around between all the LinkedIn posts on 'what makes a good leader' or 'top ten behaviors of successful people', or being told what books to read to be successful, or something like that. However, if you want my perspective on what makes solid leaders, and behaviors to absolutely stay away from because they will slow or stop your career growth as it relates to security, then read on. If you could care less and feel you are at the top of your game and don't need another person giving such advice, then skip it. I find more than other technology functions, there are some essential behaviors you need to adopt to get the company behind you in what you're working towards. You also want to avoid some pitfalls that seem exclusive to security folks that can kill your momentum, reputation, and credibility.

First, let's start by putting aside any notions that we have some authority over any aspect of the business. Nothing gets done without support from other teams and security is not a directive set by us but rather a negotiated set of terms. We absolutely recommend a direction and establish the strategy

DOI: 10.1201/9781003616528-6

that we review and get buy in for, after which we ensure compliance to. We do not, however, work in isolation and as a policing body under the auspice that we have some sort of bestowed power. Security has this reputation some times of being hard to work with because we can come off as authoritative in how we communicate. Because we are an enforcement body, there is this aura of authority but I've learned that in order to get others to work with you and eliminate friction, you need to be viewed as cooperative to the extent possible. The way we communicate is as important as what we communicate and I've been in meetings where I was the one making go/no-go decisions on a migration or integration. Everyone looked to me for approval to proceed, and in younger versions of Timur, this could have gotten to my head and I would lay down the law! I've realized that this approach can get you past the short-term objective, but folks won't have a warm feeling about working with you come the next round, and they'll remember how you made them feel the next time you need help. Frankly, I've gotten to the point where I want all of us to come along on the journey together and solve problems as a unit rather than being the guy who decides alone, sometimes at the expense of others.

My preferred approach now is to reason out the impact of the risk, ask for opinions on what we are exposing ourselves to, and with all the feedback, make a recommended decision and ask for input. Now some of you will say, Timur, you are soft, this isn't the way we work, but I've learned this is the only way I want to work for many reasons. For one, I've observed that as soon as you make the larger non-security team part of the decision, they begin to identify risks independent of you and start making pro-security recommendations on how to proceed. People appreciate being part of the solution and most times we're all trying to solve the same thing, we simply look at the objective from a different lens. Let's try and solve problems together and in doing so, we establish a foundation of trust that will only help all of us for the future. Yes it may take just a bit more time in decision-making but in the long-run, you are building a coalition of trusted partners that will speed up your journey together. Our role is not about control and authority, but about making sure someone is watching out for the security of our organization and in doing so, also securing our people's personal information. This is directly correlated to our livelihood because if we do our job poorly, the extreme could mean an impact to company reputation, revenue streams, litigation, and all of this can lead to loss of jobs. I don't want to refer to the clichés of corporate talk too much, but servant leadership must be reflected at its finest as you work to support the company's best interest, and your attitude should absolutely reflect this mindset.

If we do this right, we promote a level of openness and begin to be viewed as reasonable; boy wouldn't that be great if our colleagues viewed us as a reasonable security team that wants to make positive change? I absolutely have seen that when I had this realization and naturally began to behave in this way, my peers and superiors in the company began evangelizing security on our behalf. I'd go into sensitive meetings and come out with full support of our objectives. It took me a long time to get over myself because I'm thick headed but it allows for faster growth, and at times when you need to be firm, you'll find the impact of that is more potent because your colleagues know that what's at hand must be serious if you're drawing a line in the sand.

In developing leaders in my organization, there are a few basic themes I try to champion. For one, don't get defensive. Some folks get defensive of their team and responsibilities in a way that becomes counterproductive. They become sensitive to any conversation around the space they manage and hold things personally against others. Step back and look at things more broadly; is that critique being made against you personally, if yes, then go for it and be defensive! Okay, but most of the time you're in a leadership forum or a meeting and someone is pointing out an opportunity to do something, or they may not be completely familiar with the work being done in a specific area so they make assumptions. Don't take this personally. Respond by offering insights and clarification. If they happen to know something about that topic then listen and put yourself outside your own ego and hear what they have to say. The worst thing we can do for our own careers is to be viewed as difficult because as you work through your career, less emphasis will be placed on what you do, and more on how you do it and your approach. Don't be that person that is hard to deal with and overly sensitive about every topic. You'll quickly find your support and your own growth will stop.

Lastly, stop complaining… really, just stop. We know every company has some red tape, some politics, and some personalities that may not be easy to work with (make sure you're not one of them). Have patience but be persistent in what you're trying to accomplish. Maybe the company is not ready for whatever you're trying to do now, but keep at it and many times the conditions will change. Champion the cause and if it is urgent then get your leadership involved and push for it, but if it's not urgent but rather a best practice in the way things can be done, then incubate the idea and grow it. Along the same lines, never complain without offering a potential path forward. Leadership generally is fine if you identify gaps but when you follow it up with ways to resolve the matter, then you'll be viewed as a problem solver and not just a critic. I'd ask you to think about that one person you've run into that had an opinion about everything, and loved to call out all the issues but never offered up any resolution and never took accountability. How quickly do we pass them off and stop listening to them because we're all looking for productive partners and problem solvers; we're not looking for a bunch of whiners who have no stake in the game.

I think I'll stop there on mindset. To recap the three themes I believe are important are 1: always behave like a servant leader and let's go one step further, act like a fiduciary who has an ethical obligation to your team and your company, 2: don't get defensive and remain open to constructive criticism. Be able to recognize constructive criticism from your own self-imposed notion that it's simply an attack on you. We need to set aside our egos and be able to see our own blind spots, and 3: don't be that whiner that always complains that things aren't getting done, or it's hopeless or even that this is how we've always done it and it's not going to change. No one likes a complainer who calls out every issue but has no solution, and never takes accountability for anything. You'll quickly find yourself on the outside and if layoffs are coming, guess who's going to get hit.

6.2 YOU CAN'T DO IT ALL... SO DON'T

As you're developing your team, you want to ensure the mindset has been set as already described but you also want to ensure you yourself understand that you need to take on the challenge of security by investing into your teams development. We should do this anyway, as one of the most important jobs we have is being responsible for our team and their success, but the stakes are even higher when you're running a function that touches literally every part of the business. The best sports teams have a winning culture where there's empowerment at all facets of what they do. Every member is aligned to the common goal and they know they will be supported if something goes south. Invest in training, invest your time to speak to your team as close to individual engagements as possible, and nurture a mindset where everyone can safely and confidently make decisions at every level of the team. The formula is based on personal relationships. The formula includes transparency in decision making across the team. Bring high performing members across the team into your strategy meetings, setup an engagement team to promote team building. Share the 'whys' of what drive your decision making, and ask for the teams opinions and act on them, or at the very least acknowledge the input and let them know why you don't pursue them if you choose not to. Like the title says, you can't do it all yourself so develop a team where all of you are working actively towards the same cause.

One final point to make on my personal view of team management. I used the word fiduciary earlier to describe our responsibility to our team and the company. One of the most important responsibilities we carry as leaders is for our team members. I calculate it this way, for every member on your team, you can assume an average of two children and one significant other. So, you're responsible for 4 individuals for every person on your team, meaning, if you have a team of 100, then there are 400 people counting on you for their livelihood and sense of safety. Put everything else aside, this is enough for me to work as hard as I can to make sure we are successful together not just for the job but for the people that we work with. If you truly take this to heart, you really can't do wrong, because you will have the right values in front of you. Develop your team, grow your team, make them accountable for things they value and let's not lose the human aspect of what we do. Don't allow yourself to hide behind financial statements, and numbers to rationalize people reductions when you have alternative means to get to the same objective. The reality of corporate life is that sometimes we will face circumstances where we have no other recourse but to reduce workforce, but do everything you can to stay away from it, and then minimize the impact to the extent possible.

This means a few things. First, be very stingy on approving new headcount. Profile your direct reports and determine what they believe success looks like, and if it is a function of team size then you need to set them straight. If you have to upset your direct reports because you deny new hires, then so be it, because it's better to keep your team small than to oversize it and run the risk of layoffs that impact their families. Many times during budget planning and strategy sessions you will have the opportunity to drive this point home that you need to protect the existing team by managing workload as opposed to looking to add personnel for the ebbs and flows of workload over the course of a year. Second, and there are so many more points on this but we'll keep it to two; collect and track data around staff utilization so you can model your team size effectively and defend the size when needed. This is easier said than done but put in place a resource utilization and planning model with some sound assumptions wrapped around it so that you can articulate why your team is the size it is and what they do. Couple this with your track record for controlled hiring and you will gain credibility for being responsible with how you manage your team. Maybe adding one more point, drive your teams to look as much into automation as possible. Use this as a partial alternative to adding more staff. There are so many low-level tasks we as technology teams can automate that instilling a culture that drives towards efficiency is vital to promote the ideas noted in this section.

6.3 PARALLEL PROCESSING

We double click just a bit on the point that you can't do everything yourself. Focusing on your direct reports, you want to become very comfortable with empowering them to go out into the company and lead. Some very seasoned leaders have a tendency to control communication in and out of their organization so that they have full awareness of all interactions. This doesn't work, and stifles your team. In security, we need compliance folks to be talking compliance to Legal, HR, and every other team in the organization; for me as a CISO to get in the way will become a huge congestion point. Our infrastructure services teams need to support other departments, product security needs to be lock-step with product engineering and serve as our relationship managers to product engineering; if we had to control engagement, we would implode. Develop your team to act independently. Your job is to set a common vision, strategy, and objectives so that everyone is working toward the same thing. This does mean developing your team's leadership skills and communication. You will want to invest heavily in communication assessment and training so that your team develops constructive and mutually constructive engagements.

6.4 FULL TRANSPARENCY (CREDIBILITY IS GOLD)

Another quick-hit relates to information sharing. The more you bring your team and stakeholders along for the ride, the less misalignment there will be. The more participative in approach, the less you'll have to argue for support when difficult conversations occur. You obviously have some things you simply can't divulge because in doing so they would damage more than help your cause, but beyond these highly sensitive topics, share the plan, share the strategy, and share your personal thoughts and concerns so that your team knows where your mind is at, and the reasons why they see certain activities that without context, would not make any sense.

The quickest way to gain trust is to show your team you are human as well. When things don't work out, or you don't know something, don't try to talk around it. Security personnel are pretty intelligent folks, and they will read right through the dance. Speak plainly, acknowledge mistakes you have made or information you simply don't have. It is human nature to get behind someone who shows sincerity and root for them; if you act with sincerity, you will find that your team will begin relating to you and you'll be one step closer to developing a strong culture together.

We talked about the equation for trust in an earlier chapter. Trust that is comprised of credibility is something you need to protect as if it's gold, because it is in a corporation. When you have the trust of your team and your leadership, you'll find conversations are easier, support comes more readily and when things go wrong from time-to-time, the patience and understanding is so much more. Build up your credibility, be there when others need you even if it has nothing to do with your role or your goals. Work to build relationships that matter. By doing this, you'll grow the numerator of that equation that is C+R+I (Credibility + Reliability + Intimacy).

6.5 EVANGELISM (YOU'RE IN SALES & MARKETING)

Let's get into some of the other aspects of our job as security leaders. One aspect that initially when asked to run security operations I wasn't prepared for was the marketing aspect of it. You have to work as a promoter of security and the good work your team does needs to be marketed continuously because the rest of the organization may view you as big brother and others, simply a nuisance. You need to get past the stigma of a watcher and push for the reputation of a doer in the organization. Lobby for a reputation of partnership and not a dictator. Every Quarter you will take to the road (metaphorically of course) and do a roadshow of the message you plan to convey to the Board on security. You'll be wise to ensure everyone affected by the message has a chance to review what is said and contribute. This holds true whether you report to the Board, CEO or CFO or CIO. These are folks you need to work with and what's more, you want to be civil about the work you do and how it impacts others so while it takes time to prepare, and then review and push more revisions, the effort is important.

Second, it's important to be visible in the organization. Now those introverts like myself may have a hard time doing all of this, but we have to do it. This doesn't come naturally to me; let me first admit that but I force it because our voice needs to be heard and the message a security leader conveys will carry some weight to it. Participate in town halls, show up as a guest speaker to other departments, contribute to cybersecurity month messaging, put together short videos on security and post them on your Intranet. Believe me, my energy says I'd rather not, but my rational mind says we absolutely must. Your reputation as a subject matter 'expert' gives your company credibility so if you get a chance to speak at conventions or other security events, try to do it. You'll soon find out that your contact information is now out there (how…we are supposed to be secure?), and you'll start getting contacted to give a talk, or even be showcased on a magazine. Yes this happened to me but I didn't pursue it because I had things going on personally that had to be my priority. Take full advantage of this because again, it's good for your career and it's great for the company because they can tell regulators that their security head or CISO is well respected in the security community.

Let me reiterate; get the word out about what you do and why you do it. A large percentage of your job as a leader in this space isn't to run operations, but to champion your security brand and get support. All of our personalities are different and this will come easier to extraverts. For us introverts, the best way to cope is to institutionalize the marketing of your mission. Setup routines, recurring practices, and establish marketing campaigns in your operations support team so that some of this can get automated, because otherwise your energy will drain, that's just the nature of who you are. All of us can be effective but we may need to approach it in different ways. Last point on this, you'll read about some billionaires saying they despise presentations, and in some ways they may be right, but a big part of evangelizing what your team does is through presenting. PowerPoint, Google Slides, or whatever else you use are great tools, just know how to use them effectively as guides for messaging. In my humble opinion, there's nothing wrong with a good set of slides that aide in the messaging but the voice over is yours and not written down verbatim.

6.6 LEGAL IS VITAL

As a security leader, you want to establish relationships with Legal as soon as you can. So much of what we do is in partnership with the law department so we need to be lock step in our strategy and operational workflows. In some organizations, security reports into the Chief Legal Officer for this very reason, but no matter where security reports into, having strong connections is key. Let's talk a little bit about some of the engagements you can expect with Legal.

First, the administration of Board interactions typically flows out of Legal. They manage the schedules, coordinate participation requirements and content creation across the organization. Because you will be reporting to the Board in some capacity, you will want to be involved in any requirements for presentations that come out of the Board through Legal. Having Legal as a champion of security will potentially give you more face time with the Board and that is important because you want to ensure the Board is comfortable with your strategy and progress in your space. Prior and potentially after Board meetings, you will want to touch base with Legal to ensure the content is appropriate, and then have a retrospective on the back-end of what was learned and any action items to address before the next cycle.

Another important interaction deals with regulatory matters. Your intermediary to regulators may very well run through Legal. If you're in the U.S., any interactions with the SEC will need to be facilitated through Legal. That means you want to integrate Legal into your incident management practice so that if a security event arises, you can quickly notify them to determine if it's a reportable event. You will be responsible for incident management and Legal will take on the task to circulate to the right folks internally to deem the event material or not, and then subsequently facilitate the communication outward to the SEC, the Board, and the media if appropriate. You're in it together, so the best that can happen is that both of you see one another as an extension of your own operation.

Investigations internally will come from HR and Legal; you want to have a good practice in place to field these types of investigation requests and work through them. Investigations may deal with ethics violations, compliance, or something more serious. You are a trusted partner to Legal and HR, so you want to ensure you protect that trust and support these types of exercises that aren't fun but they are necessary. You will serve as the monitoring arm of certain oversight practices on employee activities and organizational processes. You'll work with Legal to determine the right level of this oversight to ensure protection of privacy and company interests.

One area I've been involved with in the past is crisis management. In some cases, you may we one spoke in the wheel supporting crisis management activities and in others, you'll help shape the structure and planning. No matter how your organization structures this, you have to ensure you are intimately involved in this space that usually is facilitated by the Legal Team.

We talked about incident management early; that is one aspect of crisis management.

Hopefully you don't have a lot of this, but litigation may involve you in supporting the Legal team. You'll absolutely be involved in any legal holds for data such as email of past and present employees if they are involved in any investigations. Legal may have an inhouse person who does some sort of forensics, or some outside firm. You'll be working with them to help identify data points that are pertinent for the investigation.

There's likely a process in place in the organization around new vendors and contract management. In every compliance practice in security, there should be a third-party risk assessment practice in place that ties back into contract and vendor management. This process crosses Procurement, Legal and Security meaning the three departments need to co-own the process and it's efficiency. Let me just say that this is one of the likely pain points in some organizations because it cross so many teams to get a contract out the door. I've witnessed a lot of frustration in more than one company I've worked with surrounding how fast (or slow) this process works. Keep an eye on this to see if you are a congestion point or if you need to influence improvement and assignment of service level agreements (SLAs) around each step of the process.

Both Legal and Security maintain policies specific to their areas but many times these policies cross into joint exercises. Whether it's a standard on crisis management or how you manage regulatory mandates, you'll likely be involved in developing some of this together. Where Security is interested in, well, security; Legal will make sure the body of documentation that the organization follows abide by the applicable laws. This truly is a symbiotic relationship that is essential and not a nice to have.

There are a lot of synergies across the two teams as you can see, some others revolve around training and awareness, risk management, data privacy and intellectual property protection, to name a few. I won't expand on these but know that in each of these additional spaces, the two teams are working together. Investing time to build strong connections is imperative; it will be a driver of your success going forward for all the reasons I've pointed out here.

6.7 THE CFO IS A HIDDEN KEY

As much as Legal is a partner in how we operate, Finance, and your CFO is a key to enabling your investment portfolio. It's very important to establish an understanding of strategy and your discipline in deciding on what to invest in and when, because if you gain the trust of your CFO, you will have more opportunities to do the work you need to but in a controlled manner. Things you'll learn from interacting with Finance include prioritization of security investments, conducting a cost-benefit analysis and developing a phased approach that sets short, mid, and long-term objectives. Let's not forget, especially in for-profit companies that we need to work within the confines of how the company performs financially. If you're asking for 20% increase in investment but your company is growing at 10%, that may be a red flag. It really depends on where you are in maturity and yes, what are the level of risks you are trying to address that may make this scenario perfectly fine, but you need to be aware of the financial considerations that drive the company, and the Finance Team can guide you on this.

There are other touch points here, such as controllership that may come out of Finance that ties back into regulatory considerations. There's the financial risk component to what you do that may require you to support SOX for example and work closely with the Finance Team. Fraud detection and control as it ties back into financials, and overall strategic planning are areas of interest. Having a good relationship and understanding of how Finance assesses investments and risks is going to be very important. For one, you'll learn the 'other' side of the business and make you well rounded and second, your messaging will become a lot crisper and you'll experience less friction if you speak a little bit of their language.

6.8 INTERNAL AUDIT

The language of audit is another thing entirely. Internal Audit has an important role in ensuring the company is abiding by the laws that govern it. Having an independent assessor that keeps us on the rails is not a bad thing, but sometimes, as I eluded in a past rant, the intention behind an audit can lead to complications that I have experienced personally.

There's a common theme that emerges as you see the types of engagements between Legal, Finance and IA. The same categories of activities apply, such as fraud prevention, data and privacy protection, and oversight. With all three of these teams, you are managing risk and ensuring that the organization is protected across several dimensions. The additional element with IA is tied to testing the controls we institute and validating that they are effective and meet the objectives. IA can be a good partner if you are working together to identify true gaps and drive remediation. IA can be an internal resource that can bridge the time between third party assessors to give you feedback on areas you can improve.

Many times IA reports back to the Board on the state of affairs in the company. Having insights into their findings and reporting will better prepare you for the conversations ahead. Secondly, having an opportunity to do pre-reads can help you start efforts to close gaps so that you progressively improve your posture. If you think about what IA offers as continuous improvement, then you can really benefit from their involvement. The key here is not to get defensive at findings so long as the intent is pure and there's mutual respect. Now if you know they're trying to build their brand on the back of your team then all bets are off!

6.9 CEO STAFF

These next two are probably obvious in that you need to maintain good relations with the CEO and their staff. Security is something that needs agreement and support. You never want to be perceived as big brother, and you always want to be viewed as a partner. The most influential people who can affect change are the CEO and their staff, so invest the time to build relationships. Now I have a limit; some folks just simply don't have the time to spend on matters affecting you so once you get that signal, stop pursuing. They are focused on other things and in turn, I'll move on in other spaces. Forcing something is just as bad as not pursuing genuine desire to connect. Some have their hands full with the challenge given to them that they just don't have the time to focus on something that does impact them, but it's being handled by someone else that they can defer to. That's perfectly fine. Sometime in the future, as things change, you may come back to that person in a natural way and foster a relationship but again, don't force anything, and give them their space.

6.10 BOARD OF DIRECTORS

Lastly, the Board of Directors. What an important group of folks who can coach, guide, and help establish direction. Your Board is comprised of industry leaders across various disciplines who have seen and done a lot. From an experience standpoint, they are someone you want to connect with. From an influence standpoint, they are absolutely folks you want to build strong relations with because they influence the state of the company.

Your relationship with the Board sets the groundwork for a security-conscious culture. If you build credibility, they will champion the cause of security across the company. Because security is a business objective and no longer an IT topic, the Board now has oversight requirements for security and in the U.S., the SEC calls out various practices that the Board should participate in, including reviewing security risks. You have a mandate to provide updates to the Board and share information on security trends, emerging practices, metrics for performance, and your overall health as an organization.

The age old 'what's in it for you', says that if you represent your management team effectively, and build bridges with the Board, they will become your advocate for funding security initiatives. Some of the things we need to pursue are multimillion-dollar efforts; for some companies this is no issue but for many, that is a sizable investment. By demonstrating your aptitude and proficiency, you will get support to do the big things you know you need to. Finally, you can influence the perception of security as a business enabler if you are embedding yourself into the various teams and helping them drive innovation, adopt secure technologies, and market your security capabilities as a competitive advantage.

Chapter 7

Management system

What to institutionalize

Last chapter, we spoke about a winning mindset and relationships. Let's pivot now again, to some of the structural elements that will make your practice successful. You can call it what you will, a management system, or a management operating system (MOS) or a portion of one or the other but the idea here is to establish some routines that reinforce your vision and assert discipline in the areas that drive your success. We spoke a bit about the various elements that make up the system I have instituted, and here we'll delve a bit deeper into each of them to point out intent and structure.

This book is all about what has worked for me in the past and allowed the teams I've been involved in to succeed in a demanding profession and an ever-increasing difficult threat landscape. If you have best practices that work for you in any of the areas noted here, then use them. The point here is to share the elements I've found need to be in place, and a little more on mindset so that you can cross-reference with what you're doing in case there's something you've been frustrated about and this triggers the creative juices to resolve that frustration. Figure 7.1 shows a rough sequencing of the elements described in this chapter, to give you a sense of timing. The items at the bottom happen earlier than the ones that are noted above them. In some cases you can implement parts of this in parallel, depending on your unique circumstances.

I place strategic planning as the foundation for everything else, because you will be pulling your team together right away to establish some baseline strategy that will drive the next several Quarters. Asserting discipline through a regular portfolio review will place emphasis on execution given most of security for many years will be driving new capabilities so our ability to execute needs to be a focus. Since risk is the underpinning of what we do, you should start thinking about that practice sooner rather than later, which is why it's third, and from there you can work through the thought process of the rest of the stack.

DOI: 10.1201/9781003616528-7

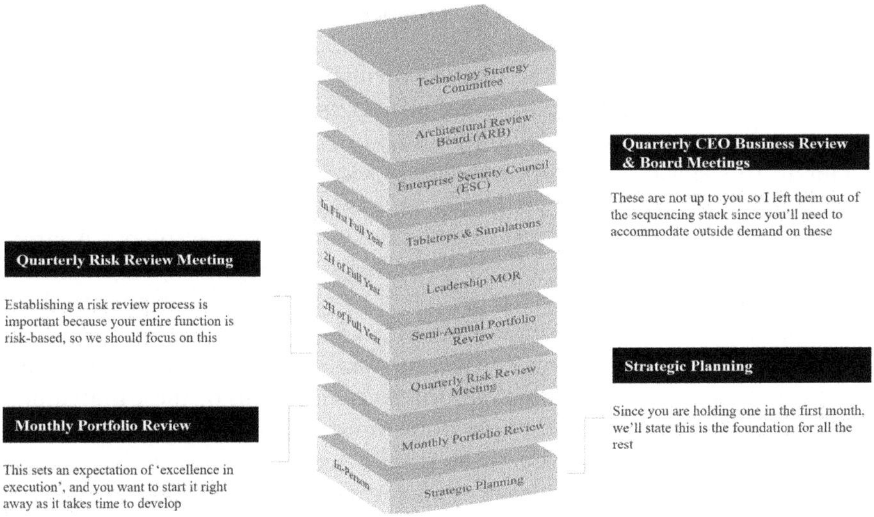

Figure 7.1 MOS sequencing.

7.1 MONTHLY PORTFOLIO REVIEW

Let's start with making a statement. I've observed that the most effective leaders are those that can map a vision to a strategy and then convert that into a set of executables. A leader that can work across the entire spectrum from idea all the way to the implementation of that vision is surprisingly not as common as you might think. There are a lot of very smart people out there in the world and many of them can see what needs to be done but not all of them can translate that into reality. Coincidentally, there are a lot of rockstars in execution that can't see the larger vision of where they want to go and you'll hear them get frustrated at little things because they're lost in a sea of tasks but don't, well, see the forest from the trees. As much as you need to be an adaptable communicator because you converse with folks from all levels of the organization, you also have to do the same in the life-cycle of executing goals.

My natural tendency is to look for 'excellence in execution', this means looking for accountability. This also means identifying who has the organizational skills and proficiency to set an idea, establish the boundaries for success, develop a plan, and act on that plan. Furthermore, the folks that do this well also know how to articulate status, pull in support for challenging times, and mitigate risks along the way. In my mind, security is more projects than operations, at least for the first five to six years of development. If you go back to the Strategic Roadmap, those work packages are not small and consume quite a bit of time, so we as security professionals need to institute execution discipline as soon as possible. The monthly portfolio review is the minimum for me, to assign governance over an emerging project management practice.

What's under the hood of a portfolio review? You need to figure out who will take charge of developing your project management practice and as noted earlier, your operations support team is that group to mature and facilitate this space. You want to identify members of your team who are project managers or have the ability and interest to run projects. In the larger IT teams, you'll find resistance from some because there's a larger operational element tied to IT, but in security, because it's predominantly project based, you'll find folks more likely to welcome this chance to drive new initiatives. Identify whom in operations support will serve as the portfolio lead, and they will be responsible for establishing templates for reporting projects and the overall portfolio top level view. This or these individuals will also facilitate the monthly portfolio review, but if I have my way, I'd actually make these bi-weekly to be frank; there's so much going on that meeting once a month just doesn't cut it for me but it's a minimum, which is why I noted it as such. Try to run it bi-weekly so you have enough touchpoints to grow this capability and mature the practice.

At first, you can't expect non-project managers to be great at cost management in particular so historically I've started with a basic four-block reporting template where they speak to accomplishments in one, next steps in another, challenges and risks or support needed in the third and a snapshot of scheduling milestones in the last. You can create some modified version of this but you're keeping it basic and something they can get behind right away. At the top you're capturing overall health across scope, schedule, cost, and maybe a fourth element of risk later. As you go forward, you'll formalize risks and risk mitigation more, and you'll want to start capturing cost information such as original budget versus burn down to see how you're doing in cost management.

This is the start of your reviews, and getting all the initiatives first identified, reporting in the same way and coaching the team to tell the story behind the initiative will take some time. Getting your portfolio leader to develop an understanding of the initiatives so that she or he can summarize at the beginning of each review and then facilitate the rest of the review will take time. Getting the team to get into a cadence of updating their information, doing quality checks and presenting in a succinct manner is a change and you want to develop this to assert discipline. You'll likely start with PowerPoints or Google Slides or something equivalent but over time, you want to pursue system-based reporting and automate as much of it as you can. The first year or maybe even the first two, your team is updating slides but you want to get the effort underway to translate the learnings and move your project management into a system such as Jira, or ServiceNow or some other portfolio and project management platform.

I have used ServiceNow in the past and front-ended it with a reporting tool like Tableau or something else to extract the relevant information and display it in a consistent fashion. The trick is to get everyone updating on a regular basis and build habits around updates so that when you extract into the reporting, it's updated and relevant. The foundation of all of this is to get folks actively identifying tasks, driving towards delivery dates, acting on issues (that are actual problems today) and risks (that are potential future problems), and taking all of this and keeping good records so that as a team, you can get together and go through the portfolio to seek understanding, awareness, and offer support where needed. Recently, I've moved more to Jira because for one, my teams have been rooted in engineering backgrounds and they used Jira, and second because the world of Agile showed up a few years ago and Jira became the go-to platform. Whatever your toolset is, move to a culture of transparent reporting, recurring reviews either bi-weekly or monthly, and a drive to automating the outputs so that you can quickly and dynamically get information on any initiative that's driving your security practice.

Eventually you want to build a center of excellence where you bring onboard a couple of top-notch program managers and maybe a couple of mid-career project managers to run the project and portfolio management practices, as well as run the large initiatives that cross teams and are most strategic and sensitive. This supplement of the rest of the team will be seen as a relief, and a source of coaching to improve their skills in running small to mid-level projects themselves. What you'll find if you open the meeting to everyone on your team is a growth in awareness and transparency and a culture driven to execution. If you handle yourself right and encourage and promote the folks that present in these meetings, you'll foster a sense of safety and interest to do more. Be careful you don't get into assessment and dissection of what is said because the team is fragile at the onset and nervous that they'll get called out. You don't want this to turn into a stressor for the team, but rather an opportunity to talk to the leadership, present to them, practice their presenting, and grow their careers. The difference between poisonous and constructive is very thin here, so be careful.

7.2 SEMI-ANNUAL PORTFOLIO REVIEW

Somewhere along the way, your team will be getting better at telling the story and demonstrating an aptitude for controlling initiatives that you'll want to open up status reporting to the broader external community and your manager. The intent behind the portfolio or PMO practice if you will, is to assert discipline and follow through on commitments. You have a lot of stakeholders that you report to so having semi-annual reviews with your stakeholders to give them a deep dive into the status of security initiatives is a good way to evangelize your security mission goals and the work being done. This gives them an opportunity to see the details, ask questions and guide you with suggestions.

As much as a semi-annual portfolio review is useful for transparency across the organization, it also allows you the opportunity to map the projects to the risks they are mitigating. The ultimate objective is to have a system designed where identified risks are rated for criticality, and mapped to your maturity model for added dimension. Then you take those prioritized risks and define initiatives to address them and convert those into projects. Doing this, as you systematically implement the projects and introduce new capabilities, you are reducing your risk exposure, improving your maturity and tying back to business objectives. Having a portfolio practice, presenting to your leadership and stakeholders, and tying everything back to your strategy reinforces a structured methodology as opposed to random investments with no view for an ultimate objective. What's more, in these semi-annual reviews, you can talk through risks that haven't been mapped to initiatives and talk through new business cases that include return on investment (ROI) profiles to get support for execution or even investment.

As it has been the case in everything, the frequency of these larger reviews is subject to your organizations appetite for such information. Some like the semi-annual while others might prefer Quarterly. Just remember that you report in many areas and in different ways so don't overwhelm yourself and overcommit where your team is constantly prepping and presenting. Find that happy medium between communication and reserving time for operational activities.

One last point on project management methodologies. You can use three different ways to run a project. You have scrum, kanban or waterfall. Kanban is more operational in nature so I'll only speak to scrum and waterfall. There once was a time when I was a program manager and all I knew was waterfall. You followed the PMBOK methodology and defined scope and subsequent requirements. You executed and prepped for the big release date or production go-live. If all went well, everyone was happy but what the project management world learned is that we tended to miss our targets quite a bit because what was delivered many times didn't match the requirements. We started labeling this a big bang approach because you plan a formal requirements document and make a one-time big release and hope all goes well. Don't get me wrong, there were many successful program and project leaders but something was missing.

Enter Agile and the world of incremental deliverables, a focus on flexible modeling and a keen focus on customer feedback. What you see now is a movement towards smaller bite-sized deliverables instead of big heavy ones so you can have small wins along the way that when integrated, result in the whole body. Scrum is part of the Agile methodology where you break the work into small time-boxed sequences called sprints that can last anywhere from 1 to 4 weeks (or sometimes more) and you run iterative cycles to delivery on key capabilities along the way, with customer feedback being a continuous injection to your assessment. I intuitively like Scrum because you can demonstrate wins along the way, adjust your plan throughout the initiative, and ensure what you're delivering is actually what the customer wants. It will be interesting what new frameworks develop in the next 10 years beyond the ones described here.

My conclusion, marry the two together into Wagile (waterfall plus Agile). The Agile purists hate this but I believe when you take the best of both worlds, you get something better than either as isolated practices. Case-in-point, if you're deploying hardware, you don't need to run it in Scrum because you know the steps and if you've done it enough times, you know the durations of each step from ordering to delivery to installation, configuration, testing, turn-up and transferring to operations. There's nothing obscure in this process. Again the Agile purists will say you can run this in Scrum, but I say why? I believe at the larger program level, running it as a Scrum project can make a lot of sense, whatever you're doing, but certain elements within the larger program can effectively be delivered using waterfall. Ultimately we are interested in getting things done, but my personal point of view, don't discard one out of bias, and allow yourself the flexibility to use either or both at the same time. Something like data protection in Functional Third should absolutely be run this way. There are too many capabilities being released and a heavy investment of time and money. You want to progressively demonstrate value and ensure what you're doing is directionally sound, so definitely run it in an Agile fashion.

7.3 MONTHLY OPERATIONS REVIEW (MOR)

Being a good partner with the business and driving value creation beyond operations is crucial because frankly, the business doesn't feel how effective you are in running an operation, it feels how you helped them solve their problems. It is absolutely vital to drive a mindset of business value creation but we can't do that if our foundation is cracked. Let's make sure we have full control over our operation so that we can invest our time and energy in helping teams solve issues and we can integrate into their areas and form partnerships. To ensure your operation is running smoothly and progressing, you really should install an operations review to 1: review the key measures across your operation to understand overall health, and 2: to assert operational discipline in your team so that they know what they do day in and day out is the basis for everything else we build on top. Operations to technology folks is our bread and butter as it should be, and for our customers, it's the invisible element that just makes things work. It's like cloud, no one knew what was 'cloud' when it first came out but everyone knew it was there…doing something.

If we're running an IT organization, we're going to look at things like incident management, problem management, request and change management. We're going to want to evaluate metrics like mean time to identify, and repair/remediate (MTTI/MTTR) for incidents. From a service management and change control perspective, we want to know how much of our queue is auto-flow, versus manually addressed. Within all these spaces, we follow the rigor of root cause analysis and permanent corrective actions as methods to understand why issues occur and then install processes to ensure they never happen again (or as close to that as possible). If you think about these topics, why don't they apply to security as well?

We run in parallel to IT and all of these are relevant. If you have an infrastructure function then you absolutely want to review these metrics over time to ensure you are under control and progressively reducing severity 1 and 2 incidents. But our objective in operations review goes further than that. We have operational workflows in Cyber Fusion, Security Assurance, and even Compliance and Architecture. You want every team you have to be able to articulate the operational integrity of their space, and be able to identify key metrics that tell them the health of their function. For some it'll come easy, like Cyber Fusion will have a bunch of metrics and KPIs but some others like Architecture may struggle at first but as they think about this over time, they'll realize that many of the lifecycles they are involved in (SSDLC, PDLC, or others), have measures for ageing and performance that are absolutely relevant.

For as much as you can, define benchmarks for measurements. For incident management, are you trying to achieve 99%, 99.9% or 99.99% based on your business and the sensitivity of what you do? Now for those who've been doing this sort of thing for most of their professional career, 99% is doable but as soon as you go into the decimal range, it becomes progressively harder and near impossible. Map the uptime to the business need and be realistic. Start by measuring your real performance and set goals to achieve what your business requires. Trying to achieve 99% when you are just standing up an operation may not be realistic, and you'll find yourself under fire if you state this; determine if it's 95% or 97% or whatever and work to that objective. The same holds true for all the other metrics. Base them on something real and then identify that performance baseline on all your analytics to see how you're trending over time.

On the Cyber Fusion side, you'll have a bunch of data at some point once your MSSP is operating and you've had time to tune your systems. The standard start of every security report shows how many logs were collected that converted to alerts and then subsequently to incidents (the funnel effect). The reason we always see this is to demonstrate the sheer volume of data that is analyzed on the back end to result in what we see, and then we map these incidents to an established severity scale of low, medium, high, and critical priority. For each of these categories, we then apply specific SLAs that increasingly get tighter. So for example, a critical event will require say, a 10–15-minute mean time to respond (MTTR) whereas a low priority event might be 8-10 hours. You might ask how do we meet a 10-minute response time? Well, if you're 24x7 then you have continuous eyes-on-glass and this is achievable but if you are less than 24x7 this will become a challenge. This is why I always recommend a SOC should be staffed continually.

My personal opinion is that this and the portfolio reviews should be open to everyone in your organization so that they can see what we're doing, understand what we're measuring, and get exposed to the conversations that ensue. It goes back to transparency and alignment, the more your team is informed and involved with the leadership team and interacting, the better your alignment will be because they'll get to ask questions, observe and participate in the key meeting that drive your operation. I have never made this mandatory other to the folks presenting and my direct reports, because my teams have historically been global and timing will not be conducive to everyone. I also don't want to make it mandatory because I don't want to drag my team into something they don't want to do. One measure of engagement will be how much involvement there is beyond the mandatory personnel.

The MOR drives a quantitative method of assessing your organizations health. Now depending on who is reading and your philosophical views, you'll either appreciate this or scarf at this because you feel data doesn't tell the whole story. Well, data doesn't tell the whole story but when you're running an organization in a company, you'll need to be data centric and measure key performance indicators. That's just the nature of what we do if we want to have control over our performance. Having said that, there are mechanisms to apply qualitative assessment and the portfolio review is one that does incorporate qualitative measures. What I'll say is don't shy away from data-driven decision making because it's a big part of how we control variance, and manage quality but at the same time, don't fixate on data and allow for interpretation and intuition to be part of the equation.

7.4 LEADERSHIP MOR

This will be short. As much as we look internal to how we're doing so that we get better, we also want to demonstrate the same to our stakeholders. Similar to what we do with the semi-annual portfolio review, we should hold a Quarterly or semi-annual MOR with leadership to demonstrate to them the controls we have in place, how we measure ourselves, and share the wins and challenges for awareness. There's nothing more powerful than to have them be part of the process from time-to-time so they understand how we look at our operation and as long as we're being fair with the good and the not so good, it will drive further credibility. There's that word again, credibility. I protect this to a fault because it's the thing that will allow us to reduce friction and maintain focus. Always look for ways to increase credibility and in turn trust and involving your leadership in the MOR allows you to do just that.

7.5 TECHNOLOGY STRATEGY COMMITTEE

Trust continues to be the theme and the thing we pursue, and another mechanism for nurturing this is through a Technology Strategy Committee (TSC). These come in different forms and in different names, but the idea is that if your organization is comprised of multiple technology teams, say multiple business units with IT organizations, or separate enterprise and product security teams or the sort that you have this top-level strategic conversation across those teams to maintain alignment. This is one of those that doesn't apply to all of us, and it's not the first thing you put in place, and you may not have complete influence on its inception and design but it can be very useful to keep close relations and have conversations across the organization at a strategic level.

There are some cases where this simply doesn't need to be in place, namely, smaller companies where there is a single IT team, and/or single security organization. This would simply be overhead and red tape and we need to be able to decipher when something is productive versus just another bureaucratic exercise. When companies are larger and have more complex models, we find there are many technology decisions, strategic plans that impact all of us. Say for example we are pursuing Functional Third capabilities in data protection; you should absolutely be talking about organizational change and transformation, and how you're all going to support the effort. You normally don't implement data protection in one business unit and not the others so this crosses (usually) structural elements, unless you're a behemoth of an organization that truly works as independent entities.

In past lives, the facilitation of TSC has been done by a corporate unit because they touch all the other teams in some capacity. This doesn't have to be the case but it's one way to do this. You can meet once per month or if things aren't changing too fast, once per Quarter. Again, this applies only to certain conditions but I have included this in my MOS because it's been very effective for me to form closer relationships with other technology drivers.

7.6 ARCHITECTURE REVIEW BOARD (ARB)

I could say some similar things about ARB that I did with TSC in that it doesn't have to be right away, and it doesn't have to be led/facilitated by security. The only difference is that I'd stress the importance of introducing this at some point and that this should not be optional. The ARB is a governing body that makes sure the technology architecture that we deploy across the tech-teams is aligned with company strategic objectives. The ARB ensures that large-scale designs that affect the company's technology direction are not done in isolation and go through some rigor of assessment to ensure what's being done fits the company goals and incorporates considerations from the major technology departments that are impacted.

In speaking of technology architecture, everything deployed should have a security aspect to it. Whether you're planning a new enterprise resource planning system (ERP) implementation, or customer relationship management system (CRM), or some e-commerce solution, all technology plans need to be vetted by security so that the implementation plan is security-minded. This is not us trying to have oversight on everything because we like to, but it's a necessity in today's growing threat landscape.

Having said all of this, I find ARB is a challenging thing to implement, at least for me. The challenge is how to win the hearts and minds of other architects to see the value? I have my strengths and my weaknesses and this is one I absolutely have to get behind because of its importance but beyond putting together the logistical elements, which I can do, getting buy-in and active participation is something of a challenge. What you find at first is that other architects aren't overly eager to have a governing body oversee or have a say in what they do. They will participate because their leadership tells them we need to, but there's some resistance that shows up in how much they contribute and their acceptance of controls tied to ARB. Look, I can't blame them because who gets excited that every time they want to drive the agenda in their domain that some body of peers needs to review before implementation? However, if this isn't done, we can have gaping security holes, we may not be ready to support when implementation comes because the other technology parties that are part of delivery may not be aware of the program, there may be duplication somewhere else where the same problem has been solved. What's more, if it's tied into your portfolio and project lifecycle, it may not be the right investment at the time given everything else the company is trying to do, and another point is if it's complex enough, you may not have all the necessary expertise to build it right and may miss some key components that will delay your plans.

Let's spend a little time on this topic to put it into context of how it can be pursued. My basis of understanding comes from the framework offered by TOGAF, which is intended to provide guidelines for enterprise architecture. TOGAF is useful for defining how to approach management of technology architecture, and the key benefits of following this is that it aligns company goals with technology initiatives. This framework goes into detail on the various phases for driving architectural decisions and change, and it provides various Reference Models to help along the way (The Open Group. 2018). Within the governance structure of TOGAF, you will find a reference to ARB.

TOGAF governance focuses on the process for decisions-making on architectural concepts, keeping business objectives in your clear line of sight. The ARB is the component of governance that assesses ideas, and approves architecture plans. There is an element of assessment and change control tied to ARB, and the identified participants work together to administer this across the organization. TOGAF is a good point of reference but where I am disconnected is again, how to win the support of teams who prior to ARB, were able to work independently? This will be your greatest challenge and I feel this is as much a function of time as it is tied to commitment from leadership to drive this concept into their teams. Find some talented folks who work in architecture and may have experience in these spaces to help develop this; get the full support of other technology leaders, and start the process. Over time, the team will go through the phases of team formation that we know to be forming, storming, norming, performing and hopefully you achieve a state of productivity and strong decision making.

I mentioned it before but a little more context around how ARB ties back into the project management lifecycle. As you're developing your project management and portfolio practices, you want to have essential checkpoints to ensure all the elements required to be successful are in place. Now I didn't use the term Gates but they are essentially gates; I am a bit reluctant to use this because the Agile supporters may baulk at the use of this while the waterfall proponents will probably be more accepting. Then you have the folks that are hypersensitive to bureaucratic oversight and see gates as a form of this, but even so, I'll share my views on this. I believe having a minimum number of gates is good for ensuring the health of a portfolio. This comes from my experience formally running a PMO and my personal opinion, but you do want to ensure on the front end that the ideas generating demand are unique and match business objectives. Somewhere before execution, you want to ensure the plan and design is sound and includes all the things we need to check, such as security, and that the financial model works and the business case is something that matches strategy and delivers some sort of return on investment (ROI).

This means I prefer two gates, one after the demand phase to formally approve the project to take shape, and the other after planning and before the consumption of funds. The latter stage may come after a procurement engagement that can be a project in of itself and is intended to define all the parameters for moving forward, but before you actually begin running sprints or however you manage it, a review should be done. This is where the ARB comes into play. They can be your sole approver at the demand stage to ensure it matches business objectives. Coincident to this, they would also be one of two approvers after planning and before execution to ensure the design is sound (the other is Finance). So as you can see the ARB can play multiple roles in key decision-making so an investment in developing this is really important.

7.7 ENTERPRISE SECURITY COUNCIL (ESC)

Another piece of your MOS could be the Enterprise Security Council. In my career, I've worked for companies that did have one of these and others that didn't and both were effective. It really depends on the culture of your organization and the way the leadership wants to govern security. In some cases, leadership likes to have personal touch points with less formality and prefer to limit the number of governing bodies that make up its oversight structure. I can completely understand this and frankly, appreciate this quite a bit. In other cases, the investment in security might have taken a high level of sensitivity for various reasons, and more careful awareness of how we are developing the security program may be of interest. Another reason why an ESC might be welcome is if security plays a core part of business value delivered to customers and shareholders, which means your business units would have a keen interest in the way security is managed.

In the event your company wants to establish an ESC, you want to ensure that certain roles are represented. The CISO or security leader (you?) should obviously be there; it seems silly if you weren't given that it's a security council. If there's a separate physical security team then the leader in that space should be there as well and you co-chair the council. Key technology participants like the CIO should be there. If your company has multiple business units with multiple CIOs then you'd want to see if it makes sense for representation from all. Your Chief Legal Officer or delegate, the risk management leader for the company, and the business unit leaders. This can be as few as 6 or 7 members to something that isn't quite as optimum as it goes above 10. As we know, the larger the team, the harder to get full engagement and unwieldly it gets but there is a certain requirement for participation that you can't get away from.

So what do you talk about in the ESC? Well, the intent of this Committee is to make sure the security strategies being implemented are aligned to the business objectives of the organization. In addition, this body also looks at the effectiveness of the security program and wants to ensure the strategies, policies, initiatives, capabilities, and operational practices are all evolving and maturing. Consequently, this governance body will review all facets of your operation and offer feedback on direction and performance. So what's in it for you? By going through this rigor, you ensure that what you're doing maps to the companies goals, but as important is that you'll come away with support from the most influential leaders in the organization for the things you're doing. Once you're aligned with intent, you will find it much easier to get the teams to contribute to the cause then if you didn't have this forum in place. You may see it as yet another place to generate content and slides for, but as I have said, a large portion of our job is marketing and communication; evangelization of our security program, so I highly recommend you develop your Operations Support Team to be able to operationalize all of this for you.

So what happens if you don't have an ESC? You can accomplish this through personal and direct relationships so where you don't have a formal Committee to engage, you will have to separately capture needs and feedback to ensure you stay connected. This may reduce the formality but does increase the effort in a more distributed, unofficial manner. Whatever works for you, but somehow you need to be lockstep with these folks.

7.8 QUARTERLY CEO BUSINESS REVIEW

Another opportunity to develop trust with your leadership and market security is if your company holds business reviews. If there is such a thing and you are a participant, you might have a recurring slot on an agenda to give a Quarterly update to your CEO and their direct reports and anyone else that is invited. Sometimes these happen prior to Board meetings so that the management team aligns with the messaging and content being presented. Other times this could be a standalone set of meetings that don't line up with Board meetings; either scenario works for us, as this is a very good way to get security in the forefront of conversation.

What you present may be tied to your security scorecard and any big happenings in your area that the leadership team should be aware of. Your metrics and KPIs may be a standing topic but you might also cycle through topics on maturity, assessments, large initiatives that the team needs to be aware of. Obviously this is not something you drive but you would be asked to participate in, so it does fit loosely in your MOS but its origin is external. The best way to go about this is to take a condensed version of what you're presenting to the Board and share with the leadership team. Things that are sensitive or changes in direction are good to put in front of this group for guidance so that when you do go in front of the Board, there are no surprises.

7.9 QUARTERLY BOARD MEETING

Here's another one that is externally defined but should be registered as part of your MOS nevertheless. Probably one of the most important meetings and you can guess why. Your Board of Directors is the highest point where strategy, direction, performance is measured. This is where the company as a whole is assessed and also where shareholder interest is represented in decision making. All the other things we talked about like compliance, governance, financial control, strategy are all rolled up to this body who evaluate all of these dimensions in various committees. We, security roll up to the Audit Subcommittee usually, unless you have a separate Security Subcommittee. This is where financial oversight, budget approvals, risk management are discussed, along with security many times.

There's not a lot to say, other than let's never underappreciate the value of this group. It's very important to be open and transparent with them, and view the members as experts in industry that can help guide and support you. These folks hold the highest roles when it comes to oversight, and they have a fiduciary responsibility to the company and promoting its wellbeing. Building good rapport and eliciting feedback from this group will give you a much broader perspective on what you do and how it impacts the organization. Many of them serve on other Boards, so they get to see things from different lenses and share with you best practices or references to other companies that you can tap into for various challenges they have already gone through. You're going to meet with them at least once Quarterly so make this count; it's very important.

7.10 QUARTERLY RISK REVIEW MEETING

Another Quarterly meeting will be something you setup and it ties back to the essence of what security is all about, which is risk management. Before you can setup the first risk review, you need to do a few things. First you want to ensure your team is actually capturing risks in a systematic way. This is done through your Governance and Compliance team and they normally consolidate these risks in a Governance, Risk, and Compliance (GRC) tool that helps you organize risks across the spaces that are applicable.

A GRC tool improves workflows and provides effective means to not only manage risks but also legal and regulatory responsibilities across the enterprise. In the space of risk management, it helps you capture risks like those in operations, finance, and information management. It then helps you perform analyze impact and likelihood in whatever manner is important to your organization. In a former chapter we described DREAD and FAIR as two methods for risk assessment. You can use your GRC to centralize all risk and apply these frameworks. A GRC goes beyond this and does all the other things you need to do including mitigation planning, and tracking of deliverables to reduce risk. For leadership, a GRC makes it easy to perform analytics that convert data into information driven by predictive measures, and heatmaps as two examples that show your current and possible future state. You can absolutely manage risks on spreadsheets, but GRC tools are great to administer your overall compliance practice, and if you use the same tool here that is used for project management, incident, and problem management then you can pursue the holy grail of associating risks to initiatives and problem resolution that then connects your entire technology footprint together.

In this manner, say you're using ServiceNow; if an incident happens and we uncover a weakness, that incident is mapped to a problem that drives root cause. That root cause triggers a demand that leads to a project that has a portfolio designation. That project is tied to a risk that is reported in the GRC module. Over time, as the project progresses, you can see the updates and progress and can roll it up to report not only in service delivery language, but also from a compliance framework. Once that project is closed out, it triggers closeouts of the project, problem, and yes the risk. If you map your operation in this way, you connect all the aspects of technology delivery. Again, you can use any platform that does something similar, I happen to have experience with ServiceNow.

So now you have risks collected across the relevant aspects of the business. You have built up your GRC, and are able to use your tools to make your team more efficient. You've determined what risk assessment approach you want to use (qualitative or quantitative or both). Along the way you want to make sure there's ownership of the risk management practice in the Governance and Compliance Team so that it improves over time and is institutionalized. That or those individuals will go to each risk owner and capture the approach to that risk and a timeline for resolution if that's what the owner chooses to do. What I mean by approach is the application of the 4Ts of risk management, which are treat, transfer, terminate, or tolerate.

Treat is synonymous with mitigating risk. You are taking an existing risk level, applying some action to reduce the risk to an acceptable level or eradicate it completely. You do this in several ways such as putting in new controls tied to things like firewalls. You can revise or create new policies or install non-security technologies that will address the risk, or you can introduce or revise existing SOC capabilities to address gaps in detection capabilities. When most people talk about risk management, they are describing treatment or mitigation, but there are other things you can do as well.

Transference is something you can do if there are reasons mitigation internally is not a viable option. Maybe the cost-benefit of treatment doesn't work out or you don't have the skills to address and treat the issue, or for some reason it just doesn't make sense and you'd rather transfer the risk. The best-known way to transfer is security insurance, more commonly referred to as cyber insurance. There are times when the investment is just not worth it so you decide to cover the potential losses through insurance. Certain data breaches may fall under this decision point. Another transfer strategy is using an MSSP. Maybe your company prefers to outsource security (I don't recommend this) so it wants you to bring in a third party to do the heavy lifting. If this comes up, hopefully it doesn't apply to you because you already have a hybrid model that works well but from a pure-play, this could be a form of transference.

You can terminate the risk. Where you see this is with legacy products as an example. You may have old products that are still being manufactured and supported. At some point the risk may be too high to continue operations so you choose to terminate production and support of that product. Alternatively, you may have a regulation that now restricts the use of that product in certain geographic areas so you selectively discontinue sales and support in those regions because the cost-benefit is not worth the risk.

Finally there's the tolerating the risk or simply accepting it. You know the risk is there, you are aware of its impact and the decision is that the remediation exceeds the risk impact so you wrap some monitoring around it and develop some contingency plans and you decide to call it a day. An example close to home could be tied to not having a 24x7 SOC. We know MTTI and

MTTR will improve quite a bit if you have eyes-on-glass all the time but maybe the cost of running a 24x7 is too high or the company is going through the lows of its operation and headcount is frozen. You decide to run 24x5 with on-call for the weekends. You know this will reduce your responsiveness but you decide it's acceptable given the circumstances.

So know you've got all the pieces you need to setup your first risk review. This last exercise got you aligned with the business risk owners on the approach and for those that are to be treated, you have captured dates and actions. You want to setup the meeting with the business unit leaders and Legal at the very minimum to go through the risk register and talk through all the high-level risks defined. Now you want to roll up the risks into general categories so that you're not going through every incremental risk because that could take forever. You roll up general themes, and critical and high risks that can be effectively reviewed with a set of folks that don't usually have a lot of time on their schedules. The intent of the risk review is to inform them of the risk profile, make them aware of the risk tied to their spaces, and ensure they are aligned with the actions and timelines if applicable. Lastly, you want them to support and sponsor the actions so that their teams prioritize accordingly.

Let's just say it, these meetings aren't fun. There are more exciting things you could be doing than going over risks, but it is important. We are all required in some way to capture risks, review them, and have some kind of control in place to address them. There has to be a rational approach and awareness all the way up to the Board. In fact the SEC has expectations defined on Board oversight of 'cybersecurity risks'. In our yearly reporting, we have to define in the United States whether or not the Board has oversight of security risks, and how they map these risks to a larger enterprise risk management (ERM) approach. This means it's in your companies best interest to have an ERM and during the security reviews, to have a cadence for risk review. This type of thing is not unique to the U.S, and the EU and other regions will have something similar.

You hold the risk review meeting and you capture changes requested by the owners. You identify when the changes were made and why and you notify the functional teams that helped define the risk of the results. You then begin tracking those that are going to be treated over the course of the next few months and that becomes the basis for the next review. Now as you make this recurring, the next time you are reviewing new risks, actions from the last review and any adjustments that need to be made. At some point, you want to roll this up to the ERM, which is why you want to do a great job describing the risks in layman's terms and in summarized form so that they can be integrated into the business process for risk management. Let me reiterate the fact that everything we do is risk, which means it should be top of mind at all times. This Quarterly risk review is important to provide the mechanism for us to manage risk effectively.

7.11 TABLETOPS & SIMULATIONS

I included this topic as part of our MOS because I didn't want it to get lost in the mix of all the other points made and it is something that needs to be institutionalized in your business practices. Every year your SOC should be conducting a walk-thru of how they would react to a potential security incident so that they can prove out their incident management playbook and understand their roles. Tabletops are useful to talk through how and why you respond in a certain way and to get everyone thinking the same way. This is a hardening process of sorts to be tested and proven for the real thing that hopefully never occurs. Simulations are exactly that, a simulated event where you could work with your Security Assurance Team to model an attack and determine 1: if your SOC sees it, and 2: how they would respond. In a simulation, you're not talking through the scenario but behaving as if it is a real event.

The same concept should be applied to your executive team to ensure they know how to react to an event if it happens. Where the SOC may do this multiple times a year, your executive tabletop and/or simulation is probably once but ideally twice a year. You have several objectives for a tabletop. For one, you want to test your organizations readiness for a security crisis. There may be a corporate crisis management plan that you roll into or you may run the security ones separately if a crisis plan does not exist. Whatever the circumstances, readiness is important and the practice on decision-making is critical so that your company doesn't lose precious time in a real event. Along the way you are noting any modifications that need to be made to your incident response procedures, and you're raising awareness of everyone's role.

You can run the tabletop yourself or partner with a third party. This is a perfect opportunity to showcase your MSSP's capabilities and partnership and they normally love the opportunity to do so in front of your executives. If you structured your contract well, you have a retainer for training and other services that can be used for this purpose. Your operations leaders devise a scenario with the MSSP and customize the scenario to possible realities for your company. Ideally you run the scenario at a management level to prove it out while reinforcing the same benefits at the functional team level before running it with the executives. For the executive tabletop, you want all the leaders of the organization to be participants including your CEO, CFO, CLO, and all the others. The MSSP and your operations lead serve as observers and capture the results that will later be reported out to the group. The exercise is loosely structured with five parts. The first is an introduction to the facilitators and the intent. The second is defining the incident and the guiding parameters. The third is the escalation path of the event and initial responses from the company. The next is how you would work through containing the incident and associated activities such as notification of the Board and communication externally. Finally there's conversations around how you recover and reset normal operating procedures. Along the way, you ware keeping an eye on regulatory requirements, outside support, impact analysis and all the other pieces that fit.

Once the tabletop is over, you get some general feedback, followed by a full report on observations that will be issued sometime in the next several weeks. Those results will tell you your strengths and opportunities, the latter will then usually convert into actions that you need to carryout to strengthen your practice. The report should hopefully talk about how your leadership is aligned (or not) and what you need to do to improve it. The side effect should be awareness and reinforcement of how events will be coordinated as well as serve as a feedback to your incident response plan for improvement there as well.

A simulation is slightly different in that rather than talking through a scenario, you are running a simulated event. You don't tell anyone the details other than to be prepared for a general timeframe for running it. You do this because the leadership involved tend to have very busy schedules and you'd be hard-pressed to just run it out of the blue. Simulations are great because you are running it as if something has happened and it's not simply a conversation. When you notify the Board, you are actually notifying the Board who should be on-Board with the idea (no pun intended). You are setting up the bridge for incident response, the SOC is involved along with all the other players and you are really working through your incident response and crisis management plan. If you can run a simulation, I'd recommend you do it but a tabletop is a good secondary if you can't. What you might do is run a tabletop in the beginning of the year to walk through how leadership should respond, as part of an education exercise, and then run a simulation the second half of the year to test their response. Whatever works for you, as long as you're doing something in this space for readiness, awareness, and alignment.

7.12 YEARLY STRATEGIC PLANNING

Final topic for this chapter and for the MOS is our yearly strategic planning cycle. Look, some of you will do this better than I have and others will have areas of improvement, but we all should be running something as a best practice in managing our organization. The purpose for me in strategic planning takes multiple paths. For one, we want to plan our strategy; that seems pretty straightforward. We want to look at what we're doing 'today', and determine if those same efforts will make sense as we go forward. We want to recertify our strategic pillars that govern our activities and if there are new demands then we need to identify them and update our underlying pillars. There are quite a few benefits beyond just the strategy aspect, to running this that are highlighted below. This is not an exhaustive list but does give you a sense of the benefits of investing funds into a yearly planning session. These events can be a bit expensive, depending on what your tolerances for expense mean to you, but they are well worth the cost if done correctly:

- **Certify the Vision:** Noted earlier, one of the first things you do when you join the company is to get your leaders together for an in-person strategy meeting to establish a base vision and accomplish a few other things described in earlier chapters. That was an initial introduction and objective-setting effort but not a full-fledged strategic planning event. Now, in your yearly planning event, you want to take a second look at what you defined as the strategic pillars for your organization and determine, based on available data, feedback, and surveys you received back, if those pillars stand up or they need to be modified. Every time we come together in this forum, we need to ensure what we believed was our top planning guidelines are still relevant and useful. Examples might be to drive secure manufacturing. Another could be to drive business value through the application of security services. Whatever they are, make sure they are still relevant
- **Capture 360 Degree Feedback and Incorporate:** Something I just alluded to is the use of surveys. I believe prior to getting together, you want to elicit feedback from all your stakeholders including the Board (if possible), the executive leadership that includes Finance, HR, Legal, Procurement, Sales & Marketing and your business unites. You want to capture feedback from other technology leaders, your own domain leads, and most importantly, the folks that work within your organization. If you service external customers then you'd want to get some feedback on what works, what doesn't work, security weaknesses, opportunities for collaboration; anything that can help you conduct a fair and equitable assessment of your practice. Very important is the feedback from your own team. They will see things on a daily basis that you will not and bubbling that up for visibility will not only help you improve your security posture, but it will also capture the voice of your team that can drive to a more positive culture.

  You take all of this information and you have your Operations Support Team summarize the findings so that in the planning, you can review common themes that will then be injected into your planning for the next period. There is a bit of effort involved in reviewing, identifying commonalities, understanding the essence of the feedback and wrapping this around something you can convert into actionable items, but this effort is well worth it. What you are now seeing is a body of work that comes from your third-party assessment results, drivers for controls from your maturity model, efforts underway from your initial strategic planning effort, ideas and demand from your portfolio practice, input from architecture and planning, and now feedback from your stakeholders. This is a lot but you are really capturing a comprehensive view of your operation. The challenge will be to reconcile the old with the new, and determine prioritization. Lastly you can't do everything so you'll have to have a method for determining what happens now and what has to wait, beyond priority of work you plan on doing. Some things you'll have to shelf for a later time.

- **Qualify Past Investments and Define Future Ones:** It's worth pointing this out one more time; you need to ensure the past decisions on what to invest are still the right things to pursue. This is similar to the goals we set in a year. Goals are not static and absolute; they can change with time. What seemed to be an obvious goal during goalsetting may no longer be relevant six months into the year. You need to be adaptable as a team to understand this and adjust accordingly. The same thing holds with investments. Do they still have merit? Is there something more important that has emerged in that time? Resolve and qualify these points so that you are doing the right things for the company.
- **Ensure Mapping of Maturity to Risks to Initiatives:** At some point your team settled on a maturity model, and we discussed the use of NIST CSF as part of that as an option to look at with associated controls from NIST SP 800-53 and you may even incorporate others like NIST SP 800-171 if you're working with the U.S. government as a vendor. Whatever your maturity model is, you want to do a short exercise to see if the controls that are identified in that maturity model are in place or if you have deficiencies. Next you want to decide if the ones that are deficient have a place in your practice or not. Not all the controls may apply to what you do, but if they do, then you want to progress in driving a systematic approach to maturing your practice while you are capturing other signals from around you on the practical things you need to do to solve things your stakeholders are experiencing. You can get lost if you don't organize this planning correctly and you may find yourself later trying to figure out what exactly are you trying to accomplish if you don't keep an eye on your maturity model and the connectivity of your initiatives to that end. Lastly, let's keep an eye on not boiling the ocean along the way. In an attempt to do it all, you may end up doing nothing well, so take it to heart that you need to prioritize, queue, and shelf some things to ensure you're spending your time wisely and driving a thoughtful agenda.
- **Resolve Organizational Conflict:** While your team wants to do the right thing, sometimes conflict will arise that can't get resolved organically, meaning amongst the team. Most of the challenges can be addressed but sometimes certain things don't get worked out, and there's a need for intervention. This can be due to adjustments in structure, reporting or simply misalignments of values and perspectives. Whatever it is, as the leader, you want to keep an eye on things that remain unresolved after multiple attempts that need you to step in and be the mediator or maybe the arbitrator if that's what it takes. This is where getting

together in-person is valuable. Set time aside in closed sessions with the involved parties and go through an exercise to elicit the essence of the issues so that you can set a path forward that is mutually beneficial. There are all sorts of techniques to doing this, but I'll leave that to you to determine for yourselves.

- **Deep Dive on Critical Initiatives:** I think this speaks for itself. If you have big plays, such as the ones we noted in Functional First, Second or Third, then this will be an opportunity to hear and learn about them if not everyone is exposed to the progress. This can extend outside of your organization and you can bring in guest speakers from other departments to speak to your team and expose them to the work being done elsewhere so we gain perspective on the things that matter to others. Having your boss come in and participate, having the business units join for a few sessions will help you tie back to what they are doing so that you can bridge your work to their mission.
- **Draft First Version of Next Years Budget:** It's never too late to start developing a view of the next year's budget. You don't want to wait until Q4 to start doing this. I usually run my strategic planning session in June or July and getting a first draft of the budget is not a bad idea. You may not have all the data points to do this fully, but you can go through the line items in your budget, determine if they'll survive going forward, project if they'll increase or decrease, and amend any potential new entries. In the capital investment discussion noted below, you'll get a view of that data point for the budget as well, and by the time you leave the planning, you'll have a working approach on what you need to do next to progressively refine this in the coming months. By the time Q4 shows up, you would have been building on this initial effort and should be ready to support the Finance Team in their rollup exercise with a very thoughtful approach that was not forced due to time constraints.
- **Draft Capital Investment Opportunities for Next Year:** Pretty simple in concept but not so easy in practice. Now that you have the feedback from the organization, and you've reconciled with your existing initiatives, you can now start talking about future investments that won't require funding and will require capital. The ones that require capital will go into your investment profile that you will develop business cases for and present to your management as part of your yearly investment planning exercise. If you look at the activities described in this section, they are building on themselves. You can't look at these investments until you know the full feedback from all the dimensions described already. You can't build a first view of your budget without having a rudimentary understanding of the investments that are tied to that feedback received prior. There's a lot of work to do, but at the same time don't expect you'll get it all done at the planning session. You are setting the work in motion, laying the foundation so that

when you all return home that you know the next steps needed to be taken.

- **Reward Top Performers with Opportunity to Participate:** This is important. Every year there are the required participants that include your direct reports, the folks doing the financial work, the folks running the portfolio, and any top-level leaders that happen to be individual contributors. Sometimes you have Director-level folks that are individual contributors that I like to include in planning. Then there's those that I like to invite who are our top performers. You can determine top performers in different ways; you can just know it, you can do a 9-block (or 9-box) that helps you measure performance against potential, or you can rely on your rating results for the prior year and invite those who were recognized as high performers. Whatever your approach, bringing in a few of them to participate is a recognition of their achievements and you get to hear from folks that are driving the engine of your organization. I use the word invite because not all of them may see this as an opportunity. Depending on their personality, some may shy away from these types of events and that's perfectly fine as well. Don't force recognition; allow it to be something they can choose and feel okay with whatever they decide.
- **Form Relationships Beyond Direct Reports:** I think the last bullet speaks to this in that you get to spend time and meet folks you may not interact with as much during normal business operations. There are folks you will get to spend time with because of the function they perform outside of your direct reports, but now as you cycle in top performers, you will see new faces and get to know them in a way that is more meaningful than being on meetings and town halls, and departmental meets and greets. Forming relationships across your organization is an important thing to do to form connections and develop trust. You can expect that at first some might be nervous but the more you interact with them, and others see those interactions, the more the team will realize you are interested in what the team has to say and you want to have active voices across all tiers. Here I'm assuming you do; maybe you want nothing like this, which is your choice of course.
- **Reinforce Existing Relationships:** The other side effect is of course reinforcing the relationships you have already. Getting all the arrows pointing in the same direction, becoming a productive unit that is empathetic to one another, setting a mindset that you're all in this together and you all have one another's best interests at heart is important. Relationships drive success more than your capabilities or technical talents. Most of us function in the same spectrum of intellectual capacity; most of us develop skills through exposure and what I can learn in that exposure can be learned by someone else just as well. What brings this whole thing together, in my humble opinion, is how effective a unit we can become. The sum of the parts does not equal

the whole. When you are an effective team, the whole operates by harmoniously optimizing every strength of the team, and compensates for any weaknesses making the unit stronger. I truly believe this, which is why investing in relationships is so important. Again, my view only.

- **In-Person Leadership Training & Awareness Opportunity:** Because we have one another's beset interest at heart, this is also an opportunity to perform some much-needed training to strengthen areas that we identify as opportunities to grow in. Maybe that's around communication, maybe it has a lot to do with emotional intelligence; whatever you discover is a challenge across more than one of you and your staff is something you can tackle together in these in-persons. In the past, I've brought in coaches, leaders, third parties to help us address these areas of opportunity. If you truly want your team to succeed, expose them to their blind spots and then reinforce awareness by using whatever means you can to help them grow in that space. We should, as leaders, strive to make our teams the best they can be so they can grow within or go out in the world and conquer new opportunities. We go back to the notion of servant leadership; our job is to make everyone else better because along the way, we'll be amazed at how that progresses our agenda to improve the business.

Last points on this topic. This is why you need a strong Operations Support Team because there's a lot to plan a lot to run and facilitate, and a lot to follow up on after the fact; and this is only one facet of their jobs. You can't do this all yourself, so again, institutionalize this within your support staff so that you can do this well and get better at it over time. There's a budget tied to this that is not small as you can imagine when bringing in 15+ folks to a meeting for a week, but it's well worth it. Plan a budget, include team development activities for the event, have a precise schedule and set your predefined outcomes so you come out of this with objectives met.

REFERENCE

The Open Group. (2018). *TOGAF® standard, version 9.2*. The Open Group. Retrieved from https://pubs.opengroup.org/togaf-standard

Chapter 8

Regulatory mandates

Over regulation is a concern for most security professionals because we all talk about how we are encumbered with regulation whereas the bad actors have no restrictions and can move swiftly and with an efficiency we cannot achieve. That may be true but then we can get into a debate on what makes us the good guys and gals? We abide by rules and guidelines designed to protect our employees, our citizens, our countries from these bad actors, so is regulation really a symbol of what we stand for, which is behaving ethically and morally? That's probably debatable so I won't get into that space because there's enough topics out there that are driving division that I don't need to add to it, but let's talk a little about the purpose of regulation.

Fundamentally, regulations are protecting data, and privacy. They protect the systems that support our way of life, our society, our economies and national security; this is also referred to as critical infrastructure. Taking this one step further, regulations are focused on ensuring our communications systems are resilient, our healthcare services are protected, our energy grid that powers our lives remain operational, and the list goes on. Anything you can think of that touches our lives are susceptible to attack and regulations set minimum baselines to ensure this infrastructure is shielded.

Data privacy has become a major topic in the digital world. I don't believe we are doing a good job protecting it. It's a feeling; how many times have you had a conversation in the same room with your spouse, or kids or someone about a topic and the next thing you know, your phone or advertisements on your computer are sending you targeted material on that very topic you were discussing in what you thought was a secure space, your home? The space of data privacy, surveillance, and monitoring is all becoming a highly sensitive topic, and I don't believe I sound like a conspiracy theorist because I have spoken to more than a few people who have experienced the same thing. I don't know about you, but it feels like there's an undertone to all of this and the only way you guarantee there's no surveillance is to remove the devices from the space you deem as private; easier said than done nowadays.

So, from my vantage point, I am for regulation to ensure corporations, governments, and private security of any sort is at least on paper, required

DOI: 10.1201/9781003616528-8

to adhere to certain privacy rules to protect our rights. So going back to the essence of regulation, it seems like a strong connection between having regulations and tying it back to what makes for good guys and gals; they abide by rules aimed at protecting common societal values. Yes, I know what one group deems as values may not be the same for others so I'll stop talking about that now.

No matter what your view on regulations, one thing is clear, today we in the security profession are more nervous than ever because of the growing body of regulations that we have to be up to speed on. In professional circles, there's this discussion around CISO's considering to leave their roles now more than ever, and regulations have something to do with it. We have to understand that our jobs as security leaders must be taken seriously because there's a lot at stake if things don't go right, and with those stakes, someone has to be accountable. Regulatory pressures are a key factor but they're not the only one; they are in a family of emerging trends that together are driving people out of leadership roles.

For one, CISO's have an ever-increasing jurisdiction and are expected to tie into business strategy more today than ever before, but these expectations are not being matched with authority to act accordingly and this is leading to many burning out because they are trying to tackle a topic that should be dealt with at the top of the company and disseminated downwards. Many CISOs are three or four levels deep, placing them in the ranks of operational personnel as opposed to executive leadership. This observation ties to increasing responsibilities and stakes while leveling remains unbalanced. Tie this to market uncertainties that reduce budgets, leaving many security teams lacking in the personnel and tools they need to effectively support the growing responsibility footprint.

The landscape has certainly become more challenging so when you place an additional burden of increased regulation such as the SEC in the United States, and the rapid increase in data privacy rules in the EU and other areas, you can see why security leaders are thinking twice; now place the threat of personal liability on top of it where they can go to jail and many will tell you the risk is no longer worth the benefits. I've said this before, the best way to combat such trends is to become hyper-efficient in everything you do, which is why I weigh heavily the notion of systematic security because without it, you are outgunned.

So, knowing that all of this is playing itself out, what do we do? We double down on efficiency so that we can institutionalize the mechanisms we use to manage the regulatory landscape. Test, test, and retest your incident management protocols. Map regulatory requirements against one another to find commonalities that can be addressed in combination and identify uniqueness that need specialized effort. Automate the practice of compliance and information and data gathering to free up team members to spend their time assessing changes in regulations. If we understand the extreme boundaries of things like data privacy, or the extreme boundaries of protecting industrial control systems or critical infrastructure, then we can work our way inward to establish controls for everything within. Having said that, let's talk a little about personal liability before jumping into some specific approaches we can take in this space.

8.1 THE WORLD OF PERSONAL LIABILITY

Once upon a time, the idea of a cybersecurity threat wasn't even a thing. In fact there are many of us that within our lifetime, the concept of cybersecurity went from not existing to exploding into something that captivates audiences on a daily basis. With that, in the earlier years, and we don't have to go too far to see this (maybe 10 years?), cybersecurity risks were viewed as part of the general business risk profile and so they were handled under the umbrella of the companies general risk management practice. That changed in recent years and increasingly, cybersecurity is being seen as a separate and unique set of risks that are now being associated with the security leaders in organizations as they are accountable for the space; that being the CISO. Today's CISO is in a similar light to a CFO for the financial integrity of a company and the CEO for the overall accountability of a company's ethical principles and abiding by them.

The transition to this new focus on cybersecurity is being captured in new and revised regulations, the most popular in our time is with the Securities and Exchange Commission (SEC) that was updated in 2023 and will likely go through some further revisions in subsequent years. But beyond the SEC, in Europe, GDPR is prominent as it relates to privacy and the California Consumer Privacy Act (CCPA) is another that both carry fines and penalties that can be directed to the CISO under personal liability provisions. We talk a lot about the EU and the U.S., but not a lot about Asia Pacific (APAC), Africa or the Middle East because in those areas such regulations are just emerging and at the time of writing this book, there were no significant pointers to CISO liability; only organizational.

Beyond regulation, you have other factors that are increasing liability for CISOs as well. Legal precedence is starting to establish a basis for CISO liability. In recent years, we've seen the case of Uber, and SolarWinds where the CISO's were directly implicated in the breaches that occurred. There are others where the CISO's did not take the hit directly but were indirectly implicated such as the Equifax breach and others that are all setting the basis for increasing liability tied to the head of security.

Liability for what you ask? Well, it can be varied and diverse but you can attempt to role it up into a few general categories. For one, regulatory non-compliance. This is a hard one because while we as security leaders are accountable, the agreement to implement and implementation of controls many times lies in the hands of other teams. You fall into the debate of business requirements versus security controls and I hate to say it but if we are being good business leaders, this argument is a strong one but the SEC won't care if something happens. The idea is we have finite resources and have to balance the health and profitability (if you're a for-profit) of the company against putting resources on securing our product and software lines. This is a tough topic indeed.

Other categories tie to your security practices and controls. If you consciously allowed vulnerabilities to exist and did not have a record of why you deferred them (not that this gives you a get out of jail free card), you can be held negligent. Now as practitioners we know that there's so much to do that it is overwhelming and when budgets are hard to come by and understanding of non-security folks lacking, it makes for an uphill challenge to deal with all that you know about. The sad truth is that while it's happening we can rationalize the decisions and record them, but when the government comes calling, very quickly you'll start hearing everyone say 'why didn't you tell us?' or 'it was your job to keep us safe', or something similar. The logic, reasoning, and restrictions will all be thrown out the window. Yet another reason security leadership is thinking seriously about an expedited exit, but we've got courage and will stand against the tide! By the way, this may not be the case in your situation and you might have some really great support, but you can very easily see how this could be the case.

Some areas where you should be held accountable are if you over-inflate your readiness and report that everything is great. Then you're asking for it and there's no one to blame but yourself. Be transparent about the current state, be open about where you need to close gaps, and always take your role as a compliance lead seriously because you should abide by the rules more so than others. If you have a body of enterprise risk, call them out. If they're in the product space, or software, or manufacturing; be prescriptive in tagging them and raising them as organizational risks. If you recall, we made the Quarterly Risk Review Meeting the third most important in sequencing? Well the difference between 1 and 3 is not a lot and the sooner you get this installed the better as part of your due diligence exercises.

There's a lot more that ties back into why you are personally liable but the message should be clear, we have a lot on our shoulders and this is not for the weak hearted. So let's talk a bit about some specific examples of how we can tackle our responsibilities. If we step back and look at what we've put in place, you are addressing the areas that can implicate you, including Functional Third that will also introduce user and entity Behavior Analytics (UEBA) that is associated with insider threat management. Your insider threat program is vital and you will want to turn your attention inward to ensure your personnel are pure of heart along with dealing with the outside world. You will tackle this once you get to this sequence of capabilities, and form joint partnerships with Physical Security (if not under your jurisdiction) to grow this space. And yes, if you don't manage insider threats effectively this can again implicate you and drive personal liability.

8.2 SECURITIES AND EXCHANGE COMMISSION (SEC)

The stakes are high as noted already, but let's look at how the SEC revised regulations play into how we adjust our operations. Full disclaimer, I'm not a lawyer and they are the ones that decipher this stuff in companies but we're going to hit the highlights so as security professionals, we understand our part. As with any time you are deciphering regulatory requirements that tie back into company reportable responsibilities, consult with your Legal department to ensure you are meeting the expectations set forth. The rules set forth are intended for publicly traded companies and they are aimed at increasing transparency. There's a mixture of rules as well as some recommended guidelines that we want to address in our definition of our compliance practice.

First, there's a disclosure component tied to cybersecurity risks and incidents. The SEC mandates that companies disclose any 'material' cybersecurity risks and incidents that may impact investment decisions (Securities and Exchange Commission, 2023). Within this requirement, public companies need to disclose current and past risks and events that may have an impact to decision making. This places a bigger burden on the security team because not only do you have to adhere to it going forward, but you need to look back and determine if any past risks and incidents could influence investor behavior. I'm not going to go into the specific sections and reporting parameters as your Legal team will help you with that, but you are responsible for defining scope of any events, the impact and the action you took, similar to what we described in the 4Ts.

In practice, there's a whole debate within organizations of what constitutes 'material'. To be safe, our security team should NOT use the word 'material' until Legal and whatever body that assesses disclosure requirements officially marks an incident or risk as being material. The reason you speak only in terms of incidents and not materiality until it's explicitly defined by the disclosure body is in cases of litigation or investigation, all your records can be subpoenaed and they will search for the word 'material'. If you used it prematurely on incidents that did not materialize (pun intended) then you open yourself up to all sorts of additional inquiries. As soon as you engage legal on a potential incident that can meet the SEC's criteria, you start marking it as 'privileged and confidential' or whatever terminology the Legal Department tells you to use.

Your Legal Team will then walk the organization through the reporting requirements and normally a disclosure is incorporated in the Management's Discussion and Analysis (MD&A) section of the periodic filings submitted. As a sidebar point of interest, there are several disclosures that companies might be responsible for throughout the course of a fiscal year. Below I attempt to describe the various disclosures for understanding (Securities and Exchange Commission (n.d.), forms for registration and reporting):

- **6-K:** This is filed by foreign companies doing business in the United States. It is filed as needed and event-driven. If something happens in your security space and deemed material, then your company is likely to file this. This is typically not audited by the SEC.
- **8-K:** is the equivalent to the 6-K only for U.S.-based companies. Note that these are not exclusively tied to cybersecurity events but any significant events that are deemed reportable that could include things in finance, changes in executive leadership or others.
- **10-Q:** this is a mandatory filing that happens Quarterly, whether anything happens or not. The filings normally consist of operational information and financial. In general, these are not audited but can be referenced in the event of, well an event.
- **10-K:** this is the big one filed yearly. It is an audited filing that reflects the business status in multiple areas of interest. Language around cybersecurity is included on how we support the SEC requirements. Let's just say your Legal and Finance Teams spend a lot of time getting this drafted every year to be nice to them at the end of the year as they are under the gun to get this out; they normally have some time after the fiscal year ends to draw this up (60-90 days from year-end).
- 20-F: This is the equivalent of the 10-K but for foreign companies as an annual filing that is audited.

It's good to understand how public company reporting works as you'll be pulled into this world as the leader of security. But let's get back to your responsibilities. What caused a stir for many when the requirements came out was that companies are required to report an incident within four business days of it being deemed material in the 8-K for U.S. companies. You will need to provide a description of the incident, and disclose any impact to the company like operational disruption, data breaches, or regulatory noncompliance (Securities and Exchange Commission, 2023).

Now we all know that in four days you know very little, and everyone is highly stressed trying to get a handle on the whole event but there are subtleties of this requirement. First, and again, you do NOT use 'material' in your language until you're told to do so by Legal. If you do before it is official, the SEC can audit and determine the company was using this designation earlier and is in violation of the 4-day requirement if you have been working on the incident already for a few days before you really knew it was going to be reportable. So make this a training requirement and drive it into everyone's heads that we talk only of incidents.

Stepping away from the high-stress incident responsibilities, companies are also expected to report on how Management oversees cybersecurity along with how the Board is incorporated in oversight and governance. The SEC wants your Board to have expertise in cybersecurity. It also wants to understand how you communicate security matters to them. At some point when these SEC rules were set, your Legal Team approached your security personnel and asked for content to include in the filings. If you're new to the organization, you want to review that language to be familiar with what's stated.

Some other quick hits that derive from the SEC include expectations that you are managing risks continuously. The SEC expects that your incident response plan is updated and being tested, that training and awareness is ongoing, and you have a mechanism for managing third party risk. If you look at these expectations, if you are following NIST CSF and the associated controls, and if you installed the Governance and Compliance function like we described, then this will be the minimum you're doing in your organization. I go back to being systematic; build the program with tie-ins to your maturity model and map initiatives and Functional projects to the maturity model and you'll be just fine. Make sure that you're keeping track of any costs associated to incidents, along with any penalties or fines you have to pay in the process. You will also need to capture as a post-mortem exercise, the impact to the companies operational wellbeing, whether it's tied to revenue loss, relationships or credibility. The SEC will ask you for this once the incident is resolved (Securities and Exchange Commission, 2023).

I'll just reiterate, talk to your Legal Department as they will define what all this means to you, and use what I have provided as informational only.

8.3 SET AN SEC POLICY

Now that we know a little bit about the SEC rules, we need to establish a basis for how we will meet those mandates. Because this involves more than just security; it includes Legal and Finance, we should set a policy for our approach. You set the policy for more than just alignment, it will be an important artifact that represents your organizational structure and commitment to compliance that will bode well for you if audited. In truth, the impact of this policy goes beyond the three teams mentioned, it also impacts the rest of the management team and the Board of Directors so you may be asked to write one by your Board if you don't do it on your own, because it's part of their oversight responsibilities.

The policy should clearly articulate roles and responsibilities. Security will be responsible for incident management but Legal will take the lead in assessing impact and taking it to your disclosure team that will determine materiality. Legal will also notify the management team and Board, and work with Finance who serve as the controller and together, collect data and file the appropriate forms with the SEC. Our job in security is to manage the incident, provide timely information to Legal, and provide expertise in the write-up and follow-ups with whomever needs additional information. You rely on your Legal Team to negotiate everything beyond the incident, which again, shows the closeness you want to have and strong collaboration with them.

8.3.1 Incident identification

Don't assume your incident management practice is equipped to handle the high-pressure stakes. You want to test it to ensure the aggressive timing expectations and protocols are followed in the most effective way possible. Challenge your Cyber Fusion Team to prove to you that the SEC requirements for incident reporting are certified in practice. Doubling clicking on this; you are dependent on other departments in technology to report incidents in a timely manner. While you now have a SIEM or are working towards it, it's another thing to know that close to 100% of all assets are being monitored. What's more, there may be environments that you don't touch like Facilities networks or life and health safety environments or something else that have their own technology teams running them. You are accountable for all security incidents which means all of these non-standards environments and shadow tech-teams need to know where to go and what to do when an event occurs.

You need to test what I term as the wheel-and-spoke model. I see IT service management (ITSM) as the wheel, and all the technology teams including us as spokes that connect to ITSM. To further elaborate, ITSM should have connections into all the technology teams regardless if they are IT-specific or not. Now this may not be the case and you need to figure out how to form connective tissue across the organization but for argument sake, let's assume this is the case. That means you need to establish expectations and SLAs with ITSM and they in turn with all the teams such that if any event occurs and there is a remote possibility it's security related that the event is routed to security.

I include ITSM because they normally have all the connections for service delivery, and run incident management for technology. They tend to field as close to all of the events as any one team could so they are triaging these and supporting in whatever way needed. You work to establish protocols between your SOC, the Service Desk, and then in turn the teams so that if anyone notices an anomaly that might be security related that it is quickly routed to the SOC. The SOC in turn needs to be fully aware of the sensitivity of reporting and immediately escalate based on whatever algorithm they use to their leader who will then get it to Legal, the security leader (you), and other members of your leadership team as informational.

I have historically placed the responsibility for debriefing Legal with the head of Cyber Fusion because they should already have a cadence with Legal on incidents anyway and this would ride that same practice only with a heightened urgency. She or he will know sooner than you will and you don't want to waste time. Along the way, you need to ensure the language is around incidents not materiality. Take note of how many people would have potentially touched this event already; coordination and alignment is something you need to establish and work out even if you already have a well-established SOC and operation. Once you have informed Legal, they will take it from there and you serve as a subject matter 'exert'.

For the policy you are not defining all of this. For the policy you are stating that security will be responsible for incident management and triage across the organization and is accountable for delivering event details in a timely manner to Legal. You are also making reference to your incident management procedure that governs your handling efforts in the policy and any other pertinent official documentation you deem appropriate. On the back-end you are ironing out all of what I stated. Note that maybe your SOC has direct ties to all the teams and you don't need to work with ITSM. Customize this to your company's structure but the essence needs to be understood on what needs to be done. Last note on this, there will be little tolerance for mistakes. Losing hours in juggling the event around will quickly result in ridicule and questions internally. This is only natural because everyone knows the seriousness of SEC filings so iron this out, test it and retest.

8.3.2 Protocol to communicate

In the Policy, you want to clearly define who communicates what in the workflow. There is the initial communication by Security to Legal that you call out but you're not going to describe all the backend elements within the technical teams. You then want to describe the Legal communication responsibilities that are to the disclosure team, the executive team, potentially the Board, and to the Communications Team if external notifications are being prepped. In addition, you want to note how Finance and Legal with specific roles involved, will notify the SEC and coordinate the write-up and filing.

All of this must be clearly noted and decision points along the way, such as when to let the Board know, and what is their role (approve notifying the SEC, maybe reviewing the filing). The more clarity you offer in personnel (not names usually but titles) roles and responsibilities and decision points, the better this policy will be. You have experienced personnel who have written these types of documents so rely on them to draft it so that it can survive personnel turnover over time. As a caveat the Policy will be co-owned by at least Security and Legal and possibly Finance for controllership reasons.

8.3.3 Disclosure decision

There is likely a group of folks that serve on some disclosure team or committee who review disclosures beyond just those tied to security who will likely review the incident you supplied to Legal to deem if it's material or not. If such a team exists, make note of it in the Policy on how Legal will take the incident to this unit, who comprises this team, and how decisions are made. Call out that it's this team that determines materiality and decides on communication next steps. In practice, Legal will go to this team, a decision will be made, and then Legal or someone designated in this team will then notify the others noted earlier; I've marked that accountable party as Legal because typically Legal has coordination responsibilities for the Board, but it could be different in your company so identify this accordingly.

Beyond this, we have already noted the Board's part in this and informing them if materiality is assigned. We have also spoken to external communications and the need to notify them of impending notifications after it's approved by the Board and management. Capture all of this and maybe include a basic workflow in the Policy to summarize the steps for clarity. At this point, you have everything you need and know exactly who does what and when so that now you can focus on ironing out the logistics in incident management as described earlier in this section.

The key to success is clearly defined steps, awareness of all responsible parties of their responsibilities, training on the process and reinforcement, and testing of your incident handling procedures to address the sensitivity of these new requirements. Training and reinforcement is important because just as I alluded to the edge technology teams not being aware, your leadership needs to also know their roles and everyone needs to know the importance of this and what's at stake. I go back to what I said earlier about personal liability. If you area efficient in what you do, and structure business practices effectively and test them, you can do this job well and when others are leaving, you're able to defiantly stand tall and take on this challenge head on. The inadvertent side-effect of this is that if there are similar mandates in the EU, UK or elsewhere, chances are the same practices apply there and you just expand the application for what we described across the board with maybe small tweaks.

8.4 EU & UK REGULATIONS

We want to spend some time on regulations affecting security in the EU and UK because there are quite a few. Right now there are even more regulations being proposed and Bills that will add to the control mandates so while we call out many of the important regulations, know that there are more out there in specific areas of interest and more to come. We could spend quite a bit of time talking about product regulations in of themselves with the Radio Equipment Directive (RED), Cyber Resiliency Act (CRA), and Personal Security and Trust Infrastructure (PSTI), and others but for now we will focus on the general regulations that apply across the board.

You can't talk about the EU (and actually UK) without talking about the General Data Protection Regulation (GDPR) that is the premiere regulation in the EU for the protection of personal data and privacy. Anyone who has worked in the EU will know about GDPR. At the heart of it, there are elements of consent, rights, communication of breach, and fines. In the data rights category, GDPR explicitly points to individuals having the right to access, rectify, and erase data that applies to them. Fines for non-compliance can be up to 20 million Euros, and this pertains to any company that manages EU resident data for any purpose. (European Union, 2016). The UK has something similar called the UK General Data Protection Regulation (UK GDPR) and it's essentially the same as the one described here, This shouldn't be a surprise because once upon a time the UK was part of the EU and then Brexit happened that will drive variance and divergence over time.

Other notable EU regulations include the Network and Information Security Directive 2 (NIS2 Directive) that aims to improve security in critical areas like financial systems and energy. You also have the Digital Services Act (DSA) that focus on online content and establishing rules around illegal content and data. I'm not going to go into these too much but know that they are there, along with a few others that you should be aware of. My recommendation is to have your compliance team inventory all the enterprise regulations you need to abide by and product and software ones and work through a pretty intensive exercise of mapping all the required controls to your existing control base to identify gaps. Then you want to convert these gaps into an initiative to close them out so as to ensure you are abiding by the rules of each Region you do business in.

The same goes for the UK, you have what we referenced earlier as the UK GDPR. There is a supplemental Act that came out in 2018 called the Data Protection Act 2018 (DPA 2018) that enhances GDPR. You have a similar Regulation to the EU NIS Directive, and one other notable one is The Telecommunications (Security) Act of 2021 that focuses on the telecom space and sets standards for security (United Kingdom, 2021). You have a heavy dosage of regulations in the US, EU, and UK, so it's important to perform that mapping and certify it every couple of years as the regulation landscape changes 'regul-arly'.

8.5 APAC, MIDDLE EAST & AFRICA REGULATIONS

Regulations in Asia Pacific (APAC) are evolving but as of the time of my writing this book, there were no regulations that explicitly called out liability for CISOs, which is why we haven't really talked about this region (or the Middle East or Africa) in prior chapters. This however is likely to change as cyber-attacks are on the rise in APAC that have resulted in more regulatory requirements, especially in Australia, Singapore, and Japan. There are already steep penalties assigned to corporations who fail to comply with existing regulations but nothing directly tied to CISOs.

In Singapore, one regulation of note is their Cybersecurity Act. This was instituted in 2018 and was intended to protect critical infrastructure. This Act also defines roles and responsibilities for communication surrounding security events, similar to what the SEC has put in place (Government of Singapore, 2018). In Australia you have their Privacy Act that carries with it severe penalties if not adhered to. This law has been around for quite some time and is similar in intent to GDPR where it sets rules for how data is managed across its lifecycle. This Act applies to institutions but not to individuals using personal information domestically. In 2018 the Notifiable Data Breaches (NDB) Scheme was released that sets requirements for organizations on notifying individuals and the Office of the Australian Information Commissioner (OAIC) of events similar to what the SEC has done in the United States (OAIC, 2018).

Switching gears to the Middle East and Africa, the same holds true in that CISOs are not personally liable but there's an emergence of regulation that may soon apply liability to CISOs. There are numerous countries in scope here, but most of them have some sort of rules to govern privacy. The United Arab Emirates (UAE) have DIFC Data Protection Law that is similar to GDPR (Dubai International Financial Centre, 2020). In South Africa you have the Protection of Personal Information Act (POPIA) (Government of South Africa, 2013). The point to take away is that everyone is hyper sensitive about privacy and the growing threat posed by cyber-attacks and we will see even more regulations emerge. If you work in a global company, you will need to have a robust Governance and Compliance Team to address these head on, and again, a strong push for compliance automation because you will likely have a limit placed on staffing.

REFERENCES

DIFC (Dubai International Financial Centre). (2020). *Data protection law 2020*. Retrieved December 15, 2024, from https://www.difc.ae

European Union. (2016). *Regulation (EU) 2016/679 of the European Parliament and of the Council of 27 April 2016 on the protection of natural persons with regard to the processing of personal data and on the free movement of such data (General Data Protection Regulation)*. Official Journal of the European Union, L 119, 1–88. Retrieved from https://eur-lex.europa.eu/legal-content/EN/TXT/?uri=CELEX:32016R0679

Government of Singapore. (2018). *Cybersecurity Act 2018*. Retrieved December 15, 2024, Retrieved from https://www.imda.gov.sg/regulations-and-licensing-frameworks/cybersecurity-act

Government of South Africa. (2013). *Protection of Personal Information Act 4 of 2013*. Retrieved December 15, 2024, from https://www.gov.za/documents/protection-personal-information-act

Office of the Australian Information Commissioner (OAIC). (2018). *Notifiable Data Breaches scheme: Resources and guidance*. Retrieved December 15, 2024, from https://www.oaic.gov.au/privacy/notifiable-data-breaches

Securities and Exchange Commission. (2023, July 26). *Final rule: Cybersecurity risk management, strategy, governance, and incident disclosure. U.S. Securities and Exchange Commission*. Retrieved from https://www.sec.gov/rules/final/2023/33-11216.pdf

United Kingdom. (2021). *Telecommunications (Security) Act 2021: An Act to make provision about the security of public electronic communications networks and public electronic communications services*. Retrieved from https://www.legislation.gov.uk/ukpga/2021/31/enacted

U.S. Securities and Exchange Commission. (n.d.). *Forms for registration and reporting*. Retrieved from https://www.sec.gov

Chapter 9

Complacency vs controlled change

Ever heard the joke about complacency?

> Why did the complacent chair lose its job?
> Because it couldn't handle any more pressure – it as just too comfortable!
>
> (OpenAI, 2024)

Getting too comfortable is a formula for all sorts of not so good things. Now on one side we say that everyone needs to calm down, slow down and just enjoy. Hey, I can't argue with that and there's truth to it. If we, however, choose to work in this field, and have an interest in career growth, or we have a protective nature in us and have this innate drive to ensure the safety and security of those around us then complacency is our enemy. The thing we need to watch out for is that complacency can creep up on us and we can find ourselves stagnant without realizing that it had been happening to us for some time. Security is ever changing as is technology, and we have to recognize that while we may have implemented all the things discussed thus far, that we need to establish a practice that injects new thinking and innovation as part of our culture.

We can either be a change agent or change will happen to us with possibly not so favorable terms. Take artificial intelligence (AI) for instance. I stayed away from this topic in this book because there are so many smart people writing about it that I deferred to them so that I am not just reiterating things you may already have heard. I will however devote a section here to discuss AI and the generative kind we are so fixated on right now because it's a large enough topic that is happening to us right now that we shouldn't overlook it. Looking beyond AI though, we will see the emergence of quantum computing and for us security folks, this can be a scary thing as it will impact the world of encryption and the broader topic of cryptography. We are a few years away from quantum computing becoming a real and present danger to how we protect our data but the point here is that as soon as you think you've solved for something, another appears that challenges the

DOI: 10.1201/9781003616528-9

foundations of what you have established. We consequently must embrace change and never become complacent if we want to continue working in this field.

9.1 AI AND THE GENERATIVE KIND

Generative AI (genAI) took the world by storm in 2024 as the hot topic that was spearheaded by the emergence of ChatGPT. I myself have borrowed a joke or two from this platform because it's got a sense of humor but nothing is funny about the potential security issues that will arise if we don't get a handle on how we govern over AI in our organizations. Think about all the risks tied to the application of AI by bad actors in their mission to disrupt operations, steal intellectual property or simply extort money. If we don't change the way we manage the threat landscape, we're going to find the attack surface just got significantly larger and if we are resting on our laurels, well we're going to go backwards very quickly.

AI now can be used to develop sophisticated malware in record time, and this malware can be written with new capabilities that can bypass security controls that have stood the test of time. Using artificial intelligence and adaptive algorithms, attacks will become harder to identify, contain and mitigate. Most of us are astutely aware that the beginning of an attack is in learning about the victim. There are existing means to do this from phishing to smishing, to sophisticated social engineering campaigns that go deep into the understanding of how companies function and what the trigger points might be.

With Generative AI, you can develop phishing campaigns faster with improved quality and in mass quantity. You can expand into the world of deep fakes, and voice cloning and impersonation that looks, sounds and feels like the real thing. For espionage, you can use AI to generate false data sets and falsified records in volume that can drive decision-making failures. All of us security folks know the value of managing vulnerabilities, well, AI can rapidly identify vulnerabilities at scale and devise automated attack patterns to infiltrate with so much ease. We used to believe that zero-day exploits came few and far between; now those can be generated in bulk, meaning all the anti-virus and anti-malware solutions become minimally effective because they don't have the updates to address them since zero-days by nature are new and never before seen.

What about all the paranoia around data ownership, data privacy and what happens when Generative AI takes data sets as inputs and creates an entirely new and unique output? Generative AI can rapidly analyze data that is in the public domain and create new works that compete with existing proprietary, copyrighted, patented intellectual property. Data privacy is a big deal in this emerging space, which is why new regulations are emerging around artificial intelligence. This is also why whole countries banned this new tech at first because of the implications tied to national security.

Let's take this even further, how easy does AI drive autonomous activities to crack passwords or carry out Distributed Denial-of-Service (DDoS)? The emergence of realistic fakes, the volumized delivery of misinformation, the impact on continuous and nonstop attacks on networks; the concern is legitimate. Complacency will kill your ability to protect the interests of the folks that work with you and the company. So using some of the same principles as we have in the past, how do we get control of AI while enabling our company for innovation?

9.1.1 Three part governance

As much as we define all the challenges and obstacles, we should follow it up with possible methods for mitigation in how we run our operation. For me, there are three levels of governance that we need to install in order to effectively manage the risks tied to genAI. The thought process around it is fairly simple as depicted in the diagram. The first we will discuss is the middle tier referred to below as where the "Operational Decisions" are made. This can be stood up quickly and requires the least amount of coordination and agreement across the organization. The objective of this function is to establish a policy or standard (however you manage your documentation) that defines acceptable use, as well as the process for reviewing any AI-based toolsets that are being pursued for use.

The operators in this mid-tier are at the very least, Legal and Security. Designees should be identified who will work with Compliance to establish the policy, publish it and follow it up with training so the organization is informed. You'll need to go on the road and perform an awareness campaign so that the organization knows where to go for support, and place the process in a prominent place like your main Intranet corporate page for easy access. Depending on your organization, you may have others who need to be involved in making decisions and driving outcomes like AI innovation team leads or others that would strengthen the decision-making and support (Figure 9.1).

Figure 9.1 AI governance design.

The mid-tier I am describing helps bring the first layer of order to managing generative AI. Ideas on new tools, usage requests and any other topics associated with genAI will be reviewed to ensure a few key things. One of the biggest concerns that companies have is to ensure they are not relinquishing any rights to their data to the providers. This applies to both the data being inputted and outputted. If you use your data in an AI platform that is say publicly available, what's there to prevent the service provider from using that data to create new models that are publicly available? This mid-tier ensures data privacy is maintained and data ownership is not inadvertently relinquished because our personnel mistakenly used data they shouldn't have in tools that have unfavorable terms and conditions.

This leads to the question of how do I know what data is safe to use and what is not? This is the connection point to your Functional Third initiatives in data protection. On the front-end of that effort, you are setting classifications for data such as public, internal, confidential, etc. Through that initiative in data protection you are tagging your data over time against these classification levels, which becomes very important for the practice we are installing for AI governance. Having a separate classification standard that has been agreed to will allow this team to define what data can be used with publicly available tools (classification of public) and what cannot (all the rest). So, you want to take the time to establish this classification standard, and marry it to your generative AI policy/standard to provide guidance to users.

Other policy considerations revolve around generated media from genAI and how that will be handled. Decisions have to be made on whether media that comes out of an AI platform needs to stay internal or can be used externally as well. There are all sorts of reasons why this comes into play that tie back to how that media was created, what inputs were used, etc. Another topic that we have spent some time on in the regulatory conversations revolves around the use of AI-generated information on personal privacy and decisions on personnel and employment (as an example). In the EU, these are highly sensitive topics and you want to ensure you are restricting the use of AI-generated data for decisions such as these. Speak to your Legal team and build a policy that addresses all these risks and others.

So the mid-tier assesses usage requests and makes decisions based on an evolving policy or standard. The downstream tier I deemed as conducting "Tactical Execution" is where you are enforcing the decisions that were made in that mid-tier. Here again I refer back to your Functional Third initiatives and frankly, it is the method by which you will gain control over genAI. At its core, you can see genAI as a very sophisticated application, and like other applications, you can manage the data that is used and consumed and generated. Your data protection initiative will tag data so that you know how to treat various sets and how they can be consumed. You will likely run a data discovery effort in this across your devices, data centers and cloud so that you can be as comprehensive as can be. You will introduce data loss prevention (DLP) capabilities for all types of data whether they're in motion or at rest. You will be able to control usage patterns with DLP and your cloud access security broker (CASB) and other tools, thus giving your enforcement practice teeth. Alongside all of this, you will introduce data monitoring that you didn't have before so that you can identify unauthorized usage patterns and address them. Prior to the Functional Third, you probably relied on your firewalls to identify what applications or tools were being used but you had little ability to manage usage and enforce a policy. With Functional Third capabilities, you now are installing the methods of enforcement.

In addition to enforcement, you are also building in the ability to audit usage as described here. This becomes important for testing the effectiveness of your practice. This quality control also allows you to provide evidence of an effective practice if the time comes when you are audited. Prior to having the third tier, which is Tactical Execution, you had no means to administering the decisions in the mid-tier.

The last and final part of the equation is the top-level strategic aspect of your governance. Like I said, the middle is easy, the enforcement is hard (Functional Third) and the strategic portion referred to as the "Strategic Planning" part of this workflow is moderately challenging. This is where you need to work closely with as many of the top executives as you can to champion the creation of an AI ethics council, committee or whatever you want to call it that makes organizational decisions and sets the direction for AI consumption for the business. You need a solid mix of individuals who represent all aspects of your business. Facilitation of this can be handled by you in security or Legal; it doesn't matter because you're in it together but having the support of the Chief Legal Officer goes a long way, and if the Chief Financial Officer (CFO) is in support, well it makes the case very strong.

The creation of this Council should start with training on the topic of generative AI, what it means, what are the pitfalls, what are the benefits, and what others in industry are doing with it. You want to arm these folks with the information that allows them to make thoughtful decisions around the future of genAI. What you don't want is out of self-interest, the person that runs development to blindly push for full access and no controls, or Finance saying we need to open up web-based platforms for number crunching carte blanche. You first arm them with awareness and then get into discussing the AI vision for the firm, and relevant use cases that will then feed into the mid-tier, driving modifications to the policy and empowering the operational folks to work in the best interest of the organization and have air cover in the event they get pressured to do something that is out of the acceptable use models.

At this time, when you get all three of these pieces in place, you now have a complete governance framework and practice to manage this emerging space. You know what you want to do, and what you don't want to do and the effect is loosening up controls that were put in place due to unknowns. Your organization should now be able to move fast in adoption of approved solutions and you can make AI a part of your competitive advantage. Your team now becomes an enabler while maintaining the security of the organization. There's a lot to do, especially in the space of data protection but in my view, that set of initiatives will give you most of what you need to enforce and control.

Something that will absolutely surface is the topic around standalone tools versus embedded ones. It's relatively easier to set usage controls over tools that are standalone AI such as ChatGPT, or Copilot from Microsoft or something else, but it becomes very difficult when AI is integrated into tools you use daily like software for productivity, for project management, or software development… you name it. How do you control those aspects?

9.1.2 Contract & third-party reviews

Another dimension to your emerging governance and control is integrating the practice of contract management and third-party assessments into the AI governance framework. We're not going to be able to control AI being embedded in platforms, nor would we want to because it would limit the capabilities. What we do need to do is re-evaluate contract terms tied to data privacy, data usage, and general terms and conditions. Vendors know that in order to continue to do business with their customers, they need to provide a level of comfort in how they will manage their customer's data so that they can continue to work together. On our side, whatever process you have in contract management and security risk reviews, you need to inject a checklist of items tied to data management and privacy so that when you decide to move forward with that supplier, you are protected. The modification you make is that any time a new contract is under review or an existing contract is coming up for renewal that AI due diligence is applied and the results are fed to the mid-tier team so that they have a quick approval path to certify the decision. In doing this, you now have a relatively complete approach to managing artificial intelligence.

9.1.3 Reinventing our operation

Complacency would kill your ability to support the organization, and everything I just described has to be actively pursued and instituted so that your security posture evolves with the changing tide. We turn our attention to applying the same mindset to our own practice; what can AI do for us? I can remember (it wasn't that long ago) that my immediate thought went towards SOC automation. As I survey the playing field now towards the end of 2024, there are emerging platforms offered by security vendors that are doing just that, promising to automate your SOC in identification, triage, containment and remediation in a way that speeds up your response times, drives high accuracy, eliminates the impact of fatigue and learns over time. We've talked about this previously but imagine being able to do these elements and create that virtual forcefield around your operation, allowing you to grow your SOC analysts into engineering functions that can supplement the other aspects of your operation. There's so much you can accomplish with generative AI in the space of technology that I'd do it a disservice to attempt to capture even a fraction of the possibilities, so we'll leave that for you to explore. The key is to make a concerted effort to explore the possibilities.

9.2 INSTITUTIONAL CHANGE

What we just finished with has an underlying theme of institutionalizing change within your organization. The entire practice around managing the introduction of AI-based tools aims to enable invention and innovation but do so in a sustainable fashion. Through partnership we have the ability to instill security focus while helping standup business processes quickly and effectively to remove fear and anxiety and ultimately paralysis to doing something different. We as technology stewards need to continuously challenge our teams to visualize different ways of doing things that have been in place for long periods of time, install disruptive capabilities in a controlled fashion and optimize.

Institutional change is a way of thinking. We drive this into our culture by the things we say and the things we do. Case-in-point, as leaders we meet with our teams in various venues pretty regularly. In those venues, making the point at the right time that your team is safe to explore will resonate with them. This followed by true support reinforces your connection to one another, meaning don't say it's safe to think creatively and when something goes wrong, make them jump hurdles to explain themselves. Hold them accountable for outcomes but allow them the space to apply their creativity. Celebrate the risks taken by teams in a sensible way even if the results weren't what you wanted. There's value in proving something doesn't work as much as proving something that does.

Your change culture starts with you as the leader and spreads across the team by doing some simple things:

- Send the message of support continuously in every opportunity you get.
- Establish an environment conducive for exploration with things like seed money for testing, and the creation of test environments for playing.
- Provide support and reinforcement of purpose for things that prove out and things that don't.
- Make an aggressive training investment to develop skills so that your team can tap into change opportunities.

- Make the process simple; don't make them write a dissertation every time they want to pursue an idea.
- Lead by example in the way you think and the things you do.
- Always relay the essence of why change is important. This is tied to messaging but with a focus on change itself.
- Participate in the change pursuit. Join the functional meetings, review the results of proof of concepts (POCs); invest your time where possible.

The process of driving a change culture is tied to the connections you create with your team. This is not about some business process or a tool, it's about investing in relationships, forming a shared vision, and driving a sense of excitement. Change can be institutionalized if it becomes a way of thinking. People don't like change because they like their comfort around the parameters by which they function. Change correlates to the unknown so people shy away from it because the mind typically assumes the unknown will be bad. If you strip this away from the mindset of your team, then you have an opportunity to keep things fresh and dynamic even if you have been around together for a decade. Full disclosure, this isn't an academic thing I'm referencing, this is simply my learning and observations. If you take one thing out of this, it is to ensure somehow, you do not become stagnant and allow the world to pass you by because soon you and your team will fall under serious scrutiny, so do it in the best way you know how.

9.3 IDENTIFY KEY THIRD PARTIES

With everything we do internally and all the emphasis on innovation and change, the reality is our vision is limited and narrow because we work for one company and see one view. Vendors see many companies across a variety of industries so they can see what's common and what's unique. They can also see what practices work and what do not because their exposure is so large. There's something to be said for spending some time in large consulting firms or in positions where you interact with customers as a supplier because you get this broad exposure. The trick here is to find those rare third parties that have unique capabilities and a culture driven to building long-term relationships. The difference between transactional and relationship-based vendors is unmistakable. Transactional vendors are looking at the current sale and positioning their next sale while the first one hasn't even completed. They are fixated on short-term gains. I have no time or patience for these vendors but I will work with them so long as there's a thing we need to buy but I'm not going to spend my time with business reviews, or in-person meets and greets, or frankly non-essential pleasantries. They come off like salesmen and I would prefer not to entertain.

You do have that additional third-party that goes beyond the transaction but is full of themselves. The type that simply can't believe you would ever pick another option over them and if you do, they get insulted, offended and start going up your chain to voice their dissatisfaction with you, the customer. These people and companies are unreal, as they fail to remember who the customer is and they are bidding for work against others at all times. The arrogance drives me to stop engaging period. These are not the type I want to build strategic relationships with.

Then you get to the relationship-based third-parties who look at the engagement as an opportunity to partner, knowing that if we partner well that money will come in time. Money and profit is always a thought but how you get there is very different with these folks than the others. These relationship-based providers invest time into understanding your business model, your people, and your challenges. They may even invest their own capital to seed development of opportunities. If you find these types, invest into the relationships, and offer them opportunities because true relationship-based third-parties who we will refer as strategic partners don't come around often. I've run into maybe a handful in twenty-five years that I can genuinely say were strategic partners and the investment was worthwhile.

These partners can embed themselves into your teams and learn about what you do and how you do it. They can identify areas of opportunity; help you build business cases and stand next to you when you give the pitch for investment. Because their core business may be operational efficiency, business optimization, IT practice development or something that isn't to your core, they will usually have a much larger pool to draw from for helping you solve your problems. Identify low hanging fruit, have them prove themselves and then grow the challenge over time.

The partnership goes both ways. As much as they help you drive innovation and yes they make a profit, you can help them develop new services with the implementation of disruptive technologies like generative AI. With the approval of your Legal organization and company compliance, you can present use cases to their customers and help them develop a brand. They in turn can offer you first rights to new platforms and discounts while also helping you continue to improve your practice. Go in search for strategic partners because they can become an invaluable source for fighting complacency and driving innovation and constructive change.

9.4 SEED INNOVATION

Seeding innovation takes on similar parameters to those noted under driving a culture that isn't afraid of change. The pursuit of experimentation and an unyielding drive for learning are underpinnings of a strong innovative spirit. In mature operations, budgets are structured to enable creative thought and seed money is set aside for experimentation, knowing that some of this money may not be recovered. For us security folks, a great source for creative stimulation is in threat intelligence. Threat intelligence and the understanding of emerging security patterns are excellent paths to driving new thinking. Having access to external professional groups, seminars and training adds to the body of information your team can tap into. Something that can't be overlooked is affiliations with other companies in the same or other industries to learn what challenges are unique to them and how they solve for those challenges.

In my case, I have spent a lot of time in manufacturing, telecommunications and wireless over the years but where I choose to tap into is the banking and financial sectors. They have a very sensitive set of problems and are very good at identity management, and implementation of advanced access controls because their business is money. If you want to learn how to structure really strong identity and access management, you go to these industries. Obviously they are more than just this and do many other things well, but be open to tapping into your network and if you work with any consulting firms, they may have ways to connect you to some of their other customers to build relationships aimed at information sharing.

Something that will help gain support for your change culture and innovative initiatives is measuring your success. At the end of the day, all of us work under some financial limits and if you continually spend money on something that seemingly doesn't result in anything quantifiable, you will begin to field questions that can lead to restrictions. We need to promote exploration but at the same time, we need to measure the outcomes of innovation projects so that we can demonstrate the body of work we are supporting to our organization and our leadership. We need to keep a good record of disruptive initiatives that change the way we do business through new capabilities, optimization, or cost reduction. The return on these investments needs to be captured so that you can translate a program into business value.

9.5 INNOVATION CAMPAIGNS

What can help get the creative juices flowing is to identify problems and to challenge your team to solve for them. You can define specific themes in innovation campaigns that follow a hackathon approach. Hackathons are time bound events that can be structured around a specific problem, or they can be open-ended. They last for a set period of time, and can be entered by individuals or small groups who come together to solve for the problem statement or promote a new concept in an open-ended tournament. These events may have multiple rounds where the idea or approach is assessed by a panel and can eventually lead to one or several finalists who can win prizes and possibly seed money to incubate their ideas.

The idea behind them is to create a fun environment where teams can step away from their daily routines and innovate. At the very least, you promote team building and engagement with top leadership. You also encourage creative thinking and the injection of new ideas that may not surface without this type of event. If it stopped there, it would already be worthwhile but the ultimate possibilities lie with maybe solving major problems in ways never before thought of. For us security folks, maybe it results in new ways to identify threats or the creation of new toolsets or processes.

9.6 STRATEGIC PLANNING

We spoke about this before but it's worth mentioning the opportunity you have to use your strategic planning cycles to drive new thinking. There are so many things you can do with these planning efforts beyond just talking about the bits and bytes of the operation and running some team development outings. Those are absolutely worthwhile but if end up inviting some of our best performers to participate then it can be the perfect opportunity to have maybe an external facilitator run an idea generation session and wrap it around specific themes so that you can break up the monotony and tap into the best minds on your team. Strategic planning can be useful to plan your next steps, build strong teams, offer training focused on leadership, communication or something similar, and incubate idea generation. I'll leave it at that but think about how you can tap into something you already do in ways that haven't been done before; be innovative in the way you plan strategically!

REFERENCE

OpenAI. (2024). *ChatGPT* [Large language model]. https://chatgpt.com

Chapter 10

Closing remarks

We're all trying to make sense of an ever-changing landscape not just in security but technology as a whole. The broader environment sees conflict between countries and posturing by political parties on all sorts of principles that each side believes justifies fragmentation. My hope with this book is to share an approach to implementing a successful security practice where we can all agree that this is important and we can learn from one another on how to address a common and universal challenge. If you're new to security, I hope you got a sense of what to expect, how to potentially think about the new role you are taking on and the pitfalls to avoid in deciding to enter this space. Security is an exciting, dynamic area to grow a career around but it has its risks that go beyond the typical risks that folks take on in most employment considerations. You have to understand the nature of personal liability and how one day you can be running through a normal day of work and the next day you're being questioned on the integrity of your security practice from inside your company and outside. Be aware of what you're getting into and build the mechanisms to make you successful, immaterial of what demands are placed on you.

The nature of institutionalizing key practices and driving efficiency are key to thriving in this environment, and maybe any large-scale business function. Be very systematic and prescriptive in your approach and your risk will be manageable. My hope is that we look at this bigger than the things we do in our own corners of the world and view the challenge of security as something that affects our families, friends, colleagues, our companies and nations. This is not a topic that will go away and you can bet that things will escalate quite a bit for the foreseeable future. What we do together can set the foundation for a cooperative and concerted effort to improve together.

The content in this book is based on experience. We can drill down on most of what was presented and get to the nuances of the topics but that exercise you'll have to rely on experiencing what works and doesn't in your area. The blueprint presented here has worked for me several times and if I were consulting, I would use the same to build a systematic approach for whomever is asking. It is important to realize that while a lot of our success is based on the work done; another big factor is tied to relationships,

DOI: 10.1201/9781003616528-10

support for our cause, and the evangelization of our security program. Build connections, avoid being seen as big brother, and stay away from believing you have some sort of authority because frankly, that is an illusion.

We work as a fiduciary to our team and our company, and we work towards a meeting of the minds for implementation of reasonable security controls. This is what I've learned the hard way in my journey and for myself, this is the way I want to behave and be seen in my role as the head of such a department. Be ultra-transparent in everything you do and have the courage to raise risks and issues in a timely manner. This is the only way you can protect yourself and gain support to remedy gaps. Your practice needs to be completely risk-focused and you need to stand up a risk management approach as soon as you can get your team organized. Be aware that as soon as you record a risk, you need to have a plan for how you will deal with it using the 4Ts we discussed in this book. Review risks, define the action plan, and track with tenacity the actions associated with those risks.

Risk management is part of your Governance and Compliance Domain, and my recommendation is to be very aggressive in developing this team as soon as you can. We have data privacy, artificial intelligence cybersecurity, and product regulations that are emerging from everywhere. If you are a global company you will have your hands full in capturing all the requirements and ensuring compliance. This Domain must be structured so it can stay ahead of all of this and keep your company out of trouble. In places where you can, drive automation including in the area of compliance. Operational efficiency as with any team really, is essential.

The challenge of what to do and when to do it can quickly overwhelm you if you're not careful. Determine what functionality makes sense to introduce at what time and sequence them. I've offered three functional groupings called Functional First, Second, and Third to help determine what can be prioritized over time. You may find some of the items identified need to run a bit sooner or later based on your own conditions and that works perfectly fine. The key is to ensure you get the things identified in, at a minimum so that you can develop a strong security posture.

Your plan for introducing controls should map to business needs, risks and your maturity model. Figure out what framework you want to use quickly so that you can then map the controls and subsequently all your initiatives in a logical way. The intent is that every three years you want to have an external auditor come in and assess your maturity; if you map your initiatives to the maturity framework then there should be no question that the next time they come to assess you that you have improved your maturity. Your maturity is tied to the controls you put in place and operational practices. Your management system will help you assert the discipline needed to drive your agenda and instill a culture around execution.

Your management system or management operating system (whichever term you prefer) is key to driving excellence in the areas that are important to you. In my opinion, you need to have an operational element because if you don't run operations well then the rest doesn't matter. You want to quickly stand up a portfolio and project management practice because much of what we do in our space is tied to projects. Another priority to put in place is your risk review process because as I said earlier, everything revolves around risk management. Beyond that there are several other pieces to your System that we covered and should be introduced at a time when each of them makes sense. By doing this, you will establish a cadence across your team and progressively get better at what you measure because of the simple fact that you're continually looking at it.

To close, this is a fun space to work in. If you are constantly looking for new challenges, this is the place to find them and it's also a place where you can make a difference. There will be plenty of people who want to help you whether you want it or not and sometimes a clear path gets covered by all the noise. Don't get encumbered by all the marketing and sales pitches that tell us we 'must' by this great tool to be secure. Follow a strategy and defined roadmap and remain laser focused. It's our job to maintain clarity when everyone around us is under the influence of unyielding information overload. Good luck and happy trails!

Index

For Product Safety Concerns and Information please contact our EU representative GPSR@taylorandfrancis.com
Taylor & Francis Verlag GmbH, Kaufingerstraße 24, 80331 München, Germany

www.ingramcontent.com/pod-product-compliance
Ingram Content Group UK Ltd.
Pitfield, Milton Keynes, MK11 3LW, UK
UKHW020203200926
475702UK00004B/593

* 9 7 8 1 0 4 1 0 1 2 7 3 3 *